PONTIAC FIERO 1984-1988

Compiled by
R.M. Clarke

ISBN 1 870642 015

Distributed by
Brooklands Book Distribution Ltd.
'Holmerise', Seven Hills Road,
Cobham, Surrey, England

BROOKLANDS BOOKS

BROOKLANDS BOOKS SERIES

AC Ace & Aceca 1953-1983
AC Cobra 1962-1969
Alfa Romeo Giulia Berlinas 1962-1976
Alfa Romeo Giulia Coupés 1963-1976
Alfa Romeo Spider 1966-1987
Aston Martin Gold Portfolio 1972-1985
Austin Seven 1922-1982
Austin A30 & A35 1951-1962
Austin Healey 100 1952-1959
Austin Healey 3000 1959-1967
Austin Healey 100 & 3000 Collection No. 1
Austin Healey 'Frogeye' Sprite Collection No. 1
Austin Healey Sprite 1958-1971
Avanti 1962-1983
BMW Six Cylinder Coupés 1969-1975
BMW 1600 Collection No. 1
BMW 2002 1968-1976
Bristol Cars Gold Portfolio 1946-1985
Buick Riviera 1963-1978
Cadillac Automobiles 1949-1959
Cadillac Automobiles 1960-1969
Cadillac Eldorado 1967-1978
Cadillac in the Sixties No. 1
Camaro 1966-1970
High Performance Camaros 1982-1988
Chevrolet 1955-1957
Chevrolet Camaro Collection No. 1
Chevelle & SS 1964-1972
Chevy II Nova & SS 1962-1973
Chrysler 300 1955-1970
Citroen Traction Avant 1934-1957
Citroen 2CV 1949-1982
Cobras & Replicas 1962-1983
Cortina 1600E & GT 1967-1970
Corvair 1959-1968
Daimler Dart & V-8 250 1959-1969
Datsun 240z 1970-1973
Datsun 280Z & ZX 1975-1983
De Tomaso Collection No. 1
Dodge Charger 1966-1974
Excalibur Collection No. 1
Ferrari Cars 1946-1956
Ferrari Cars 1962-1966
Ferrari Cars 1969-1973
Ferrari Dino 1965-1974
Ferrari Dino 308 1974-1979
Ferrari 308 & Mondial 1980-1984
Ferrari Collection No. 1
Fiat X1/9 1972-1980
Ford Falcon 1960-1970
Ford Mustang 1964-1967
Ford Mustang 1967-1973
High Performance Mustangs 1982-1988
Ford RS Escort 1968-1980
Honda CRX 1983-1987
High Performance Escorts MkI 1968-1974
High Performance Escorts MkII 1975-1980
Hudson & Railton Cars 1936-1940
Jaguar Cars 1957-1961
Jaguar Cars 1961-1964
Jaguar Cars 1964-1968
Jaguar MK2 1959-1969
Jaguar E-Type 1961-1966
Jaguar E-Type 1966-1971
Jaguar E-Type V12 1971-1975
Jaguar XKE Collection No. 1
Jaguar XJ6 1968-1972
Jaguar XJ6 Series II 1973-1979
Jaguar XJ6 & XJ12 Series III 1979-1985
Jaguar XJ12 1972-1980
Jaguar XJS 1975-1980
Jensen Cars 1946-1967
Jensen Cars 1967-1979
Jensen Interceptor Gold Portfolio 1966-1986
Lamborghini Cars 1964-1970
Lamborghini Cars 1970-1975
Lamborghini Countach Collection No. 1
Lamborghini Countach & Urraco 1974-1980
Lamborghini Countach & Jalpa 1980-1985
Lancia Stratos 1972-1985
Land Rover 1948-1973
Land Rover Series II & IIa 1958-1971
Land Rover Series III 1971-1985
Lotus Cortina 1963-1970
Lotus Elan 1962-1973
Lotus Elan Collection No. 1
Lotus Elan Collection No. 2
Lotus Elite 1957-1964
Lotus Elite & Eclat 1974-1981
Lotus Turbo Esprit 1980-1986
Lotus Europa 1966-1975
Lotus Europa Collection No. 1
Lotus Seven 1957-1980
Lotus Seven Collection No. 1
Maserati 1965-1970
Maserati 1970-1975
Mazda RX-7 Collection No. 1
Mercedes 230/250/280SL 1963-1971
Mercedes 350/450SL & SLC 1971-1980
Mercedes Benz Cars 1949-1954
Mercedes Benz Cars 1954-1957
Mercedes Benz Cars 1957-1961
Mercedes Benz Competition Cars 1950-1957
Metropolitan 1954-1962
MG Cars 1929-1934
MG TC 1945-1949
MG TD 1949-1953
MG TF 1953-1955
MG Cars 1957-1959
MG Cars 1959-1962
MG Midget 1961-1980
MG MGA 1955-1962
MGA Collection No. 1
MGB Roadsters 1962-1980
MGB GT 1965-1980
Mini Cooper 1961-1971
Morgan Cars 1960-1970
Morgan Cars 1969-1979
Morris Minor Collection No. 1
Old's Cutlass & 4-4-2 1964-1972
Oldsmobile Toronado 1966-1978
Opel GT 1968-1973
Pantera 1970-1973
Pantera & Mangusta 1969-1974
Plymouth Barracuda 1964-1974
Pontiac Fiero 1984-1988
Pontiac GTO 1964-1970
Pontiac Firebird 1967-1973
High Performance Firebirds 1982-1988
Pontiac Tempest & GTO 1961-1965
Porsche Cars 1960-1964
Porsche Cars 1964-1968
Porsche Cars 1968-1972
Porsche Cars in the Sixties
Porsche Cars 1972-1975
Porsche 356 1952-1965
Porsche 911 Collection No. 1
Porsche 911 Collection No. 2
Porsche 911 1965-1969
Porsche 911 1970-1972
Porsche 911 1973-1977
Porsche 911 Carrera 1973-1977
Porsche 911 SC 1978-1983
Porsche 911 Turbo 1975-1984
Porsche 914 1969-1975
Porsche 914 Collection No. 1
Porsche 924 1975-1981
Porsche 928 Collection No. 1
Porsche 944 1981-1985
Porsche Turbo Collection No. 1
Reliant Scimitar 1964-1986
Rolls Royce Silver Cloud 1955-1965
Rolls Royce Silver Shadow 1965-1980
Range Rover 1970-1981
Rover 3 & 3.5 Litre 1958-1973
Rover P4 1949-1959
Rover P4 1955-1964
Rover 2000 + 2200 1963-1977
Rover 3500 1968-1977
Rover 3500 & Vitesse 1976-1986
Saab Sonett Collection No. 1
Saab Turbo 1976-1983
Singer Sports Cars 1933-1934
Studebaker Hawks & Larks 1956-1963
Sunbeam Alpine & Tiger 1959-1967
Thunderbird 1955-1957
Thunderbird 1958-1963
Thunderbird 1964-1976
Toyota MR2 1984-1988
Triumph 2000-2.5-2500 1963-1977
Triumph Spitfire 1962-1980
Triumph Spitfire Collection No. 1
Triumph Stag 1970-1980
Triumph Stag Collection No. 1
Triumph TR2 & TR3 1952-1960
Triumph TR4,TR5,TR250 1961-1968
Triumph TR6 1969-1976
Triumph TR6 Collection No. 1
Triumph TR7 & TR8 1975-1982
Triumph GT6 1966-1974
Triumph Vitesse & Herald 1959-1971
TVR 1960-1980
Volkswagen Cars 1936-1956
VW Beetle 1956-1977
VW Beetle Collection No. 1
VW Golf GTi 1976-1986
VW Karmann Ghia 1955-1982
VW Scirocco 1974-1981
Volvo 1800 1960-1973
Volvo 120 Series 1956-1970

BROOKLANDS MUSCLE CARS SERIES
American Motors Muscle Cars 1966-1970
Buick Muscle Cars 1965-1970
Camaro Muscle Cars 1966-1972
Capri Muscle Cars 1969-1983
Chevrolet Muscle Cars 1966-1972
Dodge Muscle Cars 1967-1970
Mercury Muscle Cars 1966-1971
Mini Muscle Cars 1961-1979
Mopar Muscle Cars 1964-1967
Mopar Muscle Cars 1968-1971
Mustang Muscle Cars 1967-1971
Shelby Mustang Muscle Cars 1965-1970
Oldsmobile Muscle Cars 1964-1970
Plymouth Muscle Cars 1966-1971
Pontiac Muscle Cars 1966-1972
Muscle Cars Compared 1966-1971
Muscle Cars Compared Book 2 1965-1971

BROOKLANDS ROAD & TRACK SERIES
Road & Track on Alfa Romeo 1949-1963
Road & Track on Alfa Romeo 1964-1970
Road & Track on Alfa Romeo 1971-1976
Road & Track on Alfa Romeo 1977-1984
Road & Track on Aston Martin 1962-1984
Road & Track on Auburn Cord & Duesenberg 1952-1984
Road & Track on Audi 1952-1980
Road & Track on Audi 1980-1986
Road & Track on Austin Healey 1953-1970
Road & Track on BMW Cars 1966-1974
Road & Track on BMW Cars 1975-1978
Road & Track on BMW Cars 1979-1983
Road & Track on Cobra, Shelby & Ford GT40 1962-1983
Road & Track on Corvette 1953-1967
Road & Track on Corvette 1968-1982
Road & Track on Corvette 1982-1986
Road & Track on Datsun Z 1970-1983
Road & Track on Ferrari 1950-1968
Road & Track on Ferrari 1968-1974
Road & Track on Ferrari 1975-1981
Road & Track on Ferrari 1981-1984
Road & Track on Fiat Sports Cars 1968-1987
Road & Track on Jaguar 1950-1960
Road & Track on Jaguar 1961-1968
Road & Track on Jaguar 1968-1974
Road & Track on Jaguar 1974-1982
Road & Track on Lamborghini 1964-1985
Road & Track on Lotus 1972-1981
Road & Track on Maserati 1952-1974
Road & Track on Maserati 1975-1983
Road & Track on Mazda RX7 1978-1986
Road & Track on Mercedes 1952-1962
Road & Track on Mercedes 1963-1970
Road & Track on Mercedes 1971-1979
Road & Track on Mercedes 1980-1987
Road & Track on MG Sports Cars 1949-1961
Road & Track on MG Sports Cars 1962-1980
Road & Track on Mustang 1964-1977
Road & Track on Peugeot 1955-1986
Road & Track on Pontiac 1960-1983
Road & Track on Porsche 1951-1967
Road & Track on Porsche 1968-1971
Road & Track on Porsche 1972-1975
Road & Track on Porsche 1975-1978
Road & Track on Porsche 1979-1982
Road & Track on Porsche 1982-1985
Road & Track on Rolls Royce & Bentley 1950-1965
Road & Track on Rolls Royce & Bentley 1966-1984
Road & Track on Saab 1955-1985
Road & Track on Toyota Sports & G T Cars 1966-1986
Road & Track on Triumph Sports Cars 1953-1967
Road & Track on Triumph Sports Cars 1967-1974
Road & Track on Triumph Sports Cars 1974-1982
Road & Track on Volkswagen 1951-1968
Road & Track on Volkswagen 1968-1978
Road & Track on Volkswagen 1978-1985
Road & Track on Volvo 1957-1974
Road & Track on Volvo 1975-1985

BROOKLANDS CAR AND DRIVER SERIES
Car and Driver on BMW 1955-1977
Car and Driver on BMW 1977-1985
Car and Driver on Cobra, Shelby & Ford GT40 1963-1984
Car and Driver on Datsun Z 1600 & 2000 1966-1984
Car and Driver on Corvette 1956-1967
Car and Driver on Corvette 1968-1977
Car and Driver on Corvette 1978-1982
Car and Driver on Ferrari 1955-1962
Car and Driver on Ferrari 1963-1975
Car and Driver on Ferrari 1976-1983
Car and Driver on Mopar 1956-1967
Car and Driver on Mopar 1968-1975
Car and Driver on Pontiac 1961-1975
Car and Driver on Porsche 1955-1962
Car and Driver on Porsche 1963-1970
Car and Driver on Porsche 1970-1976
Car and Driver on Porsche 1977-1981
Car and Driver on Porsche 1982-1986
Car and Driver on Saab 1956-1985
Car and Driver on Volvo 1955-1986

BROOKLANDS MOTOR & THOROUGHBRED & CLASSIC CAR SERIES
Motor & T & CC on Ferrari 1966-1976
Motor & T & CC on Ferrari 1976-1984
Motor & T & CC on Lotus 1979-1983
Motor & T & CC on Morris Minor 1948-1983

BROOKLANDS PRACTICAL CLASSICS SERIES
Practical Classics on Austin A40 Restoration
Practical Classics on Land Rover Restoration
Practical Classics on Metalworking in Restoration
Practical Classics on Midget/Sprite Restoration
Practical Classics on Mini Cooper Restoration
Practical Classics on MGB Restoration
Practical Classics on Morris Minor Restoration
Practical Classics on Triumph Herald/Vitesse
Practical Classics on Triumph Spitfire Restoration
Practical Classics on VW Beetle Restoration
Practical Classics on 1930S Car Restoration

BROOKLANDS MILITARY VEHICLES SERIES
Allied Military Vehicles Collection No. 1
Allied Military Vehicles Collection No. 2
Dodge Military Vehicles Collection No. 1
Military Jeeps 1941-1945
Off Road Jeeps 1944-1971
V W Kubelwagen 1940-1975

CONTENTS

Page	Title	Publication	Date	
5	Pontiac Fiero Introduction	Road & Track	Sept.	1983
12	Pontiac Fiero S/E Road Test	Road & Track	Sept.	1983
16	P is for Plastic . . . and Performance	Autocar	Sept. 17	1983
20	Pontiac Fiero 2M4 Preview Test	Car and Driver	Sept.	1983
26	Forging the Fiero Design Analysis	Car and Driver	Sept.	1983
30	Both Ends Against the Centre Comparison Test	Autocar	Feb. 11	1984
33	Pfaff Turbo Fiero Road Test	Motor Trend	March	1984
36	American Express	Motor	Sept. 15	1984
38	Pontiac Fiero GT Road Test	Road & Track	Nov.	1984
42	Pontiac Fiero GT Road Test	Car and Driver	Nov.	1984
48	Plastic Import	Wheels	Nov.	1984
53	Flashdance	Motor	Dec. 29	1984
54	Pontiac Fiero Owner Survey	Motor Trend	Feb.	1985
56	Muscle Machine	Autocar	Mar. 13	1985
57	Motorsports on Parade Track Test	Car and Driver	June	1985
65	Pontiac Fiero GT Driving Impression	Road & Track	Aug.	1986
66	Pontiac Fiero GT Road Test	Car and Driver	Feb.	1986
71	Pontiac Fiero GT Preview	Automobile	Dec.	1986
75	Pontiac Fiero GT Road Test	Sports and GT Cars		1987
78	Sports Cars for the Real World	Automobile	Mar.	1987
90	Fiero at Last	Autocar	Oct. 7	1987
92	Fiero Formula vs MR2 Supercharged Comparison Test	Road & Track	Oct.	1987
100	News from Pontiac	Pontiac	Aug. 5	1987
101	The Gee Force Comparison Test	Car and Driver	April	1988
104	End of the Road for Pontiac Fiero	Motor	Mar. 12	1988

ACKNOWLEDGEMENTS

When we sent this book to the printer a month ago it was to form one of a trio covering the leading sportscars of the period along with Toyota MR2 and Honda CRX. Alas, last week came news from Pontiac that Fiero production was to cease at the end of the year.

It is not our task to perform autopsies, however it will become clear to readers that the Fiero started badly. The manufacturers it would seem actively followed a policy of on-the-road development by their customers. The outcome was in 1988 a worthwhile value-for-money sportscar, unfortunately not in time to save it.

A clue as to its future place in the automotive spectrum is given by Autoweek in its obituary:

"Sales of Fiero now may be bolstered by collectors. An '88 with the V6 and 5-speed may be the most highly valued Fiero for collectors 10 years hence,...".

It is our view that the Fiero will quickly go to classic status as did an earlier British 2-seater the Triumph Stag. This was killed off in 1977 for much the same reasons, and rose phoenix-like from the ashes as a collectible as the production line ground to a halt.

Ten years from now the Fiero will be greatly sought after firstly because of its rarity, shape and two-seater configuration, secondly because its fibreglass body will be free from rust and finally because most of its mechanicals will be readily available from aging Chevettes and Citations. We predict a long second life for the Fiero and have no doubt that we will have to keep this book in print for many years to come.

We have added at the proof stage an extra comparison test from Car and Driver as a final tribute to the Fiero — they summed up the '88 Formula as follows:

"It's a shame that it's taken half a decade to get the Fiero right, but Pontiac and America finally have a budget-priced sports car to be proud of. Well done."

The leading automotive publishers have for many years generously supported our series by allowing the inclusion of their copyright road tests and other articles that make up these anthologies. I am sure that Fiero devotees will wish to join with us in thanking the management of Autocar, Automobile, Car and Driver, Motor, Motor Trend, Pontiac Motor Division, Road & Track, Road & Track Specials and Wheels for their understanding and ongoing help.

R.M. Clarke

PONTIAC FIERO INTRODUCTION

The new kid on the block really wants to make friends

BY JONATHAN THOMPSON

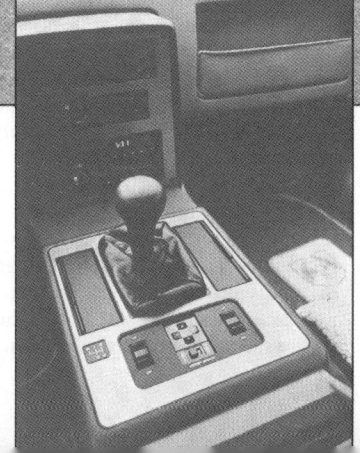
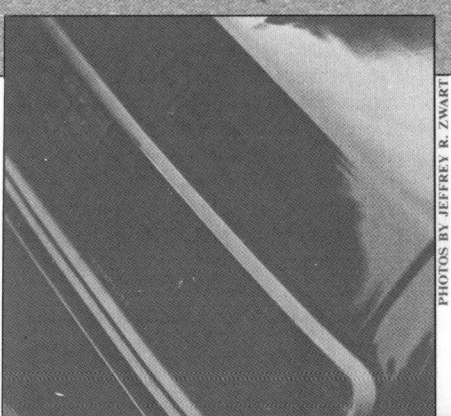

PHOTOS BY JEFFREY R. ZWART

The Fiero, Pontiac's P-car, has arrived. After a 5-year development period in which the only major problems were temporary cutbacks in project funding (twice), Hulki Aldikacti's team has brought the 2-seat mid-engine coupe in as a 1984 model, available in mid-September. And—enthusiasts give three cheers—the car is pretty much what its 49-year-old, Turkish-born creator had in mind from the beginning.

Something of a maverick at General Motors, Aldikacti (whose name is pronounced almost like it's spelled, but with the "c" sounded as a "ch") worked at Packard before joining John DeLorean's advanced project engineering group at Pontiac in 1956. The P-car project began in the late Seventies as a high-fuel-economy commuter car (to mollify GM executives during that critical period), but Aldikacti's design staff had sports car handling and performance in mind all along.

Working without interference, the P-car staff concentrated on the car's structure and manufacturing process. After deciding that it *had* to be mid-engine, for reasons of handling and (for later!) the application of high power outputs, the engineers developed an independently driveable all-steel space frame chassis, an extremely rigid structure with excellent crash-barrier characteristics. Believing that a car's success must depend upon the effectiveness of the manufacturing process, what he calls "productionizing," Aldikacti conceived a unique assembly method. Using plastic body panels of different weights and flexibility, he ensured their tight fit on the space frame by employing a large "mill and drill" machine on the assembly line. As each space frame passed under it, the huge Gilman-built machine would simultaneously mill 39 different body attachment points to the correct height and then drill them precisely. This would ensure that the molded plastic skins aligned with a tolerance of 1/64 in., despite any minor discrepancies in the welding of the basic space frame, assembled from six modular units.

The body panels were molded from two basic types of plastic. Those requiring great rigidity, such as the horizontal pieces—hood, roof, upper rear quarter panels and rear deck—were made of sheet molded compound (SMC), while those subject to frequent contact—bumpers, front fenders, doors and lower rear quarter panel—used the reaction injection molded urethane (RIM) process, also called RRIM when reinforced with fiberglass for greater strength. The entire space frame-cum-plastic body system has been seen as economic for 100,000 units annually, possibly 150,000.

While the concepts for the structure and manufacturing process were being refined, the mechanical components were under consideration. In its original guise as a commuter, the P-car had to be an economic proposition, using an existing drivetrain. The X-car's "Iron Duke" 2.5-liter 4-cylinder transverse package was chosen for the initial P-car series, although the engine compartment was designed from the outset with room for larger units of Vee configuration. The X-car axle shafts dictated the P-car's rear track at 58.7 in., while the engine and passenger accommodation called for a fairly long wheelbase at 93.4 in.

The first space frame was built by a 4-man crew at Entec, a special Pontiac facility in Troy, Michigan, beginning in October 1979. The prototype bodywork, conceived by the Pontiac advanced studio under Ron Hill, was built of fiberglass, with proportions ultimately retained on the production model but differing in many details. This first running car, of which the purpose was to convince GM executives of its viability, was completed on March 15, 1980, only five months from inception.

Followed by 16 pre-prototypes with plastic skins (also using the original body design, as seen in R&T's preview in the May 1981 issue), the original car demonstrated its promise and the package was approved on April 16, 1980 and turned over to the Pontiac production design studio under John Schinella for styling refinement on April 24. Pontiac's older Plant 8, being used for Grand Prix production, was selected as the site for P-car manufacture, requiring a complete renovation (including robot welding as well as the mill and drill machine), while detail engineering continued at the Entec facility under Jay Wetzel and, later, Ron Rogers.

Still known as the P-car within Pontiac, the car also received the code designation 2M4 (2-seat, mid-engine, 4-cylinder) and the temporary name Pegasus. The emblem, based on the Pegasus theme and barely discernable as a winged horse, was first sketched in the Pontiac interior studio by Jon Albert.

Because of the X-car track dimension, the Fiero had a wide structure and this allowed the engineers to position the 10-gal. fuel tank in the middle of the car, between the two passengers, where it would have the best protection and affect the weight distribution the least. To keep the car as short as possible, the tail was designed to house only a moderate amount of luggage. In front, T-car suspension arms were employed, using a different crossmember, of course, while disc brakes were fitted all around, a favorable result of moving the X-car front-drive layout to the back. Most of the nose was taken up by radiator and spare tire, with some room around the edges for incidental parcels.

Once the majority of production details were pinned down, 30 additional pre-pilot prototypes were assembled before pilot cars were started directly from production tooling. Full-scale manufacture began in July 1983 for a September 14 introduction.

As a product, the Fiero is still the high-mileage commuter it was intended to be, but the improving economic climate has permitted Pontiac to stress its sporting characteristics by referring to it in press material as a driver's car. As the following full road test shows, this description is completely justified.

Although the 92-bhp 4-cylinder engine doesn't propel the 2500-lb car at a startling rate, Pontiac is making modification information and part numbers available for customers wanting to bring the four up to a super-duty configuration of over 140 bhp. Three transmission options are offered: a 4-speed manual with a 4.10:1 final drive ratio, the same gearbox with the high-mileage ratio of 3.32:1 (for which Pontiac claims a highway consumption figure of 50 mpg), and a 3-speed automatic with a 3.18 ratio. The all-independent base suspension includes 13-in. slotted steel wheels, with finned cast aluminum wheels as an option, while the WS6 handling package, comprising different springs and shock absorbers front and rear, is mated with extremely handsome 14-in. cast aluminum wheels and P215/60R Goodyear Eagle GT tires.

With the stock 4-cylinder engine, the only one available on production cars for the 1984 model year, the Fiero is a 105-mph car with 0–60 mph acceleration in the 11-second class (see road test). For 1985 the 2.9-liter V-6 engine will be available, including a turbocharged version with 180 bhp, nearly double the base output, and expected 0–60 times around 6 sec. That will please the high performance enthusiast, but for now Pontiac is understandably concentrating on getting the basic car right. Considering that probably 80 percent of the estimated first-year market of 75,000–85,000 units will be composed of less performance-oriented customers, this would seem to be a good priority. The potential market for the Fiero is vast; with an expected price tag of $9000–$10,000 it should appeal to a wide spectrum of buyers wanting unique styling, good handling and a luxury interior, for commuter or pleasure driving.

After the attractive exterior, the wide, comfortable and extensively equipped interior may be the key to the car's ultimate acceptance. This comes in two configurations, the base Fiero (or entry-level, as Pontiac calls it), and the much better appointed Fiero S/E version, with 3-spoke padded urethane steering wheel,

INTRODUCTION

electric release for the rear compartment, better sun visors, tinted windshield glass and radio as standard equipment. Interior upholstery is either tan and brown or a combination of grays; for 1984 the only exterior colors are red, white, black and silver.

The Fiero is a complete breakaway from previous Pontiac—or GM—technology and marketing. It is the first mid-engine mass production car from the U.S. industry, the first with all-plastic body (as distinct from fiberglass), only the second 2-seater from GM (after the Corvette) and after the Corvair the only non-front engine car. Beyond the obvious motive of opening up a new market and making money for Pontiac, its purpose is to raise public consciousness for the division's technical expertise and to develop new manufacturing methods that combine quality improvement with increased worker morale. A visit to the Fiero plant when the first pilot cars were being built showed that the latter objectives were off to a good start; under plant superintendent Ernie Schaefer assembly-line efficiency was of a high order and the employees seemed as excited about their new product as any sports car enthusiast.

Pontiac made its first press showing to a group of 30 journalists in northern California, handing over the keys to 15 Fieros for a 100-mile run on winding roads from Burlingame, across the Golden Gate Bridge, through Marin County and then to Napa. The following day the cars were put through their paces on the Sears Point race track after instruction on the characteristics of cars and course by Bill Cooper (chief instructor for the Bob Bondurant school) and Phil Hill. Present as teasers were two Fiero specials produced by Pontiac designers, one a spider with a low windshield and headrest fairings but lacking a top of any kind, the other a full race car chassis based quite freely on the Fiero layout. Although neither is a direct precursor of a production model, Pontiac wants the public to know that even more interesting Fieros are on the way.

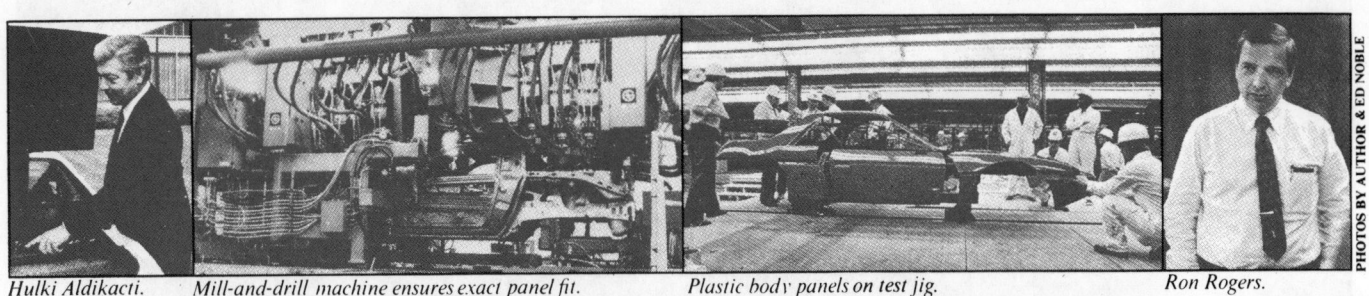

Hulki Aldikacti.   *Mill-and-drill machine ensures exact panel fit.*   *Plastic body panels on test jig.*   *Ron Rogers.*

PHOTOS BY AUTHOR & ED NOBLE

PONTIAC FIERO
TECHNICAL ANALYSIS

PONTIAC ENGINEERS MUST have had a lot of fun with this project, which appears to have been put together in the same spirit as other American 2-seaters such as the original Corvette and the original T-bird. It's as though a bunch of engineer/enthusiasts got together and said, "Okay, let's see what existing parts we've got in the bin, and how we can rearrange them into a real sports car." This is the same procedure used for building such historical favorites as MGs, Triumphs, and others. They take an existing driveline/suspension (the hard parts) and incorporate them in a more interesting package.

In an engineering analysis I find myself comparing the Fiero to the new Corvette—not because of any similarity in size or market, but because that is America's only other sports car and they share corporate heritage. In a full road test, of course, comparative cars might be the Mazda RX-7, Porsche 944, Datsun 280ZX or even the Bertone X1/9.

A consideration of the packaging of the Fiero raises the immediate question: "Why *mid*-engine, after Chevrolet just convinced us that *front* engine was proper for the Corvette?" Because the two are aimed at different markets. The Fiero was justified in the corporation largely as a mass production economy commuter/sports car. This meant that an existing unitary driveline package was required. Then, for an aerodynamic hoodline, the low seating position, short wheelbase and light chassis, the mid engine location was justified. The fact that this creates a potentially better handling competition car may or may not have been incidental.

The Fiero is very wide and short. It has almost a 2-in. greater track than other sports cars in its class, and is about 10 in. shorter in overall length. The existing X-car driveline dictated the width (this gives us another generation of "wide-track" Pontiacs). But this makes roll and handling development easier. Given a 2-seater limitation, the width also allows room for the fuel tank beneath the console, right at the center of gravity. The mid-engine design gives a moderate 56-percent rear weight bias, partly because of a relatively short rear overhang. When the proposed V-6 becomes available, however, approximately 100 extra pounds at the tail will increase the rear bias.

The 600-lb stamped-steel and spot-welded space frame is being highly touted, although it is only a slight deviation from conventional unit construction. The primary difference is that none of the steel panels makes up the exterior bodyshell. This is comprised of easily fitted plastic outer panels, as described in the main story. The concept is very similar to the Corvette's, except for the precision-fit, mill-and-drill process. The percentage of plastic in the body structure is likewise similar to Corvette with about 175 lb of sheet molded compound and reinforced reaction injection molded (fiberglass) exterior panels.

You can't get Detroit engineers to talk about chassis beaming or torsional rigidity these days. Instead they like to refer to vibration *frequencies*, which are problems perceived by comfort-minded tourists. Still, for enthusiast drivers this chassis is solid enough. The fixed steel top (no T-top is planned) provides an efficient stiffness-per-pound structure that can't be approached by any convertible sports car made. Finite element analysis and high strength steels were used extensively to produce just about the minimum acceptable mass—from a ride comfort standpoint. So it doesn't look like there will be any major weight reduction

from the base 2500 lb in the future unless some costly exotic materials are used. As for impact safety, we don't have to worry about whether the engine is up front or in back, because Big Brother's standards apply equally to all designs.

Aerodynamics may not have been a high priority consideration in the original Fiero design. With a relatively low weight and small frontal area (by American standards), good EPA mileage figures were possible without going for the ultimate in low drag coefficient. The reported C_x is 0.377, which is not bad for such a short car, but not too strong an advertising point either. One obvious problem is the notchback rear window, which is almost a necessary evil in a mid-engine car. Although it allows easy engine access and ventilation, it really disturbs the upper airflow and increases drag while reducing potential downforce from any rear spoiler. The Fiero's other problem is the nose-up leading edge of the front bumper. This design allows a good ramp angle and radiator inlet, but it also rams a lot of air down under the nose. Not only does this usually increase drag, but it also generates a lot of lift, in spite of the bottom-breather radiator inlet. Reported front lift figures were about 120 lb at 100 mph, which can be significant when the static front weight is just over 1100 lb. It also appears that the opened headlight buckets were not as well researched in the wind tunnel as the Corvette's, as they raise the C_x to 0.417. Be that as it may, the pop-off plastic body panel concept means that better aerodynamics can be incorporated easily in the future.

The engine/driveline package doesn't provide much of a story this year. Basically it is GM's transverse 2.5-liter 4-cylinder sitting on a subframe just as it does in the X-car. The cast iron overhead valve engine still puts out an everyday 92 bhp, even

INTRODUCING PONTIAC FIERO

ITS REAL BEAUTY LIES IN THE LOGIC OF ITS DESIGN.

The 1984 Pontiac Fiero is a proud new American car unlike anything else in the world. In basic concept, engineering execution, materials, and assembly technology, the Fiero represents, in many ways, what lies in store for future automotive designs.

- Fiero is the first 2-seat American production car to exploit the advantages of a mid-mounted engine, resulting in excellent weight distribution.
- Fiero's innovative space-frame chassis uses principles gleaned from modern racing car design, giving it strength without excess weight.
- Fiero's innovative Enduraflex™ panels will never rust, the front fenders, door panels and lower quarter panels "give" on minor impacts, and all other panels resist minor dents and dings.
- Fiero's interior is an artful blend of function and comfort, featuring reclining contoured bucket seats with built-in lateral restraint, and full instrumentation including a tachometer.
- Fiero is powered by an efficient* 2.5 liter, 4-cylinder engine with electronic fuel injection.
- Fiero includes a choice of standard manual or available 3-speed automatic transmissions.
- Fiero is equipped with fully independent suspension, rack and pinion steering, power 4-wheel disc brakes and a front stabilizer bar, all standard.
- Fiero offers an available WS6 performance package including special springs and shocks, 14" hi-tech cast aluminum wheels and P215/60R14 Goodyear Eagle GT radials.
- The most beautiful Fiero feature was saved for last. Because from the very start it was designed to be affordable. See why Fiero is one of the deals of the automotive world—at your Pontiac dealer today!

Fiero! A glittering showcase of advanced technology, and a brilliant example of Pontiac innovation in action!

*Pontiac Fiero Sport Coupe with available automatic transmission offers an EPA EST MPG of ㉗ and a highway estimate of 40. Use estimated MPG for comparisons. Your mileage may differ depending on speed, distance, weather. Actual highway mileage lower. Some available equipment shown. Some Pontiacs are equipped with engines produced by other GM divisions, subsidiaries or affiliated companies worldwide. See your Pontiac dealer for details.

PONTIAC FIERO
STYLING ANALYSIS

UNLIKE THE CORVETTE, which had a 30-year tradition to live up to when it was redesigned for 1984, the Pontiac Fiero is an all-new car with a personality to establish. Actually, its personality—that of a simple, efficient, slightly aggressive but very friendly and accommodating machine—was set early in the design process. Using the prevailing GM philosophy of clean, carefully controlled surfaces, Ron Hill's GM Advanced Studio spent just less than one year—December 1978 to October 1979—coming up with a tight, disarmingly simple form that expressed Hulki Aldikacti's mid-engine concept in no uncertain terms.

The concept of separate plastic panels bolted to the space frame structure was the basis for the surface treatment—using body contour lines for the panel joins. This treatment is similar to that employed on the Corvette, with the strong horizontal break line (actually a rising line from nose to tail) used as the meeting point for all the upper and lower surfaces.

A full-size clay model, covered in red Di-noc film to simulate a painted surface, was completed on May 7 and established the direction for all future development. With only detail changes to such items as headlight doors, wheel openings, rear quarter panels and taillights, this form was refined until it was ready to be released to the Production Studio on April 24, 1980. The form developed by the Advanced Studio had already been built in fiberglass and attached to a running chassis in March.

Although the proportions of the car were unlike those of the Corvette, the nose was too similar in character and the design lacked a clear Pontiac identity. When the project was turned over to John Schinella's team in Production, several basic changes were made: The windshield was moved forward, the nose shortened and twin black "bumper" pads added to the front and rear facias.

In the center of the car, attention was given to the quarter-panel detailing just behind the door glass. The Advanced design had this part of the space frame covered with black louvered panels; the Production Studio decided to give this area the appearance of window glass, an esthetic solution but perhaps the one part of the design that was not completely honest in its expression of the structure underneath. Various engine intakes were tried in the lower quarter panels, but these disappeared as the design approached its final configuration. (A much smaller intake reappeared on the left flank as the car neared production.)

First running P-car had Advanced Studio styling.

Intermediate full-size clay model in Production Studio.

In much the same way that the exterior lost its long-nosed sharpness along the path to production, the P-car interior went from a very mechanical, squared-off concept (similar to that used on recent Trans Ams) to a friendlier environment with softer radii on all components. But the modular concept first sketched by Marvin Fisher in 1979 was retained on the final interior design,

TECHNICAL ANALYSIS

with an interesting new iron head casting. A swirl-port intake that brings the fuel-air charge into the cylinder along a spiral path makes its debut in the Fiero. New combustion chamber and piston dome shapes keep the charge swirling (and mixing) until ignition. This has allowed the compression ratio to be increased from 8.2 to 9.0:1, which is surprisingly good these days for an engine without a knock sensor.

Otherwise there are very few modifications to the driveline and subframe assembly. The transverse transmission is available as either a 3-speed automatic with lockup converter and 3.18 final drive, or a 4-speed manual with top gear ratio options. Only the "performance" ratio with a 4.10 final drive is of interest to the enthusiast, as the 3.32 gear coupled with a 0.73 4th gear is suitable only for economy runs. The X-car axles are used as-is, including the constant-velocity outer U-joints.

The engine subframe, however, is not a straight interchange with the X-car. At the rear, the rails had to be kicked up to provide a better rear ramp angle. (In the front-drive X-car these rails connect to the floor pan at the firewall.) And the front rails have had the mount bushings rotated from a horizontal plane to a vertical plane. This allows the subframe to pivot downward about the front mount bolts for easier engine removal. To absorb engine torque reactions, an upper strut connects the cylinder head with a sheet metal bracket on the right rear shock tower. All of these subframe and strut mounts are well insulated with rubber bushings, which are great for isolating road and engine vibrations from the passengers, but don't do a lot for handling.

The front suspension is taken almost *in toto* from the Pontiac T-1000. Although not originally designed for a sports car, this particular short- and long-arm configuration is not too bad for this application. The major modifications were to widen the interconnecting subframe to give a 2-in. wider track and to relocate the shock absorber mounts. On the T-car, the shock mounts to the upper arm and stands very high in the wheel well. But to lower the Fiero's hoodline, the shock now mounts to an otherwise standard lower arm. Basically, this is a good design, especially with the contemporary practice of leading steer arms. But somewhere in the translation a little too much bump steer seems to have been allowed, causing more steering wheel feedback than we are used to.

Part of the feedback can be attributed to non-assisted steering—which I prefer. Early in the design it was decided that the low front weight made assisted steering unnecessary in most circumstances. The worst situation is parallel parking with the optional wide tires. In this case the effort is noticeable though not unreasonable.

At the rear, the suspension is essentially indistinguishable from the X-car's front layout. Even the trailing steer arms are there, although in the Fiero they are anchored to the subframe via tie rods that can still be adjusted for toe-in. The combination of leading front steer arms and trailing rear non-steer arms should give excellent cornering compliance understeer properties. Only a couple of really finicky evaluators have perceived a slight yaw overshoot, which could be because of lateral bushing compliance in the engine/suspension subframe. Otherwise, the handling properties are excellent, with an easily correctable drop-throttle oversteer when cornering at the limit. The reported roll angle of 3.5 degrees per g is reasonable, considering the front anti-roll bar is only 23.0 mm and there is none at the rear.

John Schinella. *Ron Hill.*

Bill Scott.

albeit in a much less severe form. The main instruments were grouped in a pod just above the steering wheel, with fingertip controls extending toward the rim at both sides. With a very wide tunnel required for the central fuel tank, the interior console was made deliberately high to provide proper armrest height.

In April 1980 the Interior Concept Studio transferred the project to the Pontiac Interior team, then led by Pat Furey. Fisher stayed with the project as a unifying influence and was thus probably the man most directly involved with the entire development. Bill Scott took over direction of the Interior Studio in 1981, his important contributions being the previously mentioned softening of all the component edges, improved seat contouring (admittedly Porsche inspired), new door panel and grab handle design, and the replacement of the dark charcoal interior color with fresher, contrasting tones in either gray or saddle combinations.

Analyzing the production Fiero's exterior and interior design, and their contributions to the car as a market entity, one can see that a fine balance has been struck between an aggressive sports car look and a more relaxed, inviting appearance that promises comfort and convenience. The car is not brutal in any way but it nevertheless looks purposeful and efficient. It doesn't directly resemble any other car on the market and therefore doesn't rely on arbitrary details for personality. (Bertone's X1/9 is an obvious choice for comparison, but the similarity is confined to the basic proportions inherent in the transverse mid-engine layout; the basically excellent Italian design, now nine years old, is sharp-edged and narrow, with many tacked-on details, while the Fiero has a wide, almost squat look with much smoother surfaces.)

Perhaps to avoid too heavy a look, the Fiero has extremely large wheel openings, which can only partly be explained as providing room for larger tires in the future. I feel that these openings are important in giving the car its agile appearance, enhanced by the extremely attractive pattern of the special-equipment 14-in. aluminum wheels. The 13-in. base wheel, with a hubcap and 18 slots around the perimeter, is just too tame, while the 13-in. aluminum wheel has a slightly dated appearance.

Obviously, the system of bolting the plastic body panels to the space frame allows almost complete freedom in incorporating future changes, whether they are detail modifications to distinguish additions to the Fiero range (such as the V-6 promised for 1985) or completely new body contours for the future. The dual nature of the car, as mentioned before, can be taken to Jekyll and Hyde extremes if the designers are given carte blanche in developing specialized versions. An example is the one-off spider produced in only four weeks by the studio as a teaser to the journalists who attended the Fiero preview at Sears Point in June. Pontiac engineers have said they don't intend to cut the top off the rigid space frame for any production models, but that won't prevent the aftermarket shops from doing it. The 1984 Fiero is a fairly basic design with immediate appeal—and all the ingredients for a long romance with enthusiasts of widely differing intentions.

—*Jonathan Thompson*

A wide track helps, naturally, but not the reported 19.5-in. center of gravity, which seems high for a car this size.

A new disc brake system also appears for the first time on the Fiero. Pontiac's adapting two existing front suspension systems to the front and rear of this car results in 4-wheel discs, but not 4-wheel calipers. Because the rear requires a mechanical emergency brake, a standard front caliper could not be used. These new single-piston aluminum calipers are essentially identical front and rear, except for the rear emergency brake clamp, and a slight variation in piston bore size for brake balance. A conventional proportioning valve limits rear wheel lockup, although the Fiero may have almost the ultimate configuration for ideal braking. Given the static rear weight bias, and the reported cg/wheelbase ratio, the forward weight shift in braking will give an excellent dynamic balance. Other braking advantages in the Fiero are the central fuel tank, central seating and minimal luggage capacity. This means that no matter how the car is loaded, the optimum brake balance will hardly vary.

In a lightweight car without a power assisted steering option, one might ask why power assisted brakes are standard. The first explanation given was a lack of space in the pedal area for the necessary mechanical leverage. A second reason was an unexpected "knock-back" problem with the 4-wheel discs, which use up too much pedal travel. One hopes this will be sorted out eventually, allowing a non-boosted system and the resultant quicker response.

The standard wheels and tires are fairly conventional P185/80R-13 steel radials on 5½-in. wide steel rims. These provide low rolling drag for fuel economy and contribute to a low base price. However, those hoping to upgrade the appearance of their Fiero will opt for the same-size turbo-finned aluminum wheels. And true enthusiasts will demand the "high-tech" 14 x 6 in. aluminum wheels with P215/60R-14 Eagle GTs. There appears to be plenty of room for expansion in the wheel wells. Pontiac engineers present at the introduction confessed that they hope to have a 50-section tire option available next year. Of course, even if the extra-wide wheels didn't fit, it wouldn't be difficult to add optional flared fender panels.

The optional Eagle GTs are the main ingredient in the WS6 special performance package, which also includes stiffer front springs, stiffer front and rear shocks, stiffer rubber mounts and bushings but no change in the standard front anti-roll bar. For quicker steering response, the steering rack is mounted more rigidly, and a rubber link in the steering shaft is stiffer.

The stated goal in the performance package was to make the Fiero equivalent in every respect to the Firebird WS6 option, but it was fairly obvious that they hadn't met that objective. The transient response is excellent, though not exactly what you might like in a true sports car. The problem in transferring handling technology from the Firebird is the basic difference in weight distribution and wheelbase. With springs and bushings selected to avoid vibrations and freeway pitch oscillation, this doesn't allow much flexibility for response tuning—so far.

Technically speaking, what Pontiac has for the enthusiast is a diamond in the rough with microscopic flaws. Remember, the stated justification for the Fiero was that it be a relatively high-volume, economical commuter car. At that, they have succeeded admirably. Now they can spend a couple of years tuning it with option packages to satisfy the closet racer. The potential is exciting. They have all the pieces in the right places, so now someone just has to come along with slightly better pieces. If there are a lot of people out there who regret not having bought (and kept) one of the first 1953 Corvettes, this is a second chance.—*Paul Van Valkenburgh*

PONTIAC FIERO S/E

Ready, willing and (pretty darn) able

PHOTOS BY JEFFREY R. ZWART

It's not often that we test a completely new car, one without any antecedents whatsoever. The Fiero is such a car, without precedent at Pontiac, only the second 2-seater from General Motors and absolutely alone as a U.S.-built mid-engine car. One could ask whether it took a lot of courage for Pontiac to put it into production, or whether its appeal and potential are so strong that the GM division is on to a sure thing. Its novel construction and method of manufacture (see accompanying articles) required a huge investment of money as well as brainpower, and it's obvious that this product is intended to meet the challenges of European and Japanese industry head-on. The sleeping giant is not only stirring, it's stretching its muscles.

Known as the P-car project within GM, as well as to the press during the several years that its development was being revealed in bits and pieces, the 2-seat, mid-engine, 4-cylinder coupe has the designation 2M4 and the marketing name Fiero. An Italian word, *fiero* means "proud" or "dignified." The first definition is appropriate, as the Pontiac engineers, designers and production staff have given their all in bringing it to market; as for the second—well, the car may be just a bit too much fun for that.

In all, R&T staff members drove seven or eight different examples of the Fiero, most of them only briefly but three of them for extended mileage in varying conditions that included race track time at Sears Point, long-distance touring and quick around-town runs. All of the Fieros were pilot machines, that is, cars assembled in advance of regular production but built at the plant from the same machinery at a slower introductory pace. As a result, we noted several problems in the fit or operation of minor components, mostly in the interior, but as none of these problems occurred on more than one car, we didn't feel they were inherent design shortcomings.

At first look, the Fiero says, "Like me." Its size, proportions and styling all generate immediate appeal and we didn't encounter anyone who disliked its appearance. Being built with the X-car drivetrain, it is a wide car at 68.9 in., considering its 93.4-in. wheelbase. This, especially when combined with the P215/60R-14 Eagle GT tires and large wheel houses, gives it a feisty appearance, but an overly aggressive impact is avoided by the smooth, harmonious body contours. (We may see a bit more brawn expressed by the exterior when the higher-performance 2.9-liter turbocharged V-6 version makes its debut, probably as a 1985 model.) The entire body is plastic, of several types varying in rigidity and flexibility; the surfaces and paint were uniformly good as was the panel fit—especially significant given Pontiac's unique mill-and-drill process for maintaining close tolerances at the attachment points. There is little visual evidence of Pontiac heritage: the Fiero badge is all new (although somewhat reminiscent of the Trans Am's hood chicken in the graphic representation of the winged horse) while division identity is confined to the word Pontiac recessed into the left headlight door and rear facia, and the triangular company emblems on the ➤

AT A GLANCE	Pontiac Fiero	Fiat X1/9	Mazda RX-7
List price	est $9000	$15,990	$10,895
Curb weight, lb	2590	2160	2445
Engine	inline-4	inline-4	2-rotor Wankel
Transmission	4-sp M	5-sp M	5-sp M
0–60 mph, sec	11.6	12.4	9.7
Standing ¼ mi, sec	18.2	18.6	17.1
Speed at end of ¼ mi, mph	72.5	72.0	80.5
Stopping distance from 60 mph, ft	150	141	151
Interior noise at 50 mph, dBA	68	73	71
Lateral acceleration, g	0.812	0.772	0.767
Slalom speed, mph	60.6	60.7	58.6
Fuel economy, mpg	25.0	27.0	21.0
Issue		1983 S&GT[1]	1983 S&GT[1]

[1] Road & Track's Guide to Sports & GT cars

B-pillars. The twin black bumper pads front and rear give a variation on the Pontiac split-grille look and avoid any confusion with Chevrolet styling practice (early P-car prototypes were dangerously close to Chevrolet character).

The pleasing exterior is followed up very well by an inviting and accommodating interior. Again, the car's width is significant; it certainly allows the amount of room that American car owners are used to, side-to-side and fore-and-aft if not in height. The low seats, with substantial bolsters for lateral support, make getting in a little difficult on the driver's side; the passenger, with no wheel to fit his legs under, has no problem. The cloth upholstery, available in either gray or tan schemes in a narrow range of tones, imparts a richness without trying to achieve a luxury appearance. The Fiero comes as either a base model (what Pontiac calls entry-level) or with the S/E package. The former is somewhat spartan, designed as a price leader, and we feel almost every buyer will want the S/E model, with significantly more truly usable equipment.

The instrument pod, positioned close to the steering wheel with headlight, interior light, rear-window heater and rear deck release switches near the driver's fingers, has large, round, traditional dials for tachometer and speedometer, with the pointers well emphasized in orange. Fuel, water temperature and alternator gauges are included but none for oil pressure, one of the several functions in the warning light display. The steering wheel has a nice fat rim and the driver's right hand drops right onto the gear lever, angled toward the left because of the great width (10 in.) of the console. The console is high, intentionally so to provide a natural armrest, and includes the electric window and mirror controls, as well as *two* ashtrays (the In joke at Pontiac engineering is that project chief Hulki Aldikacti, an inveterate smoker, required them). At the front of the console is the housing for the heater/ventilation/air conditioning controls and the Delco AM/FM stereo receiver and cassette, which has seek-and-scan buttons and a graphic equalizer. The a/c system produced lots of airflow in every mode in the best American manner, while the radio was enhanced by stereo speakers in each headrest (the signal can be moved to the two dash-mounted speakers by the balance knob).

The test car was equipped with almost every option on the Fiero list (in addition to those already mentioned): cruise control, electric door locks, door map pockets, carpeted mats, sun visor vanity mirror, tinted glass, and multi-cycle windshield wipers, the last-named with the strongest, most effective washer spray we've encountered. Items not on the car tested but which we experienced on other examples were the 3-speed automatic transmission (good enough if you absolutely refuse to shift gears), rear deck luggage rack (useful, considering the very limited luggage volume behind the engine, if somewhat spoiling the car's lines) and rear-opening/removable glass roof panel (offering as close to open-air driving as possible with the full space-frame upper structure).

The main chassis option, which we consider necessary to the Fiero's appeal, is the WS6 suspension package. This consists of stiffer springs and shocks front and rear, 14-in. cast aluminum wheels of great visual as well as technical impact, and the already mentioned 215/60 Eagle GT tires. Despite the light loading at the front (approximately 1200 lb with driver and fuel) there is a heavy steering effort when the car is stationary or moving slowly; nevertheless, Pontiac's decision not to use power assist is applauded, as the steering is very good at high speed. The turning circle is an unwieldy 38.9 ft and bump steer is really noticed on irregular roads; otherwise placement is precise and driver confidence quickly earned. Adhesion is excellent, with 0.812g recorded in the skidpad test and 60.6 mph achieved in the slalom. With moderate understeer, the technique on winding roads is to go in deep, balance the car with the brakes, and power through, all the while maintaining a high average speed. Without achieving the nimbleness of, say, the Fiat X1/9, the Fiero chassis is an excellent combination of handling and ride.

Really rough surfaces, and such things as speed bumps and Botts dots, will send jolts through the system that are mostly felt in the steering. Overall, the Fiero has a capable and confidence-building comportment with the WS6 suspension. The brakes add to this; our overall rating is very good despite a slight lockup at the rear under panic braking. The car on which we recorded the stopping distances was noticeably worse in this respect than several other examples tried later, so it is likely that these figures would be better for most Fieros.

It's good that the Fiero behaves so sportingly when flung about, because the engine (the old "Iron Duke" 2.5-liter 4-cylinder in X-car transverse configuration, moved to the back) is just barely powerful enough to please. The 92-bhp unit only revs to 5000 rpm and there are only four widely spaced gears, so you can't get any thrills running it up to redline and snapping it into the next gear. In fairness, there is enough torque, a respectable 134 lb-ft at 2800 rpm, available through a wide enough band to keep the car moving along strongly without a lot of shifting. When you do lose speed and come down a gear there's a short band of usable revs before you have to shift up again. The initial feeling is one of frustration just as you get the thing going, but after awhile you tend to rely on the good torque to provide a steady if unspectacular reprise.

Although notchy, the shift lever worked well; reverse is hard to find until you learn to shove it forcibly to the left. Acceleration from zero came out a full second slower than Pontiac promises with the standard 3.32:1 final drive (0–60 mph in 11.6 versus a quoted 10.5) so we really don't recommend the high-mileage ratio of 2.42, which allows Pontiac to estimate a highway consumption figure of 50 mpg (a nice round number) and help its CAFE standings. We achieved an overall average of 25.0 mpg in our fairly strenuous use, including a best run of 28.5 cruising at 70–75 mph; probably 30–32 mpg could be achieved at an average nearer 60. Again, this is well below Pontiac's projected EPA number of 42.

As a commuter car (its original rationale when conceived in the late Seventies) the Fiero is already an attractive proposition, with the looks, comfort and quality to reach a wide range of buyers. (One can easily imagine, for instance, a long-time Pontiac owner approving it for a college-age son or daughter when the thought of a Fiat makes him shudder!) Young working couples without children might find it ideal, while it could appeal to almost anyone as a second car for runabout and pleasure use. High performance enthusiasts have two choices: get Pontiac's super-duty engine preparation booklet and the appropriate over-the-counter parts for 140–160 bhp modifications, or wait for the 2.9-liter V-6 versions, one of which is a turbo with 180 bhp and claimed acceleration to 60 mph in the 6-second range. The V-6s are expected for the 1985 model year. In the meantime, we think Pontiac was wise in concentrating on getting the basic car right; we found few serious objections to its concept or operation and welcome its addition to the ranks of affordable machines for enthusiast drivers.

How affordable? Pontiac has been talking about an approximate $9000 base price, although it had not committed to any exact figure by press time. We would also have to estimate the cost of the S/E version and the various desirable options on our test car at $1500–$2000; we would certainly be pleased if a fully equipped S/E came in under $11,000. If so, Pontiac has a winner. The Fiero doesn't compete directly with any other car, but the Mazda RX-7 and Fiat (sorry—Bertone) X1/9 have to be considered. The former has much better power and more of a sports car feel; the latter is an extremely agile driver's car without a lot of power. What the Fiero provides is an extremely desirable base for any of a number of exciting 2-seater applications; as its originator Hulki Aldikacti said, it is good athletic raw material waiting to be trained for special uses. One can easily imagine what doubling the horsepower will do for it; certainly Corvette, Ferrari, Porsche and other high performance car engineers can expect a major challenge.

ROAD TEST PONTIAC FIERO S/E

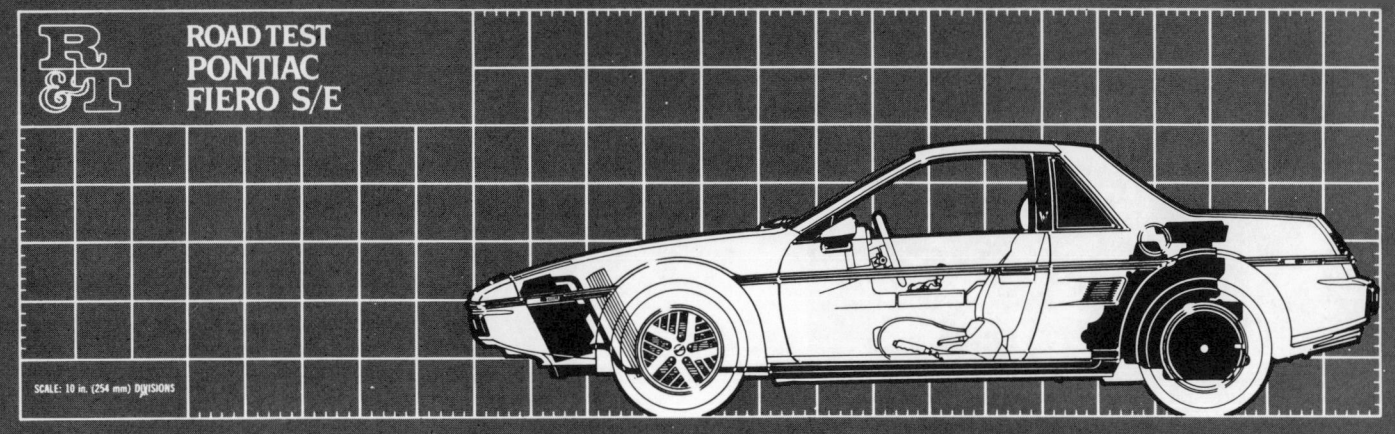

SCALE: 10 in. (254 mm) DIVISIONS

PRICE
- List price, POE Detroit .... est $9000
- Price as tested .... est $11,000
- Price as tested includes air conditioning, handling package (alloy wheels, P215/60R-14 tires, heavy-duty springs), elect. window lifts, leather and sheep-skin seat covers, AM/FM stereo/cassette, central door locking, elect. adj mirrors.

MANUFACTURER
Pontiac Motor Division, One Pontiac Plaza, Pontiac, Mich. 48053

GENERAL
- Curb weight, lb/kg 2590 1176
- Test weight 2770 1258
- Weight dist (with driver), f/r, % 44/56
- Wheelbase, in./mm 93.4 2372
- Track, front/rear .... 57.8/58.7 ... 1468/1492
- Length 160.3 4072
- Width 68.9 1750
- Height 46.9 1191
- Ground clearance 6.0 152
- Overhang, f/r .... 36.2/30.7 ...... 920/780
- Trunk space, cu ft/liters 6.8 192
- Fuel capacity, U.S. gal./liters .. 10.2 39

ACCOMMODATION
- Seating capacity, persons 2
- Head room, in./mm 36.5 927
- Seat width .... 2 x 18.5 .... 2 x 470
- Seatback adjustment, deg 40

ENGINE
- Type .... ohv inline-4
- Bore x stroke, in./mm ..... 4.00 x 3.00 .. 101.6 x 76.2
- Displacement, cu in./cc 151 2471
- Compression ratio 9.0:1
- Bhp @ rpm, SAE net/kW .... 92/69 @ 4000
-   Equivalent mph / km/h 83/134
- Torque @ rpm, lb-ft/Nm .... 134/182 @ 2800
-   Equivalent mph / km/h 58/93
- Fuel injection .... GM TBI
- Fuel requirement .... unleaded, 91-oct
- Exhaust-emission control equipment: 3-way catalytic converter, oxygen sensor, exhaust-gas recirculation

DRIVETRAIN
- Transmission .... 4-sp manual
- Gear ratios: 4th (0.81) 3.32:1
-   3rd (1.24) 5.08:1
-   2nd (1.95) 8.00:1
-   1st (3.53) 14.47:1
- Final drive (rear axle ratio x transfer ratio) 4.10:1

INSTRUMENTATION
Instruments: 85-mph speedometer, 6000-rpm tach, 999,999.9 odo, 9999.9 trip odo, coolant temp, voltmeter, fuel level
Warning lights: oil press., handbrake/brake system, check engine, door ajar, rear deck ajar, upshift, seatbelts, hazard, high beam, directionals

CHASSIS & BODY
- Layout .... mid engine/rear drive
- Body/frame .... separate; fiberglass panels/steel unit chassis
- Brake system ..... 9.7-in. (247-mm) discs front and rear; vacuum assisted
- Swept area, sq in./sq cm 343 2212
- Wheels .... cast alloy, 14 x 6
- Tires .... Goodyear Eagle GT, P215/60R-14
- Steering type .... rack & pinion
-   Overall ratio 19.2:1
-   Turns, lock-to-lock 2.9
-   Turning circle, ft/m .... 38.9 .... 11.9
- Front suspension: upper and lower A-arms, coil springs, tube shocks, anti-roll bar
- Rear suspension: Chapman struts, lower A-arms, tie-rods, coil springs, tube shocks

CALCULATED DATA
- Lb/bhp (test weight) 30.1
- Mph/1000 rpm (4th gear) 20.7
- Engine revs/mi (60 mph) 2900
- Piston travel, ft/mi 1450
- R&T steering index 1.13
- Brake swept area, sq in./ton 248

ROAD TEST RESULTS

ACCELERATION
Time to distance, sec:
- 0–100 ft 3.4
- 0–500 ft 9.6
- 0–1320 ft (¼ mi) 18.2
- Speed at end of ¼ mi, mph 72.5

Time to speed, sec:
- 0–30 mph 3.2
- 0–50 mph 8.0
- 0–60 mph 11.6
- 0–80 mph 23.2

SPEEDS IN GEARS
- 4th gear (5000 rpm) 103
- 3rd (5000) 68
- 2nd (5000) 43
- 1st (5000) 24

FUEL ECONOMY
- Normal driving, mpg 25.0

HANDLING
- Lateral accel, 100-ft radius, g ... 0.812
- Speed thru 700-ft slalom, mph 60.6

BRAKES
Minimum stopping distances, ft:
- From 60 mph 150
- From 80 mph 289
- Control in panic stop .... good
- Pedal effort for 0.5g stop, lb 21
- Fade: percent increase in pedal effort to maintain 0.5g deceleration in 6 stops from 60 mph 43
- Parking: hold 30% grade? .... yes
- Overall brake rating .... very good

INTERIOR NOISE
- Idle in neutral, dBA 51
- Maximum, 1st gear 84
- Constant 30 mph 64
- 50 mph 68
- 70 mph 73

SPEEDOMETER ERROR
- 30 mph indicated is actually 30.0
- 60 mph 59.0
- 80 mph 79.0

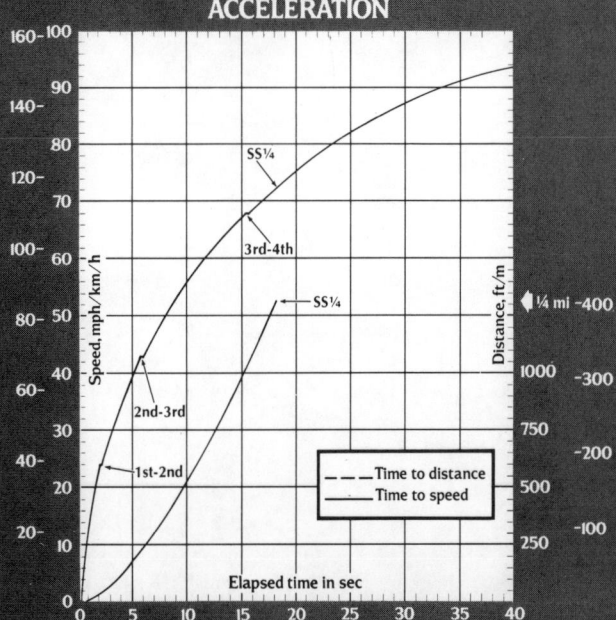

P is for plastic
...and performance

Pontiac's Fiero P-car breaks the Detroit mould with plastic panel body and engine in the middle

by John Lamm

IT'S THE automobile we were beginning to think would never be built. The design was complete and there were running prototypes, but Pontiac's P-car seemed in danger of being stillborn. General Motors' upper management wouldn't give the go-ahead to build a mid-engine sports car at a time when it had to update its product line for the 1980s despite shrinking sales and cash flow. Pontiac countered that it needed an image change to separate it from Buick and Oldsmobile — let them have the large cars for their older buyers and allow Pontiac to produce smaller, sportier machines for a younger market. Eventually the Corporation agreed to let Pontiac make its mid-engine vehicle on the premise that it was really a commuter car.

That pretence disappeared quickly and what Pontiac really has is a sports car, pure and not so simple . . . . the first new mass production, two-seat American sports car since the Thunderbird was introduced in 1955.

Obviously Pontiac took a long look at Fiat's X1/9 and then increased its dimensions slightly for the P-car. While the Italian car is 156.3 inches long on a wheelbase of 86.7 inches, the American measures 160.7 inches overall and 93.4 inches between wheel centres. Height and width for the X1/9 are 46.5 and 61.8 inches, while the Pontiac is 46.9 and 68.9 inches.

Pontiac chose a mid-engine configuration because it wanted to produce an innovative design that could be developed into a serious driver's car — bold thinking in an automotive city

Left: Attractive styling of the Fiero shows a lot of European influence. Inset, left: Very little forward stowage under the bonnet after spare wheel and ancillary equipment is accommodated. Slim rear boot area behind engine compartment (inset, right), is also strictly for soft bags. Driving compartment (centre) is cosy

that spent years trying to satisfy drivers by separating them as completely as possible from the act of driving. The basic philisophy behind the Fiero, as the P-car came to be known, is demonstrated in the interior. There is plenty of room for both driver and passenger. Instrumentation is complete and segregated on a panel ahead of the driver. Non-essential-to-driving controls are mounted at the front of the centre console. The seats are comfortable and offer good support. Everything is so well placed, the car could be Italian if the steering wheel wasn't so logically located.

With the mid-engine layout, the men who shaped the exterior of the Fiero went for a somewhat softened wedge design. The low nose is a "bottom breather", taking in its cooling air below the bumper. And that isn't a bumper in the classic sense, but one that is integrated into the design and covered with the softest of the exterior plastics used on the car, Reaction Injection Moulded Urethane. Other panels, such as the front wings, doors and rear quarter panels, are also made of this more dent-resistant material. Larger panels that need more stiffness because of their size and purpose — front bonnet, engine cover, roof and such — are done in harder Sheet Moulded Compound.

All round the car at its widest point is protection against dents and scratches by some form of moulding or soft plastic. Even the placement and design of these pieces was tested and refined in either Lockheed's or GM's wind tunnel. The final drag coefficient comes out to 0.37, which may not seem too good in light of big Mercedes and Audi saloons but is impressive when you consider it's difficult to streamline smaller vehicles . . . . like trying to catch the air as it flows off the roof without having a rear deck spoiler so high it obstructs rear vision.

That Fiero styling isn't so much a plastic body as it is a collection of panels attached to a spaceframe that is not unlike a rollcage in a racing car. This welded frame approximates the shape of the Fiero, with a floor pan, front and rear structure, door frames and a roof frame. The front suspension is added by way of a subframe, as are the rear suspension and the drive-train.

Making up the front suspension are unequal-length upper and lower control arms, with coil springs and an anti-roll bar. Many of the pieces are adapted from GM's parts pool and provide both the handling Pontiac wanted and the possibility of a low nose profile for the wedge shape. At the back is a MacPherson strut suspension, with the lower arm connected to the rear subframe that doubles as an engine cradle

Left: Basic Fiero steel space frame surrounded by the plastic panels added to create the sleek body style. Larger panels — front bonnet, engine cover and roof are made of harder Sheet Moulded Compound for added stiffness

Left: Pontiac took a close look at Fiat's X1/9 when deciding dimensions for the Fiero

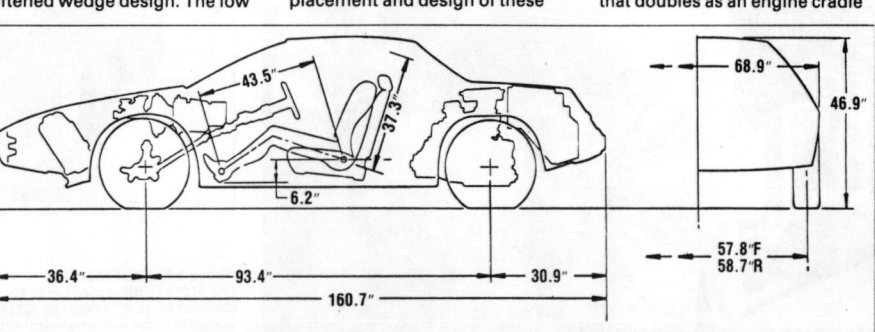

P is for plastic
continued

and is mounted through bushings to help isolate engine noise and vibration. This is essentially the engine cradle from the corporation's front-drive X- and A-models (such as Chevrolet's Citation and Celebrity) moved to the rear, with the steering tie rods now controlling toe-in. There is an optional suspension with slightly firmer springs and shock absorber valving and 14-inch aluminium alloy wheels with P215/R60-14 Goodyear Eagle GT tyres instead of the stock P185/80R13s.

With no engine weight in front, the 19.1:1 ratio rack and pinion steering does not have power assistance. Disc brakes are used front and rear, with aluminium calipers and semi-metallic pads.

As different-for-Detroit as much of the Fiero may be, the engine is pure Motown: GM's standard cast-iron, overhead-valve, 2.5-litre in-line four. This is a rugged, reliable engine that only suffers by comparison to the image of the remainder of the Fiero. With a new cylinder head and a number of computer controls on the engine — including a form of throttle body injection — the engine now produces 92 bhp at 4,000 rpm and 134 lb-ft of torque at 2,800 rpm. And that's low-rolling power, with no point in running well up the red range, where the engine gets noisy and feels overburdened and uncomfortable.

Like the engine cradle that carries it, the engine/transmission package is essentially from the X- and A-cars, so the Fiero suffers their limited transmissions choices: a four-speed manual or a three-speed automatic behind an engine that needs an extra cog in each of those gearboxes. One 4-speed version has a "high mileage" final drive gear and Pontiac claim that one will get 50 miles per US gallon in the US government's high mileage test, and 37 mpg when the "feds" average city and highway mileage numbers. Unfortunately, Pontiac also admits to needing 12.5 seconds to get that Fiero to 60 mph. With the "lower" final drive ratio, the 4-speed Fiero is a 60 in 11.5 seconds and has a combined mpg figure of 31 mpg. The automatic transmission version does 0-60 in 12.7 seconds.

There are already the pieces available to modify the four cylinder for more horsepower. A some point in the future (at least two years away) there will be a V6 version of the Fiero, possibly with a sleeveless aluminium block, à la Mercedes' and Porsche's V8s. And there's talk of turbocharging.

But even without the extra power the Fiero is, with the new Corvette, one of the most interesting new cars from Detroit in the past decade.

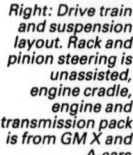

Right: Drive train and suspension layout. Rack and pinion steering is unassisted, engine cradle, engine and transmission pack is from GM X and A-cars

Making a Fiero

THE MANNER in which the Fiero is manufactured is about as unconventional as the car itself. The basis for the spaceframe "underbody" is six major components including the floor, door frames, roof and front and rear structure. These and all the other bits that go into the frame are welded in place, 40 per cent of that done by robots or other automatic welding devices.

Over the 600lb spaceframe are bolted the plastic body panels that make up the exterior of the Fiero. Using the old methods, the mounting holes for the body panels would have been drilled before the spaceframe was welded together. With the distortion in welding and then the need to fit and adjust the panels, the system would have been tedious and not necessarily have produced a quality fit and finish.

Pontiac's answer is a huge "mill and drill" machine. Each Fiero spaceframe is fed into the device to have the 39 mounting pads for the plastic panels drilled for the mounting screw holes and then milled down to the corre

Above left: Steel spaceframe meets up with the engine/suspension pack on the line at the Pontiac plant. Above: Adding the roof panel. Honeycomb in nose is covered by soft "design integrated" bumper panel. Special drilling rig ensures accurate fit for bolt on plastic seen (right) at a pre-production trial fitting

Driving the Fiero

JUST FIVE years ago Pontiac would have introduced its new Fiero sports car on the company's own turf: its massive proving ground north-west of Detroit. But with several years of hard times, GM's corporate attitude has changed, and is less insular than in the past. So Pontiac sent its new Fiero and the men and women who would write about it up the California coast from San Francisco, then inland to Sears Point Raceway to give the car a real world test. The company even brought along former World Champion Phil Hill, who did some consulting work with Pontiac during the final stages of the car's ride and handling development. My, how times have changed!

One of the first things you notice when getting into the Fiero is how easy it is to do just that. Once in, it quickly becomes obvious that the men who planned, engineered and developed the Fiero know what it takes to provide a real driver's car. All the details are about right: the steering wheel is at the proper height and angle, leather-wrapped for a good grip and with spokes for a correct 3 and 9 o'clock grip. You can heel-and-toe with the pedals. The seats offer good lateral support, so you won't risk falling out of them when cornering hard.

And that's something you can do with the Fiero. The basic handling trait is mild understeer, but the driver won't be hindered by it as in many past Detroit automobiles. If you like you can take it to a neutral attitude or even mild oversteer, but never into trouble unless you cause it yourself. Phil Hill makes an interesting comment that this is one of the rare American cars that has equally good manners and abilities on both a race track and the open road .... including rough surfaces, long a nemesis for Detroit products. Motown has had a tendency to equate upgraded handling with firmer springs and shock absorbers and thick anti-roll bars, which then lead to a correspondingly firmer ride. Not so with the Fiero, which has a very supple, comfortable ride. Even with the optional WS6 handling package it remains quite smooth.

The steering, which feels heavy when you first drive off in the car, ends up having a very acceptable effort and very good road feel for an American car. The brakes are more than adequate for a car of the Fiero's accelerative abilities.

Which leads to the one disappointment on the Fiero, and that's performance. As a commuter car to get around town the 2.5-litre engine offers enough power, but not if you like to get off into the country and put your boot in it.

Once past the problem of power, however, the Fiero becomes the most enjoyable GM car this side of a Corvette. It's not only good looking, but comfortable, with surprisingly little noise when you consider the engine is just over your shoulder. □

Left: Handling of the Fiero is neutral with a touch of mild oversteer

height. Those mounting pads are sheet metal blocks ¾ inch square and ½ inch high that are filled with an epoxy compound. Once the last holes have been drilled in the frame, it goes through its various anti-corrosion treatments.

Next, the front suspension and rear suspension/drive-train sub-frame are added, as is almost everything but the interior and the exterior panels. The result is a naked-but-driveable chassis.

While all this is happening, the body panels are sent through the paint booths in a fixture that has them mounted in the same relative position they will be on the car to assure an even look to the car's finish once the panels are on it. The last coat sprayed on is a clear one that Pontiac claim will equalize the way the paint looks when new and how it will weather on the different plastic panels.

Finally, the panels are bolted to the spaceframe, unlike the similar Matra Murena, to which most of the body panels are glued. And the Matra is virtually a handbuilt car, while Pontiac expect to produce 100,000 Fieros each year.

Taking a lesson from the Japanese, Dr W. Edwards Deming, the American statistician and management consultant, was hired to help make the Fiero factory as efficient as possible. Pontiac even altered the social structure inside the factory. No more executive park places or dining rooms are used, and management is even encouraged to dress in casual clothes. Quite a change for General Motors. □

Left: The mid-engined Fiero is claimed to have a ride quality that is good on the rough and the smooth. Above: Instrument display is limited to speedometer, rev counter, coolant temperature and fuel contents guage

PREVIEW TEST

Pontiac Fiero 2M4

Lighting a pilot under burning desire.

Fans of the new and different, rejoice. The P-machine is here at last. Although Pontiac's progeny does bow to convention with seats, doors, a roof, and four wheels, you should be prepared to buckle up for a sharp break from tradition. Consider the particulars:

• The Fiero 2M4 is the antithesis of the corporate-committee car. One man, Hulki Aldikacti, a Turkish-born GM engineer, conceived it as a turning point for the Pontiac Division. He also helped sell the idea to corporate management, directed the design (in an around-the-clock crash program purposely sequestered from Pontiac engineering), supervised the building of the prototypes, and guided the car through the development process.

• The Fiero 2M4 is a mid-engined, rear-wheel-drive two-seater. Detroit has for years toyed with such a layout but has never before manufactured one for sale to the public.

• The Fiero 2M4 is a true sports car. Now that America has two to its credit, the terms "personal-luxury car" and "sporty two-plus-two" will never be quite the same.

• The Fiero 2M4 has bolt-on plastic fenders and an engine bay that is large enough to accommodate a wide variety of powertrains. This combination makes it an ideal blank canvas for future alterations, both inside the factory and outside in the ever resourceful aftermarket.

• The Fiero 2M4 is a thrill to look at, a joy to ride in, and a ball to drive. Its visceral appeal will doubtless teeter the loftily perched Corvette.

Be forewarned that this impressive list of character references must be taken with two grains of salt. First of all, our experiences to date are limited to pilot-built cars, which are never a perfect forecast of what the assembly line will deliver. Second, you should realize that the Fiero burns with a steady flame under the engine lid, but it's nothing even close to a raging inferno. There is 92 net horsepower to work with for the time being, clearly not enough to blast this 2600-pound machine into the acceleration record books.

As luck would have it, though, the Fiero does boast several strengths to carry it through the first year of its life while it awaits the significant horsepower upgrades it so richly deserves. Nowhere else can you buy the true exotic look for less than ten grand. What's more, the Fiero is blessed with its share of that all-important factor, fun-to-drive, even though the power factor isn't what it should be. There's also a purposeful exclusion of practicalities. This good-time Charlie is quite happy to entertain you and a buddy while carrying a bag or two of beer and pretzels in the back, but don't ask it to bring the kids or move that piece of furniture for the mother-in-law. The Fiero deals in charisma, not cargo.

Aldikacti's intention at the very beginning was a sharp departure from the sterile economy cars that sprang forth during Detroit's knee-jerk response to two close-coupled energy crises. For once, the end product of all the high-minded planning sessions has hit the target, if not the bull's-eye. To sell the corporation on this much fun, there were but two prices to pay: early Fieros would have to deliver exemplary fuel efficiency, and, to keep the base price well below $10,000, all would have to be built with as many existing components

(engines, transmissions, suspensions) as possible.

Once Pontiac sealed the bargain with the preposterous-sounding promise of 50 mpg on the EPA highway test, the division's talented Turk was off and running. He filled his shopping cart with Pontiac's own 2.5-liter engine (a.k.a. Iron Duke), two X-car transaxles (a three-speed automatic and a four-speed manual), one front suspension from the Chevette, another from the X-car, seat hardware from the J-car, mirrors from the Firebird, etc., etc.

A few inventions were also necessary. The mill-and-drill process (*C/D*, August) of attaching plastic body panels to a sheet-steel unit-construction underbody is the most important one; Aldikacti claims this was the solution that made plastic competitive in cost with steel at the anticipated volume of 100,000 cars per year. Beyond this, the P-car is really just a very shrewd shuffling of off-the-shelf components. What's so smart about it is that ordinary front-drive hardware has been reassigned to rear duty, creating a sports car that is both exciting and quite different from any other American-made product.

Of course, it's been done elsewhere before—by Fiat with the X1/9 and by Lancia with the Scorpion. If anything, Detroit should be scolded for not having picked up on the plan sooner, particularly when you consider that local assembly lines have been pumping out the proper ingredients—transverse four-cylinder powertrains—for the last six model years.

Even with plenty of time to consider the mid-engined adventure, not all was sweetness and light along the road to invention. The Iron Duke is a faithful but heavy servant, as its cognomen suggests. It wears a throttle-body fuel injector on top, but the rest of this engine is right up there on the sophistication scale with anvils and boat anchors. Moreover, the transaxles are much

PONTIAC FIERO

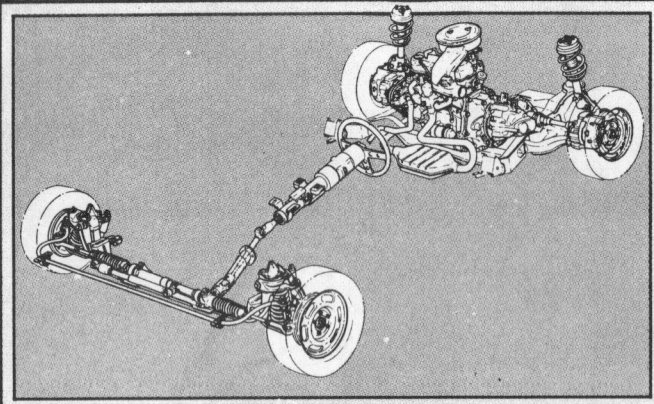

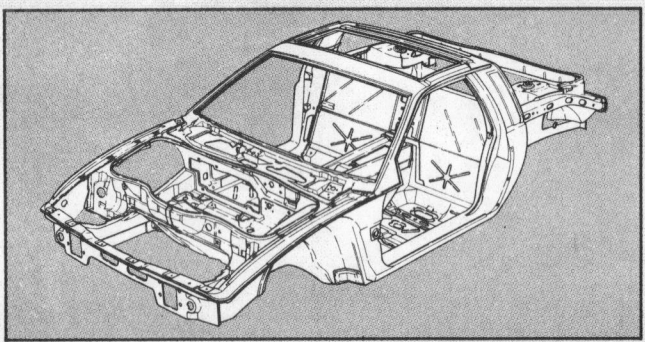

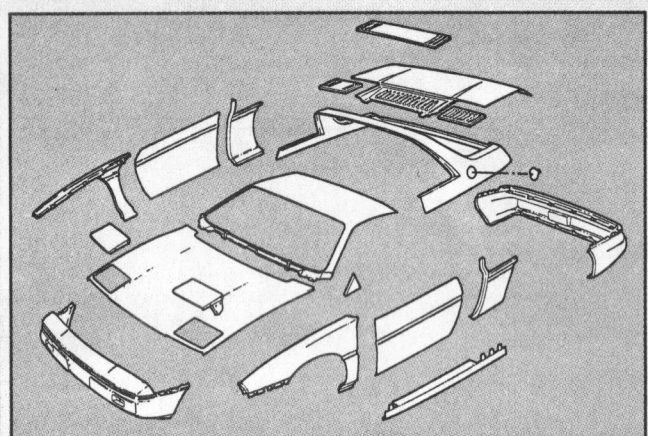

Pontiac's revolutionary building blocks include an X-car powertrain and suspension, a modified T-car front suspension, a unitized steel underbody, and a dozen major molded-plastic body panels.

heavier than Aldikacti would have liked, and he can only dream of a fifth gear somewhere off in the misty future. Such is the lot of an engineer who must pick and choose from shelves that are sadly behind the times.

Still, the beauty here is that the Fiero is not another front-drive floorpan with the back seat lopped off and a pointy nose tacked on. Weight distribution with the back-motor design is a satisfying 43.5 percent front, 56.5 percent rear, and the control-arm front suspension from the Chevette should do well with the 60-series Goodyear Eagle GT tires (originally developed for the Citation X-11). The MacPherson-strut rear suspension has new spring rates, shock valving, and rubber bushings, but is otherwise unaltered from the original X-car configuration. Since there is no steering obligation in back, the tie rods are simply anchored to pivot points on the P-car's perimeter subframe.

As you might imagine, this package is not the epitome of space utilization. The nose is long and low to cut aerodynamic drag (Pontiac spots the drag coefficient at 0.377). The fuel tank is located inside a tunnel that bisects the body, and engine-coolant lines run to the front-mounted radiator along the outer sills. While the mid-engine design might suggest the possibility of two trunks, the forward compartment is chockablock with hardware, leaving room for no more than a small duffel bag. In back, you'll find a well that's wide and deep but very pinched in the fore-and-aft dimension. Pontiac claims it will swallow two regulation-size golf bags; if you wish to carry conventional luggage, you'd be well advised to pack lightly in soft, flexible cases.

Something has to go when the roofline is squeezed down so low (to 46.9 inches, matching the Corvette's overall height), and Pontiac wisely sacrificed luggage room instead of interior space. In fact, the Fiero's cockpit seems all the more inviting because it hugs the road. The knee-high door handle demands a bit of bending, but there's absolutely no aggravation on entry, because the opening is wide and the doorsill is just a micron or so above the pavement. The optional tilt steering column is a great aid to a smooth entrance. Leg space is generous and straight ahead, and a dead pedal has thoughtfully been provided to brace the left foot. Joy upon joy, it's a snap to heel-and-toe without a permission slip from your podiatrist. The mas-

sive doghouse down the middle seems a bit overpowering at first, but it soon becomes an acceptable (if not particularly welcome) shelf for elbows; at least the door-side armrests lie at the same elevation. The shift lever is a bit too far forward for our taste (the knob reaches the wheel plane only at the bottom of the H-pattern), but the feel through the lever is surprisingly transmissionlike, in spite of the fact that cables are actually doing the shifting.

We're not particularly thrilled by the instrument cluster. Although the necessary information is available (except for velocities above 85 mph), the main dials are too small, the designers have selected an awkward mix of round and square openings, and the whole array is spotted a good three inches too low. (Clearly, those who handled this phase of the creation could profit from a crash course at the Porsche school of instrumentation layout.) Otherwise, the interior is pure function wrapped in tasteful trim. Go for the up-level SE interior, and you get a nifty leather-covered steering wheel, genuine pigskin upholstery, and lamb's-fleece inserts down the middle of the well-contoured bucket seats. Step up to the Fiero's killer sound system, and you get a pair of stereo speakers in each headrest.

One might fancy that a simple turn of the key and a punch of the right pedal would snap this illusion of sports-car supremacy into reality, but such is not the case. Escape velocity may be scheduled for next year, but for the time being the Fiero is a victim of its 50-mpg obligations. The best you can do is select the "performance" set of transmission and final-drive gear ratios (which drops the EPA highway fuel economy to 42 mpg). This boosts eagerness at low speeds to nearly acceptable levels, but the combination of short gearing and an engine that goes breathless at 4500 rpm produces more frustration than acceleration. Shift early and wait patiently for the 2.8-liter 60-degree V-6 that's just around the corner.

This year's four-cylinder does, in its own time, deliver you to the point where handling fun begins. The Fiero all but begs to be molded to your under-, over-, or neutral-steer preferences. The nose drifts out mildly as cornering forces build, but it's a simple matter of lifting off the gas pedal for an instant to cut back smartly on the understeer. And then the Fiero is yours to play with as you drift across life's apexes with the greatest of ease. Stiction levels are excellent at 0.81 g.

The steering has much less feel than it should, but the ratio is satisfyingly quick. A power assist is not yet part of the deal (it will be later), but Pontiac has added a hydraulic damper to its rack-and-pinion steering gear in an attempt to limit kickback through the wheel over bumps. This ploy has been only partially successful to date; we found the Fiero's wheel busy over wavy terrain, although the ride is exemplary.

Development is far from finished, so we'd prefer to sit back and watch the Fiero fight its way through the trying stages of early production before passing final judgment. It's clear, however, that there will be some disappointment over the feeble power-to-weight ratios that will hit the streets this fall. Even so,

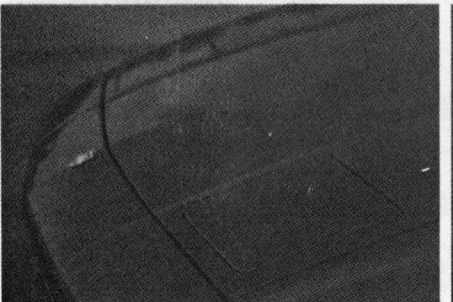

the Fiero's price, gas mileage, handling, and pure sex appeal should carry Pontiac's assault on road boredom to success beyond the General's wildest prognostications. That will set the stage for phase two, when massive horsepower injections will put some fire into the Fiero. So don your Nomex and man the extinguishers: Pontiac's incendiary bomb is aimed squarely at the Japanese, at Porsche, and at the Corvette.

—Don Sherman

Technical Highlights

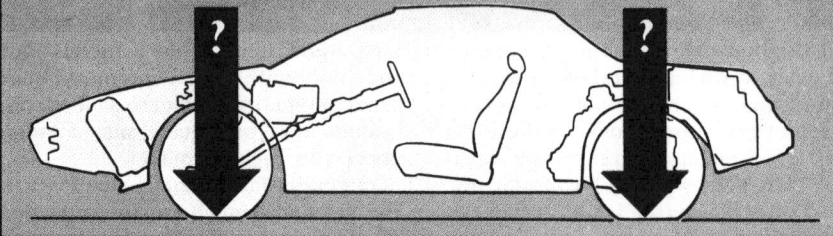

• Although the mid-engine configuration with its attendant rear weight bias is universally accepted as optimal for race cars, a 50/50 weight distribution still has the magic ring when it comes to high-performance street machines. Pontiac has chosen the racing layout for the new Fiero, so it's appropriate to take a hard look at the conventional wisdom.

Since overall performance in any car is dependent on the forces that can be exerted on the pavement, an examination of any aspect of vehicle dynamics must center on the tires and their loading. The simplest case is acceleration. Hard acceleration depends on traction, and traction is a result of vertical forces pressing the tires to the pavement. Obviously, rear-heavy, rear-drive cars and front-heavy, front-drive cars have the advantage. But rear drive holds the edge once the car is in motion, because load transfer during acceleration increases the vertical force on the driving wheels. Conversely, front-drivers lose vertical loading and traction with acceleration.

During braking, optimal traction— and therefore the shortest stopping distances—result from equal loading of all four tires. Although 50/50 seems like the obvious solution, dynamic load transfer must also be taken into account. In the case of the Fiero, with its 93.4-inch wheelbase and 19.5-inch-high center of gravity, about seventeen percent of the total vertical tire load is transferred from the rear to the front tires during a hard (0.8 g) stop. Thus vertical loading changes the weight distribution from the static 43.5 percent front/56.5 percent rear to 60.5/39.5 percent. Although this transfer results in far from equal loading, it's much better than the 67/33 distribution a 50/50 car would have under the same circumstances. Obviously, a nose-heavy, front-drive car would suffer even more. All other parameters being equal, a rear-heavy car has far greater stopping potential.

An extensive General Motors study has shown that 50/50 distribution is best for steady-state cornering in a rear-drive car, although slight variances from perfect balance (say, 51/49 to 49/51 F/R) were not found to be significant. Front-drivers, of course, do not fall within this narrow window, since packaging necessities place too much weight up front.

Most cornering is not done at steady speeds, however, but is combined with acceleration or braking. The result is far more complicated vehicle dynamics. According to the handling experts

we consulted, tire and suspension characteristics are more important than static weight distribution under these circumstances. The engineers report that excellent performance can be achieved over a wide range of weight distributions in both front- and rear-drive configurations.

While the evidence seems confusing at first, certain conclusions can be drawn. The optimal static weight distribution for simultaneous braking and cornering cannot be determined. A strong rear bias with rear drive is far and away the best design for acceleration and braking. Equal front and rear distribution is best for pure cornering, no matter which wheels are driving. When we add up the pluses and minuses, our conclusion is that the best layout for overall performance is rear drive. The ideal weight distribution is impossible to specify to the third decimal, but it lies somewhere between a small rear bias and the long-revered 50/50. —*Csaba Csere*

Vehicle type: mid-engine, rear-wheel-drive, 2-passenger, 2-door coupe

Price as tested: $11,000 (estimated)

Options on test car: base Fiero SE; WS6 special performance suspension; air conditioning; cruise control; power mirrors, windows, and door locks; Delco electronic-tune radio; fleece and pigskin bucket-seat upholstery; tilt steering wheel.

Sound system: Delco AM/FM-stereo radio/cassette, 6 speakers, 7 watts per channel

ENGINE
Type . . . . 4-in-line, iron block and head
Bore x stroke . . . . 4.00 x 3.00 in, 101.6 x 76.2mm
Displacement . . . . 150.8 cu in, 2471cc
Compression ratio 9.0:1
Fuel system . . . . 1x1-bbl Rochester throttle-body fuel injection
Emissions controls . . . . . 3-way catalytic converter, feedback fuel-air-ratio control, EGR, auxiliary air pump
Valve gear . . . . pushrods, hydraulic lifters
Power (SAE net) . . . . 92 bhp @ 4000 rpm
Torque (SAE net) . . . . 134 lbs-ft @ 2800 rpm
Redline . . . . 5000 rpm

DRIVETRAIN
Transmission 4-speed
Final-drive ratio 4.10:1

Gear	Ratio	Mph/1000 rpm	Max. test speed
I	3.53	4.8	24 mph (5000 rpm)
II	1.95	8.7	43 mph (5000 rpm)
III	1.24	13.6	68 mph (5000 rpm)
IV	0.81	20.9	104 mph (5000 rpm)

DIMENSIONS AND CAPACITIES
Wheelbase . . . . 93.4 in
Track, F/R . . . . 57.8/58.7 in
Length . . . . 160.7 in
Width . . . . 68.9 in
Height . . . . 46.9 in
Frontal area . . . . 18.6 sq ft
Ground clearance . . . . 5.4 in
Curb weight . . . . 2581 lbs
Weight distribution, F/R 43.5/56.5%
Fuel capacity . . . . 10.2 gal
Oil capacity . . . . 3.0 qt
Water capacity . . . . 13.7 qt

CHASSIS/BODY
Type . . . . unit construction with 1 rubber-isolated powertrain cradle
Body material . . . . molded plastic

INTERIOR
SAE volume, front seat . . . . 51 cu ft
  trunk space . . . . 6 cu ft
Front seats . . . . bucket
Recliner type . . . . ratchet
General comfort . . . . poor fair good **excellent**
Fore-and-aft support . . . . poor fair **good** excellent
Lateral support . . . . poor fair good **excellent**

SUSPENSION
F: . . . . ind, unequal-length control arms, coil springs, anti-sway bar
R: . . . . ind, MacPherson strut, coil springs

STEERING
Type . . . . rack-and-pinion with hydraulic damper
Turns lock-to-lock 3.2
Turning circle curb-to-curb . . . . 39.9 ft

BRAKES
F: . . . . 9.7 x 0.4-in disc, aluminum calipers
R: . . . . 9.7 x 0.5-in disc, aluminum calipers
Power assist . . . . vacuum

WHEELS AND TIRES
Wheel size . . . . 6.0 x 14 in
Wheel type . . . . cast aluminum
Tire make and size . . . . Goodyear Eagle GT, P215/60R-14
Test inflation pressures, F/R . . . . 30/30 psi

CAR AND DRIVER TEST RESULTS

ACCELERATION .... Seconds
Zero to 30 mph 3.4
  40 mph 5.5
  50 mph 8.4
  60 mph 10.9
  70 mph 16.7
  80 mph 23.6
  90 mph 33.6
Standing ¼-mile . . . . 18.1 sec @ 74 mph
Top speed . . . . 104 mph

BRAKING
70–0 mph @ impending lockup . . . . 210 ft
Modulation . . . . poor **fair** good excellent
Fade . . . . none **moderate** heavy
Front-rear balance . . . . poor fair **good**

HANDLING
Roadholding, 282-ft-dia skidpad . . . . 0.81 g
Understeer . . . . minimal **moderate** excessive

FUEL ECONOMY
EPA city driving . . . . 26 mpg
EPA highway driving . . . . 42 mpg
EPA combined driving . . . . 31 mpg
C/D observed fuel economy . . . . 23 mpg

INTERIOR SOUND LEVEL
Idle . . . . 52 dBA
Full-throttle acceleration . . . . 78 dBA
70-mph cruising . . . . 73 dBA
70-mph coasting . . . . 72 dBA

DESIGN ANALYSIS

Forging the Fiero

The pride of Pontiac design.

BY JEAN LINDAMOOD

General Motors design-studio chiefs Ron Hill and John Schinella have seen the dream of a lifetime come true. They have designed a sports car for the masses.

The Pontiac Fiero started life, however, with an altogether different mission. In December 1978, when the project was assigned to Hill's ten-member GM Advanced Design Three studio, the P-car was to be a high-mileage commuter car that would showcase a nonsheet-metal skin and revolutionary construction methods. Hill's team did not have an all-new sports car to design, but it did face the challenge of creating a new and completely different kind of vehicle. "We weren't making a new Corvette or a new Firebird," explains Hill, a 28-year veteran of GM design, "so there were no family-identity problems. It was a completely new thing; therefore, we were able to put it together relatively unbiased and without a lot of people around with their fingers in the pie."

The Fiero was especially exciting to Schinella and his staff of fifteen designers, clay modelers, and engineers at the Pontiac Two studio, whose job it was to give the Advanced Three study a distinct Pontiac identity. This was one project that would not be shared with any other GM division.

GM's design staff apparently does its best work when there are only a few fingers in the pie. It took the two studios just thirteen months to roll out a running prototype, and in another two and a half months the production design was completed. In comparison, Firebird/Camaro gestation lasted six years.

When Advanced Three first got the

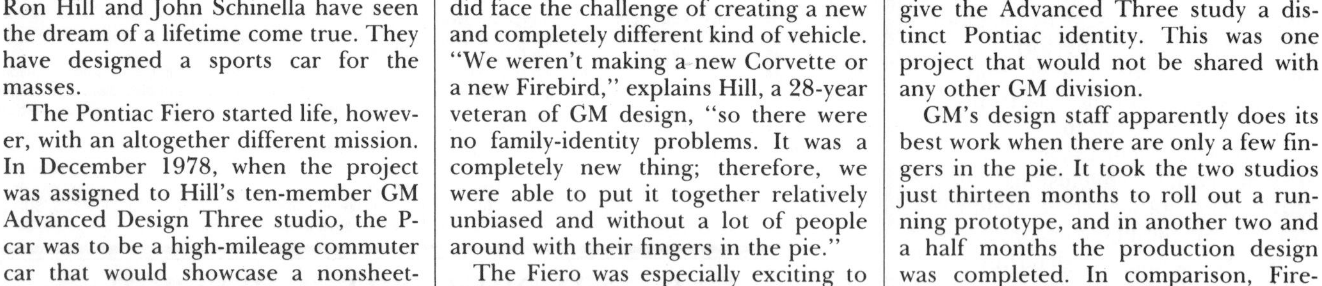

Advanced Design Three's early Fiero model posed outside of the GM Design Center with the competition in 1979: a TR7, an X1/9, and an RX-7.

Feat of clay: Advanced Design Three's full-size clay model of the mid-engine P-car project in one of its earliest developmental stages.

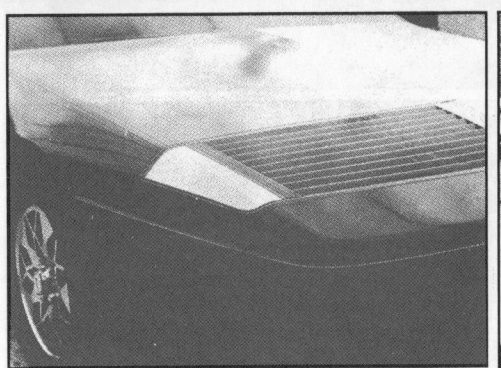

At one point, Advanced Three considered wraparound parking and turn-signal lamps (above), hood-located air intakes, and a flying-buttress rear end (right).

The bubble back (left) was desirable from an aerodynamic standpoint but too expensive. Another Advanced Design study (above) sported windowless B-pillars and a heavy cut line around the car's middle.

Fiero project from Pontiac's Advanced Vehicle Concepts group, the drivetrain and suspension configurations, and consequently the width, had already been established. Seating was also worked out, since the engineering group had decided to house the fuel tank and the service lines in a central tunnel.

Three critical design issues remained to be addressed. First, should the Fiero have a fastback or a notchback? Although some sleek fastback designs were considered, Hill's group was forced by cost and weight constraints to go with a notchback, the most practical design for exhausting engine heat away from the passenger compartment.

Second, Pontiac's new "spaceframe" underbody construction technique necessitated cut-lines between the car's main body panels. Instead of trying to make the Fiero appear seamless, Advanced Three carefully incorporated the cuts of the deck lids and doors into the overall design.

A third problem sprang from engineering's plan to use two different materials in place of sheetmetal: reaction-injection-molded urethane (RIM) on the car's upper half, and thermoplastic olefin (TPO) on the bottom. (The production car actually makes use of *four* different plastics: RIM, TPO, sheet molding compound, and reinforced reaction-injection-molded urethane.) Advanced Three avoided a potentially sloppy meeting of the plastics by carving a deep crease around the car's middle to divide the RIM panels from the TPO panels neatly and decisively. Later in the program, the mix of materials changed, and the crease was toned down with a black rub strip.

According to Hill, a consensus on the Fiero shape was reached quickly. Instead of the usual proliferation of scale models, just one was made and sent to

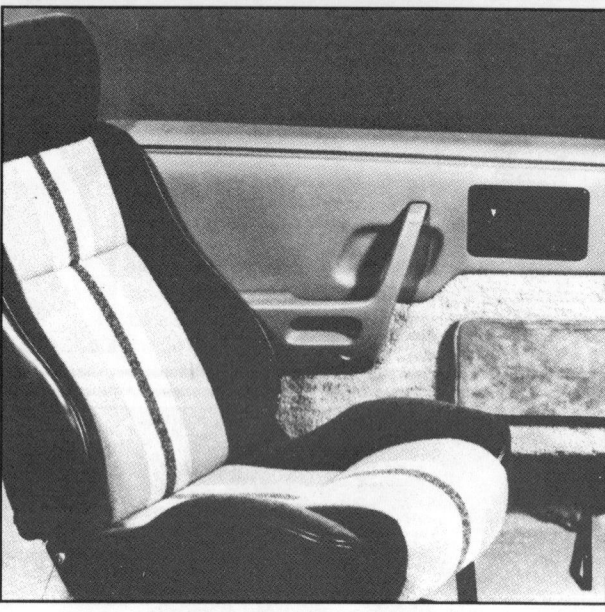

Upper left: Interior Concepts studio's first attempt to work out a general positioning of the Fiero controls. Instrumentation begins to take shape (upper right) in this early foam-core mock-up. First clay-model interior (left) from Pontiac Interior studio shows more refined surfacing, unique Fiero instrumentation. Bill Scott's group refined seats, doors (above), and added A-car armrest.

the Cal Tech wind tunnel for testing. The bulk of the design work was done over the course of nine months in dozens of small sketches, in eight or ten full-size tape drawings, and on one constantly changing full-size clay model. On September 21, 1979, Advanced Three sent its proposal to Hulki Aldikacti, project manager, chief engineer, and godfather of the Fiero.

Aldikacti, bound and determined to see the Fiero in the hands of the public, decided that the only way to sell the corporation on his mid-engined two-seater was to build a running prototype that the top brass could see, touch, and drive. He broke form, blew the budget, and ordered a roller model from Entech, an outside fabrication shop. Six months later, a drivable Fiero was presented for corporate review. Aldikacti's bold strategy worked, and on April 24, 1980, Schinella's studio received the go-ahead—and a six-week deadline—to get the Fiero ready for 1982-model production.

In the meantime, John Shettler's Interior Concepts studio and Pat Furey's Pontiac Interior studio were already eight months into the program. A look at some of their earliest aircraft-style hardware and floating-pod-instrumentation proposals indicates each man's involvement in the 1984 Corvette and 1982 Camaro/Firebird interiors.

Until another Corvette principal, Bill Scott, took over the Pontiac Interior studio in 1981, the color scheme for the Fiero cockpit was basic black, with a limited amount of color in the seats and the doors, the objective being to avoid a proliferation of parts. Scott's main contribution was to lighten up the cabin with a choice of two-tone brown or two-tone charcoal materials, in deference to Pontiac's expected Sunbelt market. Scott also brought the Fiero's instrumentation and controls in line with the rest of the Pontiac range, refined the Fiero's contoured seats, and scrapped

FORGING THE FIERO

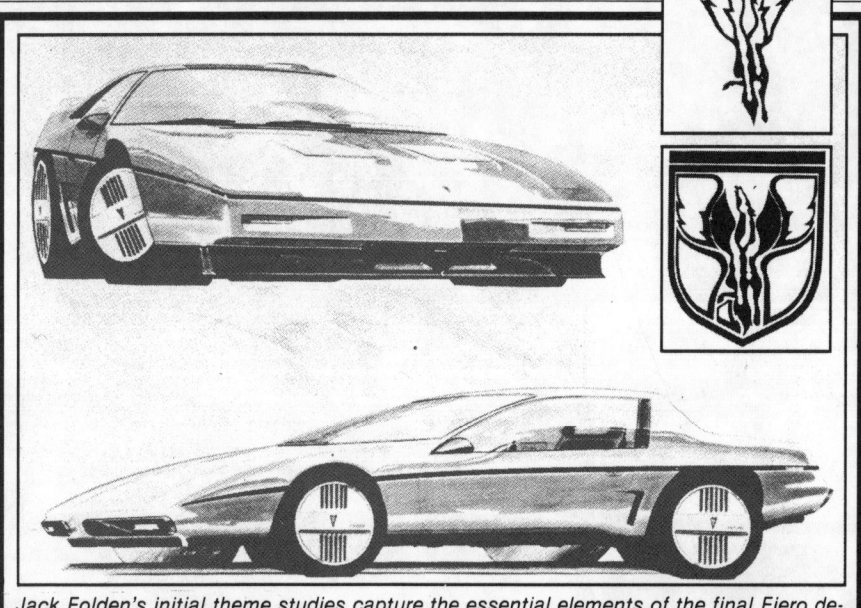
Jack Folden's initial theme studies capture the essential elements of the final Fiero design. Insets: Evolutionary work on Fiero crest done by interior designer Jon Albert.

Rear-end review: The solid taillamp strip in lower sketch inspired the 1984 Fiero rear.

Pontiac Two design team, from left: assistant chief designer Jack Folden, Bob Menking, and chief designer John Schinella.

Chief design executive Jack Humbert chose this bold, thrusting Jack Folden sketch to epitomize the hot-blooded personality of the new Fiero.

the pull strap on the door in favor of the combination armrest and grip from the Pontiac 6000.

"When we got the Fiero from Advanced Three," says John Schinella, "it was an exciting concept, but it didn't have a Pontiac face." In a flurry of sketches, Schinella's Pontiac Two group lopped five inches off the front of the Fiero, shifted its cockpit forward to emphasize the mid-engine design, raked back the windshield, and tipped the entire wedge shape forward for a more pleasing overall proportion.

"The original beltline of the car swept up to the hood from the sides, which was a counterthrust to its basic wedge shape," says Schinella. "We put more wedge in the beltline so it dived toward the front." The taillight area was also moved forward so that the rear bumper would neither add to the length of the car nor look like an afterthought.

"We wanted the car tight and lean," continues Schinella. "All the details are integrated into the rub strip: the side turn-signal markers, the door handles, and the lock cylinders. When Fisher Body balked at the potential for fit-and-finish and trim-alignment problems, I told them that was the way the Europeans did it—but I never did find a European example of this hidden-hardware idea." The rear end was treated the same way: reflectors were integrated into the bumper pads, and the taillights were stretched out behind an unbroken, neutral-density strip across the rear.

Pontiac's part in the Fiero design was over in a mere six weeks. "It was an incredible thing," says Schinella. "Everyone said, 'Yeah! That's it!' when they saw our first proposals. There wasn't a hitch in the system." Schinella credits Jack Humbert, GM's chief design executive, with establishing the Fiero's final overall theme: "Jack is from the GTO era, when Pontiac had flair. He was the Wide Track person. He felt the Fiero should be strong, and when he chose sketches, he chose the ones with the strongest feelings: nose-down, wheels-close-to-the-body stuff." Schinella also says that Humbert chose the twin bumpers front and rear to project the traditional twin Pontiac theme.

When the price of gasoline dropped and the car market started to shift back toward performance, the Fiero introduction was delayed, giving Pontiac time to retrench and reevaluate the Fiero's commuter-car image. A host of spicy ingredients was baked into the product: a new suspension option with fourteen-inch wheels, the latest plastic-panel manufacturing techniques, a broader assortment of interior-trim levels, and a new intake for engine-cooling air. The finished product is, without a doubt, Pontiac's most important car to date. Says Schinella, "There was a tremendous amount of emotional excitement in the studio during the course of the program, because everyone knew they were creating a car that they wanted to buy, that they could all relate to."

What started life as a lowly commuter car is now brimming with performance potential. We can relate to that, too. ●

Both ends against the

THE PRETTY little mid-engined car was standing nose-to-nose with the turbocharged front-wheel-drive coupé. The prices, no doubt, would be similar, but the cars could not have been more different.

In Europe, or here at home? Not at all. We were taking pictures of two very important new models inside the vast General Motors Technical Centre, north of Detroit – and one of the cars was a Chrysler! It was quite unreal. For a moment, I was even reminded of the White Queen, in *Alice Through the Looking Glass*: "Why, sometimes I've believed as many as six impossible things before breakfast!"

Impossible? Well, if not, it was highly improbable... For one thing, the mid-engined sports car came from General Motors, and the turbocharged coupé was from Chrysler, who might have gone out of business only a few years ago.

Five years ago, I'm sure, either car would have been unthinkable. GM were still a monolithic concern building millions of mass-market saloons and showed little tendency even to understand small, nimble, good-looking two-seaters; Chrysler, the third-biggest US car maker, were staggering from financial crisis to financial crisis; their cars were boring, and conventional, and their market share was slipping away.

We can thank the Arabs, and the second oil price upheaval of 1978/1979, for the revolution which has overtaken Detroit in recent years, and remember that the energy-conscious US government in Washington reacted as you would expect. In recent years American cars have become much smaller, rather slower, and closer in many ways to the European and Japanese competition. The problem was that sales, and domestic market share, fell away as fast as the new cars lost weight and inches. Eventually Detroit had to face it – the swing to interesting imported cars was permanent.

Even so, the arrival of cars like the Fiero and the Laser/Daytona is atonishing by any previous American experience, and they made their respective debuts just a few days apart. The P-Car (as Fiero was known throughout its development period) unashamedly faced up to imported cars like the Fiat X1/9, whereas Chrysler's G24 (which became Laser/Daytona) was Lee Iacocca's answer to the Mustangs and Capris built by his old company, Ford of Detroit.

In basic form, the Fiero and the Laser/Daytona models will appeal to a similar class of US motorist – who will want European standards of handling, compact dimensions, a full range of equipment and a price tag of less than 10,000 dollars (7,000 approx.) – though they seek to satisfy it in completely different ways.

The white Pontiac Fiero meets the black Chrysler Laser nose to nose. The Pontiac's pop-up headlamps and smooth bonnet line are in contrast to the Laser's more conventional appearance. Only the 2M4 versions of the Fiero have the rear spoiler, which is standard on all Laser versions

centre

Prize fight — mid-engined Pontiac Fiero v. front-drive Chrysler Laser. Two European-inspired American sporting cars that break Detroit traditions

By Graham Robson

Let's look at the Chrysler Laser/Dodge Daytona models first — effectively these are the same cars, but with different badging, decoration, wheels, and aerodynamic packages. Their very existence can be credited to chairman Lee Iacocca, who arrived at Chrysler in 1979, having been ousted from Ford, by Henry Ford II, a few months earlier. Chrysler, not to mince words, were staring bankruptcy in the face, and not only needed massive financial aid (which the US government eventually provided), but needed interesting new models to transform their stodgy image.

There was no one better than Lee Iacocca to tackle this job. In the 1960s, of course, he had masterminded the evolution of the original Ford Mustang, and the development of Ford's "Total Performance" image. He was a fighter and, more important still, he was known to like sporting cars.

The Laser is a transverse-engined front-wheel-drive machine. That, in itself, was not new to Chrysler (the original Horizon, Simca/Chrysler/Talbot based, was announced in 1977, and the basic engine chosen had been a new design in 1980), nor was the fact that it was a generously-dimensioned 2+2 seater coupé with a lift-back (for there had been Dodge Omni coupé derivatives of the Horizon since 1978). What *was* new was the combination of so many features — smart new styling, suitably tarted up for the more expensive (Dodge-badged) cars, a very modern facia layout littered with electronic aids, and a turbocharging option for both Chrysler and Dodge models.

For the record, the engine is a single overhead-cam 2,213 c.c. unit, offering 98 bhp in fuel-injected form, or an excellent 142 bhp in turbocharged guise. Naturally they have "end-on" transmissions, a choice of three-speed automatic (found on most cars, including the Laser I sampled) or five-speed manual transmissions. Quite a lot of the detail engineering comes from Chrysler's latest E-body saloons, the pressed-steel unit-construction body shell, the MacPherson strut front suspension, and the "dead" rear axle being entirely conventional in that respect.

By comparison, the Pontiac Fiero is not conventional at all. Pontiac management, so the legend goes, got approval for P-Car by calling it a commuter car, but that doesn't fool people for too long. The GM management are not so foolish as to miss its real significance — as a real image changer for Pontiac, who were in need of a showroom boost.

They make no bones about looking closely at the Fiat X1/9 for their inspiration. They didn't need Italian help to style the body (which was done at the Tech Centre, where all GM cars take shape), even though the

Laser v. Fiero
continued

Fiat's packaging was obviously a real guide to save them time. Like the Fiat, the engine/transmission/suspension cradle is essentially that of a front-wheel-drive car (in this case, GM's X- and A-body models) transplanted to the rear, while the engine/transmission installation is that used, in front-wheel-drive form, in several other GM cars, such as the Chevrolet Citation and the Pontiac 6000.

Pontiac don't like you to realise that the only engine available in the exciting looking Fiero is the very basic, cast-iron, 92 bhp "Iron Duke" — a four-cylinder overhead-valve lump of 2,471 c.c., with a very long history, and original birth as a half of a Pontiac V8 — for which there is no option at the time of writing. One day, they say, turbocharging may appear, or even a new lightweight V6 engine more suited to the car's character.

On the other hand, they are extremely proud of the car's looks, and of its body construction. Every skin panel bolts into place and carries no stress and different types of plastic, mostly injection moulded materials, are used for each of them.

It's a two-seater, pure and simple. The Fiero looks as if it ought to be as quick as a Lotus Esprit or a Ferrari Mondial, but has a lot of trouble keeping up with the more powerful Detroit saloons. It also looks as if there ought to be a Targa roof, but nothing can be removed. It looks as if it should be built in Italy — but it is built in the industrial grime of Pontiac, Michigan.

Though both have sporty pretensions, neither the Fiero nor the Laser behaves like a tuned sports car. The Fiero (especially with automatic transmission, fitted to the car I drove) is simply not fast enough to make much of a fuss (one would make mincemeat of it with an MG Metro, I'm sure . . .), and the Laser is too civilized, too tamed, to stir up the adrenalin. On the evidence of a day's driving, the Laser XE (the XE referring to the 142 bhp engine tune, complete with turbocharging) is a much quicker car. The Fiero's engine behaves as I would have expected a normal Detroit-iron unit to behave — reliably, without fuss, without character, and without sounding at all like a thoroughbred; on the plus side, however, very little noise gets into the passenger compartment, which is often a bug-bear of mid-engined cars.

The turbocharged Laser has quite a bit of get-up-and-go. There is a bit of turbo lag, but not nearly as much — say — as on the highly tuned Mustang SVO; my feeling is that, like Saab, Chrysler have chosen a relatively small turbo, and made sure that it begins to work well down the speed band of the engine.

The Fiero handles — well, exactly like you'd expect a good mid-engined sports coupé to handle. There is no power-assisted steering on the car — very strange, this, on a modern American car — but apart from the need for handling at parking speeds, that is not a drawback. The tendency is for the car to understeer slightly, but it changes direction easily, and instantly, with very little roll, and no "rubber" in the chain of command.

Part of the trick, of course, was to provide a compact (93.4in.) wheelbase; the other, for sure, was to offer 215/60R-14 Goodyear Eagle GT tyres, which look, and feel, just like like the NCTs on my own Capri 2.8i.

Laser handling is less thoroughbred, obviously front-wheel-drive, but still very well-balanced, flat-riding, and controlled by all previous Detroit standards; this confirmed my immediate impression when arriving in North America in 1983, that apart from the attitude to spirited driving, the motoring was becoming much more "European" with every year that passes.

On the Laser XE, the same trick has been applied, but this time the Goodyear Eagles are of 195/60R-15 section. It means that unless you are caught out — or foolhardy — grip seems limitless, and you merely have to point the car where you want to go. No wallow, no squash, no need to "aim-off" by a couple of feet.

On this car there is power-assisted steering, and I guess it was essential to take care of the front end weight. There was noticeable "shunt" in the drive line when going from power-on to power-off conditions, and on the sort of long, long corner you encounter when clover-leafing off an urban freeway, to back off the throttle meant that the nose tucked in again noticeably, if not sharply.

In the Laser, though, it was not the way the car went, but what it provided, which took our attention. A lot more space than the Fiero, naturally (2+ seating is at least as spacious as that of a European Capri), a well-equipped instrument display, electrical button release of the hatchback lid and the fuel filler flap. Unfortunately there was also one of those do-gooding electronic voices to remind about everything (including, if the engine stalled: "Your keys are in the ignition" — Gosh, thanks!). To our joy, we found a way of shutting him up by pressing the right sequence of buttons to get "Mute Engaged" on the electronic display.

Attractive to Europeans? Why not. The Fiero would do nicely if it could be made a little more lively, and the Laser/Daytona would appeal to the same sort of motorists who buy cars like the sporting Toyotas and Datsuns. Take your choice.

My own? Surprising, no doubt, but I found the front-wheel-drive Chrysler, with its 2+2 seating and hatchback, far more practical, and just as appealing, than the mid-engined two-seater Fiero. □

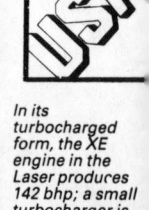

In its turbocharged form, the XE engine in the Laser produces 142 bhp; a small turbocharger is used in order to get good low-speed response

There is nothing very sophisticated about Pontiac's ever-faithful "Iron Duke" 2.5-litre engine; the Fiero may one day get a new lightweight V6

The Laser's electronic trip computer is backed up with a synthesized voice system which, thankfully, you can switch off

Could this be the Fiero we have been waiting for?

Pontiac Fiero Turbo

by Ron Grable

PHOTOGRAPHY BY RICH COX

Overheard at enthusiast magazine watercoolers around the country:
"Needs more power."
"Great car—downhill."
"Mundane performance."
"Please, Pontiac—a bigger engine." "Excellent, except for the anemic engine."

Enthusiast appraisal of the Pontiac Fiero has been uniformly critical of the engine power. The Fiero's aggressive appearance promises performance, with 2-seater, short wheelbase, mid-engine, aerodynamic flair—then delivers straight ahead on a par with your basic run-of-the-mill J-car. It is downright embarrassing to be handed your lunch (at a stoplight GP) by a Nissan Pulsar NX Turbo.

This scenario is tailormade for aftermarket wizards to jump in with a cure for the horsepower-deficiency blues. Many have done so and offer any number of different methods to increase the power of the Pontiac Fiero—from exhaust headers to nitrous oxide. Naturally, there are plenty of turbochargers in this mix. Turbocharging offers many advantages, since it retains the basically standard engine, and doesn't hurt fuel economy too drastically (unless the boost is used all the time). Bolting on a turbo and twisting the wastegate screw until it makes a million horsepower is an approach used by some aftermarket companies, but as soon as the customer gets one block from the shop with his Fast-Fiero, they won't be able to remember his name—and warranty is a dirty word.

Pfaff Turbo Systems, of San Jose, California, is doing two things to make it a little easier for the person considering voiding his factory warranty and then living with the ominous Quotation that must legally accompany noncertified aftermarket turbo installations in California: "Legal in California only for racing vehicles which may never be used upon a highway." First, Pfaff has applied for certification for its Fiero turbo kit. If it meets the requirements and is granted certification by CARB (California Air Resources Board), then its Fiero installations will be legally exempt from the "racing only" requirement. This means cars with the Pfaff kits will be legal vehicles (sellable, able to pass a smog check, etc.) in California. It could also mean the kits will be offered as options by Pontiac dealers who will install them at dealerships and include the kit cost in the purchase price. More on this later.

Second, to address the warranty question, Pfaff will offer a service contract, included in the Turbo-Kit purchase price, which will duplicate the OEM (Original Equipment Manufacturer) powertrain warranty. Such repairs will be handled by any dealership (but preferably the installing dealer), exactly as if they were OEM warranty claims. Could be a hell of a deal, *if* all the pieces fall into place.

The turbo system itself is quite sophisticated for an aftermarket kit and features a separate electronic control module that shares the control load with the Pontiac ECM. A cast iron exhaust manifold feeds the IHI (Ishi Kawajima Harima) turbo and the high-pressure air from the compressor discharge feeds into a cast aluminum plenum fitted to the Pontiac throttle body injector. Early in the development program, it became obvious that the stock TBI could not flow enough fuel (58 lb/hr for roughly 100 hp) to handle the increased engine demands, so two Bosch D-Jetronic mechanical injectors were fitted to the intake manifold. The increased fuel-flow capability (40 additional lb/hr) raised the potential of the engine to the 150/160-hp range.

The Pfaff ECM pre-empts the Pontiac unit at a certain boost level—in our test car it was set to take over as the boost reached the positive scale. After taking over from the stock ECM, the Pfaff unit begins to use the Bosch injectors to flow fuel as a function of both boost and engine speed. The Pfaff ECM also determines spark advance requirements based on the boost/vacuum and engine speed relationships. The Pontiac ECM retains control of the TBI fuel flow, as well as all the engine control func-

Pfaff is giving the consumer a little more pizzaz for his Fiero

tions, at any condition below positive boost.

Our test car came to us straight from some CARB testing, and was fitted with a manual spark control (shades of the old Model T Ford) and an electronic motherboard for determining fuel/air ratios at various engine speeds. We didn't use the mother-board, but found the spark control almost as much fun as a boost knob. The turbo A/R ratio (area of the turbine inlet divided by the radius of the turbine wheel) has been well chosen to give a responsive, low-lag power curve. At full throttle, manifold pressure will go positive at approximately 1800 rpm and reach its maximum boost of 7 psi at 2600 rpm.

The added power completely changes the character of the Fiero, and finally it is what it should be. Straightline performance is now in the Nissan 300ZX/Ford SVO/Pontiac Firebird/Dodge Daytona Turbo Z arena—0-60 in the low 8-sec range. The added power highlights the lack of a 5th gear, and engine redline in 4th gear comes all too quickly, but the passing performance at freeway cruise is great. Passing on twisty two-lane roads is no longer a terrifying gamble, because a little preplanning—to get the boost up before pulling out to pass—reduces your exposure time into the 5/6-sec bracket. After driving the Fiero for a while, we developed an acceleration technique that entailed partial throttle (one half to three fourths) until the boost came up to approximately 5 psi followed by throttle modulation to maintain the boost at the desired level. This allows control of engine power without getting into the wastegate cycle, which occurs at full throttle, and makes for much smoother and more progressive operation.

Performance Comparison		
	Standard Fiero	Turbo Fiero
0-30 mph	3.23 sec	2.70 sec
0-40 mph	5.75 sec	4.06 sec
0-50 mph	7.86 sec	6.24 sec
0-60 mph	10.86 sec	8.49 sec
0-70 mph	13.89 sec	12.10 sec
Quarter mile	17.91 sec/73.8 mph	16.55 sec/81.3 mph
Lateral acceleration	0.78 g	0.79 g
Slalom	6.71 sec	6.68 sec

Driving this rig deep into a corner requires nerves of steel and a "necker knob"—remember those?

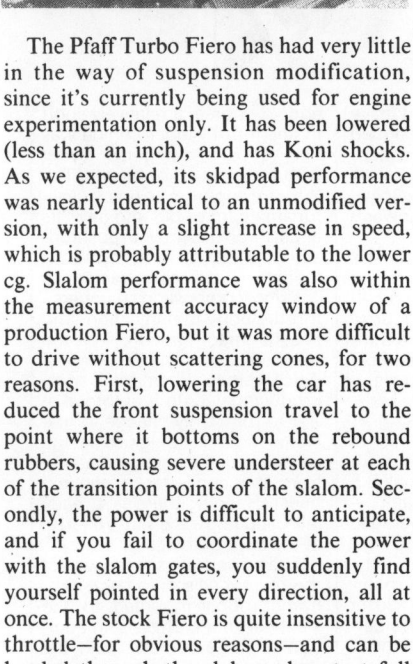

The Pfaff Turbo Fiero has had very little in the way of suspension modification, since it's currently being used for engine experimentation only. It has been lowered (less than an inch), and has Koni shocks. As we expected, its skidpad performance was nearly identical to an unmodified version, with only a slight increase in speed, which is probably attributable to the lower cg. Slalom performance was also within the measurement accuracy window of a production Fiero, but it was more difficult to drive without scattering cones, for two reasons. First, lowering the car has reduced the front suspension travel to the point where it bottoms on the rebound rubbers, causing severe understeer at each of the transition points of the slalom. Secondly, the power is difficult to anticipate, and if you fail to coordinate the power with the slalom gates, you suddenly find yourself pointed in every direction, all at once. The stock Fiero is quite insensitive to throttle—for obvious reasons—and can be herded through the slalom almost at full chat, once the correct entry speed has been established.

The standard Fiero has a condition called dropped-throttle oversteer, which describes a corner entry situation requiring sudden throttle closure, and a resultant vehicle oversteer which can be unstable. Dropped-throttle steering is the rear wheels undergoing toe-in changes as the engine torque reverses direction (sudden throttle closure). The toe changes are attributable to rear suspension geometry and the compliances associated with the engine/transaxle cradle. The increased engine power of the Turbo Fiero magnifies the compliance effects, and driving this rig deep into a corner requires nerves of steel and a "necker knob"—remember those? Seriously, folks, the increased torque moves the engine around so much that the cast aluminum intake plenum is banging into the electronic ignition module mounted on the firewall—a good 4 in. away. Stiffer bushings in the suspension and engine mounting system would help reduce these effects and make the car more linear and predictable.

So, the way this all works out, not too surprisingly, is that more power requires better suspension. Then the increased cornering capability will allow still more power, which in turn requires better suspension, and so on and so on and so on.

Anyway, the Pontiac Fiero offers a natural platform for increased engine power. We are already seeing a great deal of interest from the aftermarket manufacturers, trying to get to market with a good, reliable, cost effective method to give the consumer a little more pizzaz for his Fiero. We personally think exhaust turbocharging is the best approach to the job, and consider the Pfaff Turbo a well-thought-out system, considered in the narrow sense of what it does for engine performance. The folks at Pfaff have addressed the question of reliability with their Service Contract, and if the proper certification is forthcoming from CARB and they are successful in lobbying the Pontiac dealers to market the system through the dealer chain—the sky's the limit. But as we noted earlier, improvements in engine performance are going to have to be accompanied by suspension upgrades for the Fiero to realize its true potential.

Pontiac division is watching with interest—from afar—and sees the whole situation as negotiations between two independent business groups (Pfaff Turbo and the PMD dealers). PMD cannot officially endorse any aftermarket company, but you can be certain that responsible parties are monitoring the progress of all the many companies making goodies for their little jewel. Pontiac is rightfully proud of the Fiero and doesn't want anybody bolting on anything that can possibly tarnish the image. Sort of like the Queen of England worrying about Koo Stark and Prince Andy. /MT

SPECIFICATIONS

Pfaff Turbo Pontiac Fiero

GENERAL
- Body type .... 2-pass., 2-door coupe
- Base price $9695

ENGINE
- Type & displacement .... Transverse L-4, 2471 cc (151 cu in.)
- Bore & stroke .... 101.6 x 76.2 mm (4.00 x 3.00 in.)
- Induction system .... Rochester throttle body fuel injection, IHI turbocharger
- Max. power (SAE net) .... 140 hp (est.) @ 4000 rpm
- Max. torque (SAE net) .... 155 lb-ft (est.) @ 2800 rpm
- Recommended fuel .... 91 RON unleaded

DRIVETRAIN
- Transmission .... 4-sp. man.
- Final drive 3.32:1

CHASSIS
- Front .... Independent, coil springs, anti-roll bar
- Rear .... Independent, MacPherson struts, coil springs
- Brakes, f/r .... 9.7-in. discs, power assist
- Steering type .... Rack and pinion
- Turns, lock to lock 4.1
- Wheels .... 14 x 6.0 in., cast aluminum
- Tires .... P215/60VR14, Goodyear Eagle GT

DIMENSIONS
- Curb weight .... 1123.4 kg (2480 lb)
- Wheelbase .... 2372 mm (93.4 in.)
- Length .... 4072 mm (160.7 in.)
- Width .... 1750 mm (68.9 in.)
- Height .... 1191 mm (46.9 in.)
- Power to weight ratio .... 17.7 lb/hp
- Fuel capacity .... 38.6 L (10.2 gal)

American Express

Above: light and airy feel. Good passenger accommodation but no glove box. Left: neat instruments well laid out but appalling reflections on the glasses

AS THE Midday heat pushed the ambient temperature up into the high twenties we cranked up the air conditioning on Pontiac's stylish mid-engined sports car and headed off in the bright-red Fiero towards Belgium's Grand Prix circuits — Zolder, and the famous road track at Spa. Argue that road cars always disappoint on the track if you like, but we were keen to get to know this American-born baby supercar in exciting surroundings.

Over the brow and past the mass of black rubber streaks on Zolder's compact starting grid, the Fiero manages 85 mph on the short straight before we brake hard for a sharp, slightly banked left bend. The car turns in without drama. Was this — General Motors' most ambitious attempt at a sports car — *really* developed in Detroit, home of mushy handling, slushy autos and super-light power-steering?

The bend opens out but the "Iron Duke" engine behind the seats has little punch to offer. Still, the revs climb to the 5,000 rpm redline and the automatic gearbox takes third as an open righthander appears. Accelerating, the Fiero feels impressively secure but the sting in the tail of the bend has yet to be tackled. Deep into the corner, straighten the steering wheel momentarily, dab the firm brake pedal, tug the T-bar back into second. The bend tightens markedly yet, foot to the floor, it is still possible to clip the apex with surprising accuracy. Grip is excellent. There is little body roll to make you feel uneasy about learning a strange circuit (driving clockwise) in a left-hooker. And the steering is a revelation: it communicates the slightest loss of grip from the front tyres as they cope with lap after lap of vicious cornering.

Alan Jones went off at the next righthander when leading the 1981 Belgian GP. Accelerating in third, the Fiero takes it at 75 mph, underlining the competence of its chassis by allowing the driver sufficient time to place the car with inch-perfect precision. The Fiero holds its line neatly through the second-gear corner that follows, and then the road climbs over a rise. The break in the black tarmac ahead is filled with sand, but when almost upon it the tight zig-zag chicane comes into view across on the left. Lauda and friends make it look like a simple left-right flick before their speed climbs to 140 mph for the sweeps that follow. The Fiero was immeasurably slower, for sure, but its grip and agility demanded throwing caution to the wind, with the car hugging the right side of the track, a stab on the brakes, into second and wrench the steering wheel left and then right. The Pontiac responds superbly, threading a path between the ludicrously high kerbs with the throttle pedal already buried in the carpet. The excellent grip from the chunky Goodyear Eagles ensures that first one side of your rib cage, then the other, is jammed against the seat bolsters. A little braver each lap maybe, but the Yankee sports car never looked like losing its footing. By the crest of the brow that follows, the unsophisticated "Iron Duke" is howling and demanding a higher ratio. The Fiero gathers speed around the long sweep left where Villeneuve crashed tragically. The fast righthanders that follow blend into each other, while presenting the challenge of a steadily worsening adverse camber. The track feels narrow and — suddenly, in retrospect, Silverstone resembles the M1! Again, it is the Fiero's steering and super chassis balance that impresses.

Even with the speedo needle hovering at 80 mph as the road falls away, the steering remains wonderfully meaty, losing none of its medium-speed weighting and feel — never heavy enough to be awkward but always demanding to be driven, in every sense of the word, with a firm grip from both hands. Accepting the significant difference in power between the Pontiac and the Lotus Esprit S2 it is, surprisingly, the Fiero which achieves the better balance of front and rear grip. Helped by a good 44/56 front/rear weight distribution compared with 41.5/58.5 for the Lotus, the Pontiac manages to convince the driver he is between two equal partners, with the front displaying fine grip and control. In the Hethel car — like other top class mid-engined machines — the levels of roadholding may be higher, but while the rear end is glued to the road, the front can be less reassuring, particularly in the wet.

The lap at Zolder is not over, as the track cuts through the trees to present the driver with a view like that familiar to rallymen facing a firebreak in the forest and wondering which way the road turns. As the rows of chickenwire catch fencing approach ever closer the Boldervergbacht hairpin, with absolutely no camber to help the suspension, is there to the right. The Fiero's brakes work reassuringly well, the four-wheel discs pulling the car up true and square even after half an hour of punishment. Taken at sensible speeds there is little trace of understeer and, again, the steering suffers no disarming lightness. Accelerate when you should still be braking and the nose will edge out steadily. Easing the throttle quickly restores grip to the front tyres.

There is only a chicane left before we arrive back at the finish and the Fiero dismisses it with ease as the uphill gradient damps the pace of this underpowered car. With our Fr350 hire fee spent (and half a tank of fuel used!) it is time to retreat to the pits. The Fiero had impressed without doubt, its chassis more satisfying than we could have fairly expected for a car designed for America's 55 mph speed-limited roads, yet the question which goes unanswered is "What would it be like with the power it deserves?"

And from the Grand Prix stars who hurtle around Zolder at twice the Fiero's speed? Unqualified admiration! From your armchair in front of the TV on a Sunday night you have no idea how narrow and tight the circuit is — and as for overtaking . . .

With these thoughts in mind, and after refilling the Fiero's small 8.5 gallon (Imperial) fuel tank — absurd, on a car which averaged only 17.7 mpg on our 400-mile trip — we set off for Spa via the Belgian motorways and A-roads. The "Iron Duke" engine is a loser on two major counts — no performance, and no refinement. The Pontiac may manage a feeble 100 mph max speed, but above 85 mph the drone from the engine is certainly unwelcome, and too wearing for long journeys. Except for the engine it wouldn't be a noisy car, and on poor road surfaces the bump-thump is particularly well contained.

The choice of engine goes back to the time in the early 1980s when General Motors' planners decided to aim the car at both the enthusiast and the buyer who wanted no more than a stylish two-seater to commute to work in. Outright performance was not top of the list of priorities — with a manual gearbox it manages 0-60 mph in about 11.5 sec. More important was the ability to keep down the cost of developing the car by using existing major components.

In 1979 the original plan to make the car front-engined was ditched because the bonnet line was too high for a sleek nose and, of course, a relatively short in-line four-cylinder engine was fine for a mid-engined layout with transverse power unit. The 2.5-litre engine is an unsuccessful amalgam of old and new. Its all cast-iron design, with pushrod-actuated valves and hydraulic tappets, has been treated to "swirlpot combustion chambers", throttle body fuel injection, and programmed ignition. Yet the result is a measly 91 bhp at 4,400 rpm in US emission spec, producing 132 lb ft of torque at 2,800 rpm. Only change for the Fieros sold in Belgium is the omission of the catalyst material from the converter in the exhaust. Happily, there is already talk of putting a 2.8-litre V6 turbo in the boot of the car.

The powertrain sits forward of the rear wheels on a large sub-frame rubber-mounted to the steel backbone chassis. In addition to the automatic, with the advantage of a lock-up on the top ratio, there are 4-speed manual and 4-speed "economy" transmissions.

The rear suspension is effectively a non-steered front-wheel-drive set-up, with MacPherson struts located by pressed steel lower wishbones and the steering arms used as tie rods to determined the rear wheel tracking.

Struts at the front were ruled out as too tall, so the engineers opted for an existing unequal-length wishbone design, simply widening it to suit the Fiero's 57.8 in track, the same happening to the low-mounted steering rack which is unassisted but boasts a damper to reduce kickback. There is an anti-roll bar at the front only.

The American sales brochure for the Fiero is typical hyperbole, proclaiming the newcomer to be "Dramatically innovative. Exclusively Pontiac". The worst comes when it says that "Fiero's innova-

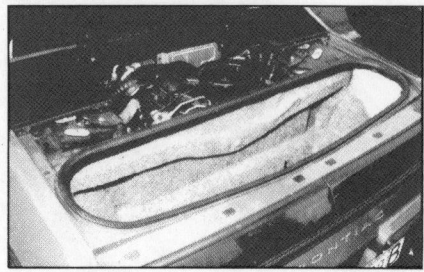

Pausing by the La Source hair-pin at Spa. Left: Could you really get two sets of golf clubs in the boot? Certainly not when they replace the Iron Duke with a V6

tive space-frame chassis uses principles gleaned from modern racing car design, giving it strength without the penalties of excess weight." Fine — as long as you don't believe it! The "space frame" is a conventional inner steel structure merrily welded together by robots. Without any outer skin panels it looks strangely like a TR7 coupé. The body is built up, with all the mechanical parts, until it is entirely driveable, whereupon the plastic body panels are bolted on. Apart from the integral front and rear bumpers, the wings and doors are also made from plastic, which will cope with minor impacts without damage. The clever part about the way the Pontiac is made is that each plastic panel sits on special locating pads which are machined (all 39 of them) in one operation to overcome the problem of variations in the dimensional accuracy of the base metal structure affecting the final panel fit. The result of all this "lightweight" design is a compact two-seater weighing about 22 cwt — certainly no lightweight and no better than plastic rivals like the Lotus Esprit or TVR Tasmin. To its credit, the car does have an excellent solid feel even on the roughest roads, and the plastic panels are well finished to give the Fiero a commendable "quality" look — not bad for a car that has a sticker price starting at $7,999 (£6,200) in America.

Seen in the flesh the styling works well, helped greatly by the absence of frills and chrome. The front is reminiscent of a narrow De Tomaso Pantera, the back is neatly executed but suffers from a similarity with the later twin-cam Lotus Europas. The slim black rubbing strake around the whole car is a super touch as it neatly incorporates the "side marker" lights and the door handles and locks. Below the nose the deep air intake for the front-mounted radiator is barely visible. The days when American cars had acres of bright red lights covering the rear end are disappearing and the Fiero has semi-high-tech lamp covers that appear dark grey unless viewed from just a few feet away.

Left alone, the rear deck at least looks uncluttered but the top models in the Fiero 2M4 range (2-seater, Mid-engined, 4-cylinder) have black plastic strips and a tiny wing which give it the look of a pick-up. The drag coefficient claimed for the car is 0.377, suggesting something goes wrong with the airflow after it passes over the clean-looking nose.

Walk up to the Fiero in a car park and it will appear surprisingly small. It is, in fact, almost four inches shorter than a TR7, but two and a half inches wider and three inches lower. Despite being the shorter of the two overall, the Fiero's wheelbase at 93.4 in is longer by more than eight inches. Its low and, wide form is emphasised in the comparison with the Lotus Esprit, which is only four inches wider and three inches lower.

Climbing into the Pontiac is easier than expected, as the doors are big and the seats not mounted too low. The driving position is excellent, with the seat well positioned for a good view over the dipping bonnet while tilt adjustment (optional) is a bonus, as the steering wheel is already in the right place. Yet the most impressive feature is the cockpit's light and airy feel and excellent forward visibility — a marked contrast to most two seater coupés. Of course, the thick rear pillars create a few problems when pulling out of junctions.

The seats are well shaped and provide plenty of lateral support but the edges of the side bolsters are so rigid they jab you in the back as you drop into the seat. The instrument binnacle is isolated from the facia to create more interior space, which it certainly appears to do, but the good positioning of the instruments is marred by the use of ordinary vertical glass over the dials. Inevitably, they suffer from constant reflections — unacceptable, even in cars of two decades ago. What a strange blunder. And perhaps, in America, enthusiasts like to see the screw heads that secure the instrument panels, and even the cluster of switches, but it doesn't look very clever on this side of the Atlantic.

While the overall concept of the interior is generaly good it is let down by certain faults. The large facia moulding which sweeps around under the big screen to blend into the matching door panels is a dated-looking white plastic which is distinctly inferior to the advanced soft-feel, leather-look mouldings found in European cars. And the packaging is really no better than that of a Lotus Esprit. There is not even a lockable glove box in the cab, just small elasticated pockets in the doors and one facing the passenger, while the single stowage space behind the engine is a peculiar shape and not large, despite the claim that it will take two sets of golf clubs. Nothing can be put under the front "hood", while the designers actually anticipate people pushing the passenger seat forward in order to stand a suitcase behind it. As they say in the blurb, the Fiero "must be packed like a small sail-boat".

The 100-mile-plus run to Spa from Zolder provided an opportunity to assess the Fiero's ride over the notably poorly-maintained Belgian roads. Even the motorways have the occasional ridge of tarmac the size of a sleeping policeman. At low speed, the car is not disgraced. Though inevitably firm and well damped, it never jars occupants, the relatively long-travel suspension coping well with the worst pot-holes. Yet the driver is aware of some body shake, and kickback through the steering. At speed, the small imperfections in the road surface are absorbed, making long journeys no chore. Poor surfaces cause the car to squirm, though it holds its line well when hitting bumps when cornering.

Seeing Spa for the first time was more exciting than I had expected. One moment you are winding your way slowly through the nearby town, the next facing the famous La Source hairpin surrounded by pits and grandstands and miles of Armco barriers with huge advertising hoardings disappearing into the distance. We move off down the hill, past the pits, towards the kink at the bottom, before leaving the road circuit briefly before the road climbs up the long, long hill to the peak where the old and new circuits part company.

The old one has all the atmosphere of a ride in the country. The road is very fast indeed, as it leads down from the peak into a long righthander where the surface is rough and the deep camber tricky even at 80 mph. We glance at the field that Moss ploughed into as the Fiero noses down the valley to the section of the circuit that is no longer there because of the new motorway. We soon find the old road again and the notorious Masta kink comes into view. Certainly fast — but returning the next morning at 6 am confirmed how hazardous the thick Belgian mist can be on a road where run-off areas don't exist. Soon the road swings to the right, ready to take the heroes of an era gone by back through a mile or two of fast sweeps, up the hill to La Source. It is easy to be overawed by the size — 8.8 miles long — and challenge of the old circuit.

It is an easy car to like. Rush down the hill. Round bends that go on forever as they switch back on themselves. And, as the downhill straights demand a courageous blast on the throttle, the excitement builds.

This year, up to 20 Belgian buyers will pay about £13,000 for a well-equipped Fiero. Me, I think I'll wait until the "Iron Duke" is dead and buried — and then stand eagerly in line. It will be worth the wait.

PONTIAC FIERO GT
Sleek, slick and powerful

AHH... HAPPINESS IS a Fiero with V-6 power. Since Pontiac's cute 2-seater hit the market a year ago, we have learned to love most facets of the car's warm personality. But we had to bide our time in anticipation of the performance that a more powerful engine would provide. Yet, in its first year on the market the Fiero achieved everything Pontiac expected and more. It attracted international acclaim for its unique design and manufacturing process, and it is selling well ahead of Pontiac's first-year projections. So it doesn't seem to matter that the car's performance was somewhat limited by its venerable 2.5-liter inline-4. But nestling a V-6 into the engine compartment has transformed the Fiero in a major way.

That transformation has come via Chevrolet's 2.8-liter 60-degree V-6 that Pontiac tailored to the Fiero's mid-engine configuration. The intake and exhaust manifolds as well as the calibration of the port fuel injection system are unique to this installation. Besides providing a high-tech profile, they are there to do a job. The cast aluminum intake manifold features individually tuned runners, as does the stainless steel exhaust manifold. All told, the engine (designated the L44) develops 140 bhp at 5200 rpm and 170 lb-ft of torque at 3600 rpm, a considerable step up from the 92 bhp and 134 lb-ft of the 2.5-liter four. Nicer still, the dual exhaust ends in two Ys and four resonators, which provide a pleasantly restrained growl when you put your foot down. Yet it idles with a mellow burble.

The V-6 engine is available as an option in the Fiero S/E and comes standard with a new model, the GT. The GT features the soft nose that first appeared on the Indy Pace car, a new rear panel (for the dual exhausts) and rocker panel extensions. There

AT A GLANCE	Pontiac Fiero GT	Mazda RX-7 GSL-SE	Nissan 300ZX
Price, base/ as tested	est $11,200 est $13,500	$15,295 $16,295	$16,199 $16,199
Curb weight, lb	2740	2640	2990
Engine/drive	mid/rear	front/rear	front/rear
Transmission	4-sp M	5-sp M	5-sp M
0–60 mph, sec	8.4	8.5	8.2
Standing ¼ mi, sec @ mph	16.5 @ 84.5	16.4 @ 84.0	16.4 @ 84.0
Stopping distance from 60 mph, ft	158	157	148
Interior noise at 50 mph, dBA	67	70	67
Lateral acceleration, g	0.817	0.858	0.822
Slalom speed, mph	60.3	61.1	62.3
Fuel economy, mpg	est 22.0	18.5[1]	18.0[1]

Fiero GT: V-6 power means a Fiero with performance to match its looks.
RX-7 GSL-SE: Nimbler handling and more power rejuvenate an old friend (3-84).
300ZX: With power and poise, the latest Z is the most refined yet (3-84).

[1] trip fuel economy

PHOTOS BY JOE RUSZ

is also a rear deck bulge to help clear the V-6, but this will be a standard features on all Fieros. Some of us liked the GT's revised styling and some of us didn't. But we all agreed that it comes closer to looking like a real race car than just about any other car on the market . . . and it's sure to generate excitement. The wing? How did we forget? It's an option.

For those aerophiles among our readers, the following will be of more than passing interest. The original Fiero with 13-in. wheels and tires has a C_x of 0.377; add 14-in. wheels and tires and that figure climbs to 0.406. With the pace car nose and 14-in. wheels and tires the coefficient of drag drops to 0.372 and falls still further to 0.350 with the addition of the rocker panel extensions and the rear wing.

So how do the V-6 and the GT work together? Very well and very nicely. The V-6's flexibility allows it to pull slowly but smoothly from 1000 rpm in 4th, which is a good indication of the low-end torque available. But there's more to it than that—the midrange torque is also improved and the V-6 engine (with its 50-percent greater power compared with the 4-cylinder) exhibits the sort of smooth, free-revving performance we have hoped for in the Fiero. Our 0–60 mph time of 8.4 seconds is 2.5 sec quicker than the 4-cylinder Fiero's. And it's 1.7 sec and 12.0 mph faster in the quarter mile. That's performance. And at all speeds but idle (maybe you better make that a loud mellow burble), the V-6 Fiero was quieter and virtually vibration-free compared with the inline-4. The V-6 engine makes even the automatic transmission a joy to drive, and, yes, the manual transmission (still no 5-speed) shift effort and precision have been improved. The only drawback to this engine is its 22 mpg city/26 mpg highway EPA ratings combined with a smallish 10.2-gal. fuel tank. With any amount of spirited driving you'll be stopping to fill up about every 200 miles.

Our skidpad (0.817g) and slalom (60.3 mph) handling numbers are virtually identical to what we got before. But you have to consider that the installation of the V-6 added 150 lb to the car (now 2740 lb curb weight), and it uses the same size wheels and tires as the 4-cylinder so those numbers actually represent an improvement. This was made possible by several suspension changes all Fieros enjoy, including toe links that have been lowered 5 mm to reduce roll steer. (We call them tie rods but Pontiac prefers toe links because of the possible association of tie rods with steering; these links are at the rear.) And this, according to Pontiac, reduces roll understeer from 8 percent down to 1–2 percent, resulting in crisper, more responsive handling in abrupt lane-change maneuvers. In addition, the front suspension lower control arm has been redesigned to provide 0.5 in. more travel. On top of that, the GT's sportier handling package (RPO WS6 on the S/E) includes higher rear spring rates and firmer rear strut valving, which not only reduce body roll but also change the ride frequency, resulting in less pitch.

Whether on the road or track the Fiero GT is in its element. In addition to our full road test we were able to assess its abilities at Waterford Hills, a tight 1.5-mile road course north of Detroit. And we found the GT to be a consistent and predictable handler. The car almost seems to have an intuitive sense of what you want it to do. Turn into a corner at speed and it initially understeers, but as you turn more, you can get the rear wheels to slide. Lift at this moment and it develops trailing-throttle oversteer, which disappears the instant you get back on the power. There just aren't any severe or abrupt transitional changes with quick power on/off inputs. Very impressive (and safe).

Overall, the brakes are well modulated, with just a hint of premature rear lock. And panic braking distances are better: 9 ft less from 60 mph and 19 ft shorter from 80.

One annoying aspect of the car is an inordinate amount of steering kickback on bumpy roads and hard turns. Even more annoying was how the steering wheel would rattle in this situation. We also think most Fiero drivers would appreciate an increase in steering quickness and a reduction in low-speed effort. Both could be accomplished with power assisted steering. Hint, hint, Pontiac.

Where Pontiac will price the Fiero GT hasn't been announced at this point. Nor do we have any indication what the V-6 option in the S/E will cost. We would estimate that the GT's added performance will command a price increase of about $1500. But if our road test results and the car's current sales pace can be used as any sort of barometer, you better get in line right now. Let's make it official. The debate is over. The Fiero isn't just a nice, 2-seat commuter car anymore. It's a world-class sports car.

ROAD TEST PONTIAC FIERO GT

SCALE: 10 in. (254 mm) DIVISIONS
DRAWING BY BILL DOBSON

PRICE
List price, FOB Detroit .... est $11,200
Price as tested .... est $13,500
Price as tested includes std equip. (V-6 engine, GT bodywork), air cond (est $730), AM/FM stereo cassette (est $450), sunroof (est $250), rear wing (est $250), elect. window lifts (est $185), cruise control (est $175), rear-window heat (est $135), central locking (est $125)

MANUFACTURER
Pontiac Motor Division, One Pontiac Plaza, Pontiac, Mich. 48053

GENERAL
Curb weight, lb/kg 2740 1244
Test weight 2910 1321
Weight dist (with driver), f/r, % 43/57
Wheelbase, in./mm 93.4 2372
Track, front/rear .... 57.8/58.7 ... 1468/1492
Length 165.1 4194
Width 68.9 1750
Height 46.9 1191
Ground clearance 6.0 152
Overhang, f/r .... 41.0/30.7 ... 1041/780
Trunk space, cu ft/liters 6.8 192
Fuel capacity, U.S. gal./liters ... 10.2 39

MAINTENANCE
Service intervals, mi:
  Oil/filter change 7500/7500
  Chassis lube .... none
  Tuneup .... na
Warranty, mo/mi 12/12,000

ENGINE
Type .... ohv V-6
Bore x stroke, in./mm .... 3.50 x 2.99 .... 89.0 x 76.0
Displacement, cu in./cc 173 2837
Compression ratio 8.9:1
Bhp @ rpm, SAE net/kW .... 140/104 @ 5200
  Equivalent mph / km/h 121/195
Torque @ rpm, lb-ft/Nm .... 170/230 @ 3600
  Equivalent mph / km/h 84/135
Fuel injection .... GM multi-point
Fuel requirement .... unleaded, 91-oct
Exhaust-emission control equipment: 3-way catalytic converter, oxygen sensor, exhaust-gas recirculation, air injection

DRIVETRAIN
Transmission .... 4-sp manual
Gear ratios: 4th (0.81) 2.96:1
  3rd (1.24) 4.53:1
  2nd (1.95) 7.12:1
  1st (3.31) 12.08:1
Final drive ratio (rear axle ratio x transfer ratio) .. 3.65:1

INSTRUMENTATION
Instruments: 85-mph speedometer, 6000-rpm tach, 999,999.9 odo, 999.9 trip odo, oil press., coolant temp, voltmeter, fuel level
Warning lights: oil press., handbrake/brake system, check engine, door ajar, rear deck ajar, upshift, seatbelts, hazard, high beam, directionals

CHASSIS & BODY
Layout .... mid engine/rear drive
Body/frame .... separate; fiberglass panels/steel unit chassis
Brake system ..... 9.7-in. (247-mm) discs front and rear; vacuum assisted
Swept area, sq in./sq cm 343 2212
Wheels .... cast alloy, 14 x 6
Tires .... Goodyear Eagle GT, P215/60R-14
Steering type .... rack & pinion
Overall ratio 19.2:1
Turns, lock-to-lock 2.9
Turning circle, ft/m .... 38.9 .... 11.9
Front suspension: upper and lower A-arms, coil springs, tube shocks, anti-roll bar
Rear suspension: Chapman struts, lower A-arms, tie-rods, coil springs, tube shocks

ACCOMMODATION
Seating capacity, persons 2
Head room, in./mm 36.5 927
Seat width .... 2 x 18.5 ..... 2 x 470
Seatback adjustment, deg 40

CALCULATED DATA
Lb/bhp (test weight) 20.8
Mph/1000 rpm (4th gear) 23.3
Engine revs/mi (60 mph) 2570
Piston travel, ft/mi 1281
R&T steering index 1.13
Brake swept area, sq in./ton 236

ROAD TEST RESULTS

ACCELERATION
Time to distance, sec:
  0–100 ft 3.2
  0–500 ft 8.9
  0–1320 ft (¼ mi) 16.5
Speed at end of ¼ mi, mph 84.5
Time to speed, sec:
  0–30 mph 2.5
  0–50 mph 5.8
  0–60 mph 8.4
  0–70 mph 11.3
  0–80 mph 14.7
  0–100 mph 27.0

SPEEDS IN GEARS
4th gear (5300 rpm) .... est 125
3rd gear (6000) 93
2nd (6000) 59
1st (6000) 35

FUEL ECONOMY
Normal driving, mpg .... est 22.0
Cruising range, mi (1-gal. res) ... est 200

HANDLING
Lateral accel, 100-ft radius, g 0.817
Speed thru 700-ft slalom, mph 60.3

BRAKES
Minimum stopping distances, ft:
  From 60 mph 158
  From 80 mph 271
Control in panic stop .... very good
Pedal effort for 0.5g stop, lb 20
Fade: percent increase in pedal effort to maintain 0.5g deceleration in 6 stops from 60 mph 20
Overall brake rating .... very good

INTERIOR NOISE
Idle in neutral, dBA 53
Maximum, 1st gear 77
Constant 30 mph 64
  50 mph 67
  70 mph 72
  90 mph 76

ACCELERATION

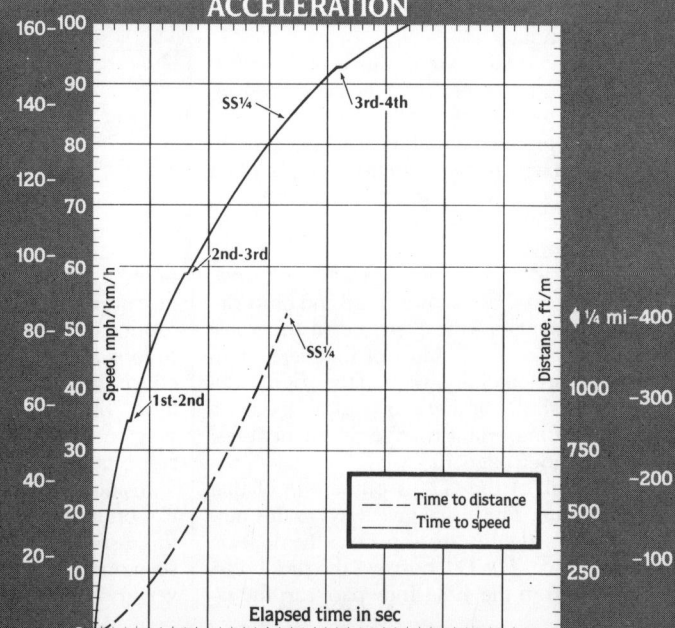

Pontiac Fiero GT

How to succeed success?

• It may be that nothing succeeds like success, but then success doesn't succeed as well as it used to. Take the case of the Pontiac Fiero. It was obvious from the start that the Fiero was going to be a winner. The plastic-over-steel sportster was the right car at the right time. We applauded it as one of the Ten Best Cars of 1984. As this is written, Pontiac has already built 100,000 Fieros—as many units as the factory has been able to pump out. By any measure, this car is a hit.

These days, though, the competition is so tough in the car business, there's no such thing as leaving well enough alone. This is especially true if you happen to be the manufacturer of popularly priced mid-engined two-seaters. Toyota will have such a car on the market by spring. Rumors abound that numerous other carmakers are on the same wavelength. In other words, it's a jungle out there.

The Fiero GT is proof that the Pontiac division understands the rules of the game. The GT, which will go on sale at the beginning of the year, is the first evolutionary step for the Fiero line. It's also a move that about halves the distance between the original Fiero 2M4 and our ideal of the true driver's car.

Clearly, help was needed. The Fiero 2M4 was plenty good for the first time out of the box, but it was a far cry from perfect. After some time in the saddle, it became apparent that, on the 1984 scale, the Fiero was an underachiever in both performance and handling.

To a certain extent, this is understandable. You may recall that the Fiero was conceived by a handful of Pontiac engineers as a low-priced commuter car that would share a host of components with other GM car lines. Its front suspension, for instance, is basically made from Chevette pieces. The standard four-cylinder engine, transaxle, and rear suspension are front-drive X-car parts. Only toward the end of its development did the Fiero begin to evolve into a sports car. Most of the Fiero engineers are painfully aware of the original design's shortcomings, so you can expect a slew of important changes in the next few years. (See page 46.)

Think of the GT as phase one of that program. The visual giveaways to this new model's identity are as plain as the nose on your face. The GT borrows the slick bodywork from the 1984 Indy pace car: the tapered fighter-plane snout, the rocker-panel extensions, the rear-deck spoiler (optional), and the rear bumper reshaped to look as though it has Indy-car ground-effects tunnels. Only the GT model will have this bodywork, which reduces the drag coefficient from a lackluster 0.41 to a respectable 0.35.

Inside, there are few clues to this model's brand-newness. A beautifully crafted, three-spoked sport steering wheel (last seen on the 1984 Firebird Trans Am anniversary edition) is the most important revision. Ardent Fiero watchers may notice that the racing stripes have disappeared from the sport seats, that an oil-pressure gauge has been added, that the graphic markings on the instruments are new, that several control buttons are now soft-touch designs, that the shift lever is a tad longer, and that the radio is ever more complicated. But that's it.

The real news is what you see when you pop the deck lid: blood-red paint and gleaming polished aluminum adorning a new port-fuel-injected 2.8-liter V-6. Gone

is the feeble Iron Duke (reworked yet again this year and renamed Tech IV), which will remain the base motivator in all other Fieros. (The V-6 is also available as an option in non-GT Fieros.)

The new V-6 is actually based heavily on the 2.8-liter high-output unit we've seen and driven over the past four years in everything from Citation X-11s to 6000STEs. The new-for-1985 edition breathes freely, thanks to the H.O.'s cylinder heads and camshaft, a new ram-tuned intake manifold, and a low-restriction exhaust system. Fuel is delivered by six Bosch injectors managed by the engine-control computer. Although both Chevrolet and Buick are moving aggressively toward mass-airflow sensors for their injection systems, Pontiac has chosen a speed-density strategy: the theoretical intake-air mass is *calculated* from measurements of various parameters (engine rpm, air temperature, intake-manifold pressure, etc.). Pontiac offers two reasons for this choice: a mass-airflow meter wouldn't fit in the space available in the Fiero's engine compartment, and Pontiac engineers were far more familiar with the speed-density scheme, having used it extensively in both throttle-body and port fuel-injection systems.

To this Chevrolet-built engine (coded L44) Pontiac adds its own custom-tailored exhaust system, consisting of fabricated sheetmetal headers, carefully routed pipes, and a low-restriction muffler. The net result is 140 hp at 5200 rpm—from five to fifteen more horsepower than any other GM division is squeezing from this powerplant—and 170 pounds-feet of torque at 3600 rpm. While these figures represent only a 5-hp gain over last year's carbureted H.O. engine, there is a solid seventeen-percent jump in the torque output. This fatter torque curve backs up the rumors that the sophisticated fuel-injection system was added to the V-6 primarily to improve its fuel mileage. (The corporation's average fuel economy has been sliding badly as the public's interest has surged toward more powerful engines.)

The 2.8-liter is handicapped somewhat by having to work through the same old four-speed manual transaxle that was introduced on the X-cars nearly six years ago. Unfortunately, GM still doesn't have a five-speed gearbox stout enough to handle the torque of this V-6. Shame, shame. At least Pontiac put the Fiero's balky cable shift linkage through a thorough tuneup, something you can feel at the first throw of the elongated lever.

Everything so far qualifies as improving the breed. Unfortunately, though, this year's training program stopped short of working the suspension into shape. The low-ball commuter-car pieces will eventually be scrapped for a higher-performance design, but for now the engineers could only work with what they had—which is to say, not enough.

FIERO GT

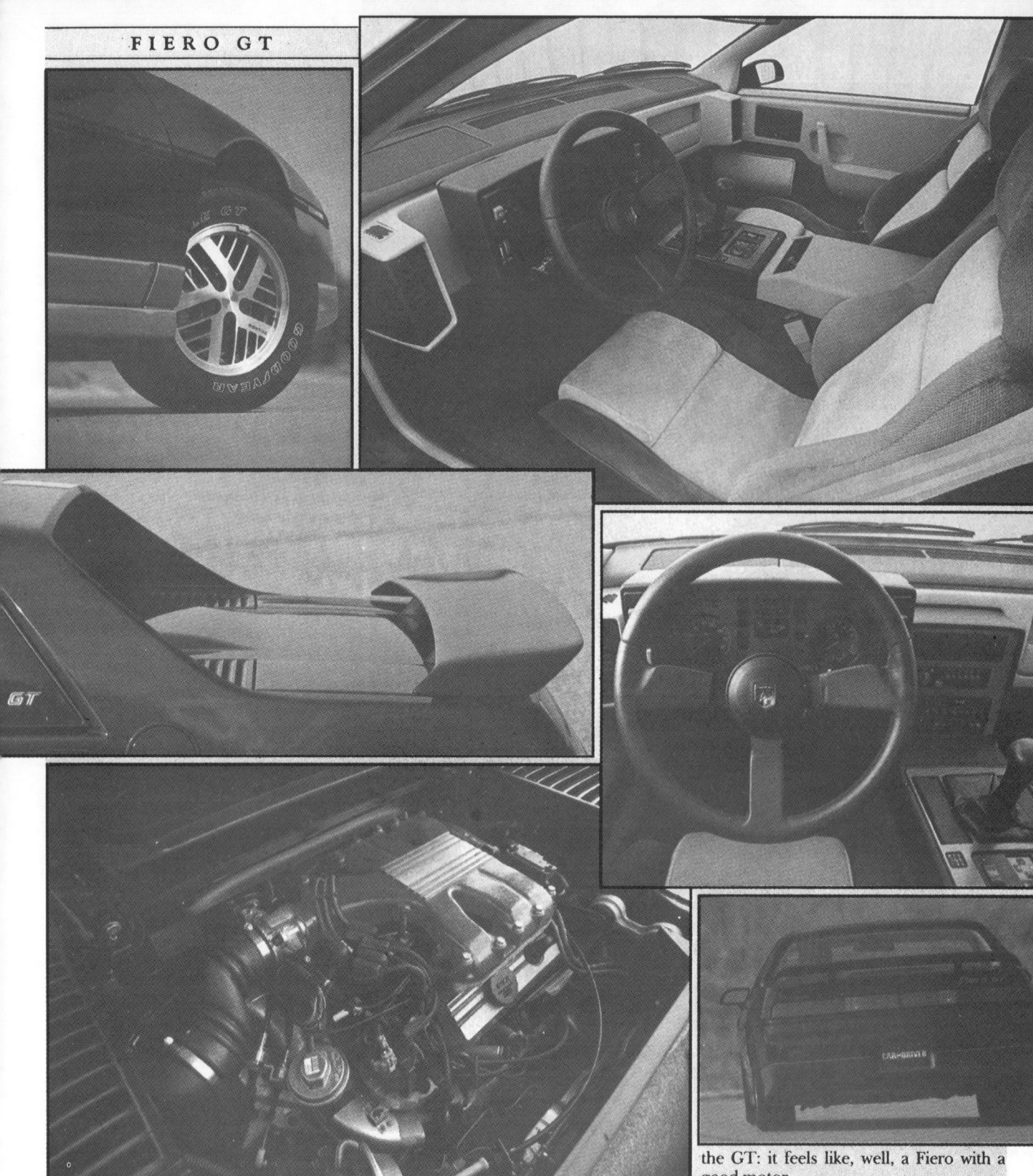

The changes to the chassis are subtle, and they apply to all Fieros—four-cylinder or six—equipped with the WS6 handling package. The front lower control arms have been revised to provide an additional half-inch of travel. At the rear, the spring rates were upped by ten percent, and the shock absorbers were revalved. There are also revisions to reduce rear-suspension steering effects created by body roll in cornering; the intention was to diminish tail wag during emergency lane changes. In addition, we're told that the brake balance was shifted more toward the front during 1984, at least in part because of our complaints about the Fiero's tail-end jitters during hard braking.

Those are the hard facts of the case. But is there any poetry here? After putting all the pieces in motion, we have to answer with an unqualified "no." If you've ever driven a Fiero, you won't be surprised by the GT: it feels like, well, a Fiero with a good motor.

If only the rest of the car were as good as its engine. The new exhaust note is a beautiful rasp, and the V-6 is smooth and sweet all the way to the 6000-rpm redline. The GT's 8.2-second 0-to-60 time and 119-mph top speed (Pontiac's claim) make it about three seconds quicker and fourteen miles per hour faster than the Fiero in four-cylinder trim. Those stats slot it into the same speed class as the Dodge Daytona Turbo, the BMW 325e, and the Volvo 760GLE Turbo—pretty good company—

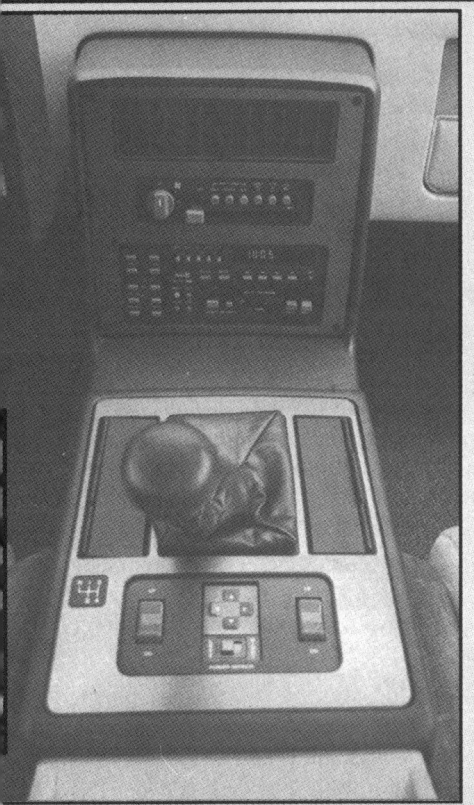

yet in the real world it doesn't seem really "fast." Nevertheless, the new energy level is more than enough to eliminate one of our two major complaints about the original Fiero.

Get the GT out on a stretch of meandering two-lane, however, and little is different. If your favorite run is as smooth as a satin ribbon, you'll find the GT fairly competent. The roads most of us must cope with, though, bring out the worst in this car—at least when you drive athletically.

COUNTERPOINT

• The Fiero was born a commuter car and will carry on throughout the 1985 model year as a commuter car, V-6 or no. Last year it was a *slow* commuter car, and this year it's a much faster one (with the L44 engine), but don't expect this machine to make your heart sing: a pleasant ride to and from work is pretty much the upper limit to the joy that's available in Pontiac's two-seater.

What we have here is a sports car on the installment plan. Last year we got the looks. This year comes more power. Pontiac claims the check's in the mail for the rest of the parts we'd like to see.

But don't expect overnight delivery. Nobody within GM is hurrying, because the Fiero is Pontiac's biggest hit in some time. A review of past sales figures does indeed reveal that the legendary GTO never cracked the 100,000-cars-per-year barrier in its distinguished eleven-year run, an accomplishment the Fiero enjoyed right out of the box. So what's the rub, Pontiac asks. Their customers love the Fiero and are still bidding against one another to get one. If Confucius were here to comment, he might advise: "If the public wants commuters, give them commuters!" —*Don Sherman*

This car has a displacement problem, but not in cubic inches. When you're running quickly, a big bump in the middle of a corner will displace the Fiero several feet. It takes the bit in its teeth and lunges off helter-skelter. And, in the midst of wrestling grimly with the sharply kicking wheel, your elbow can strike the exposed release button on the shoulder-harness latch, whereupon the tang pops right out of the buckle. Now there's a comforting feeling.

Furthermore, although anesthetics are normally administered in milli-somethings, that's not how it's been done by Pontiac. The Fiero's steering has been Novocained until stuporous. It feels okay heading down the smooth boulevard from the GM Proving Grounds, yet once in the real world it looms up to swaddle most of what you want to know. But worse even than the steering is that suspension. Hustle the Fiero GT, as buyers of the bigger engine surely will, and it only arrives at its suspension problems at a higher rate of speed. The car bounds and flails and does mostly what it pleases. Which ain't at all pleasing. —*Larry Griffin*

How embarrassing. Every time a Fiero goes by, my head goes into full swivel. Never mind its Iron Duke wheezer of a four-banger. Never mind its floaty, floppy suspension. Never mind its drugged steering and muddled shift linkage. I look every time, even when several Fieros go by within minutes of one another (a fairly common occurrence around Detroit). What a waste of good sports-car flesh.

Thankfully, Pontiac makes Fiero lust less sinful in 1985, with the addition of an optional 2.8-liter V-6 engine, an improved shifter, and sexy Indy-pace-car-type bodywork for the GT. The plastic body still squirrels around on its corners under braking, over rough road, and especially when cornering. And the three-two downshift is still a thought provoker. And there's no five-speed with the V-6. Still, the punch of the six-cylinder is enough to reduce the charge for Fiero watching from a felony to a misdemeanor. —*Jean Lindamood*

FIERO GT

Lumps and bumps, even when taken straight on, make it dart nervously. Creased pavement in the middle of a fast sweeper sets the GT hopping and sends shock waves back through the steering wheel. And when the suspension really gets exercised, you can even hear the plastic body panels clapping against one another. Around town, the steering is heavy. This is definitely not the stuff of thoroughbred GT cars.

The upshot is that the Fiero is not yet ready to take its place among the world's better road cars. Oh, it lopes through the day-to-day routine well enough, but it's not the kind of car that begs you to take it out

Future Fiero Tech

The greening of Pontiac's protagonist.

• Yes, sports-car fans, Pontiac does have a future in mind for the Fiero; one that goes far beyond this year's V-6 engine bolted to last year's chassis. It will take time to materialize—far more, in fact, than you or we might like—but at least it is Pontiac's stated intention to purge the Fiero's soul of all its commuter-car characteristics. After persistent needling, the engineering department has admitted to the following timetable:

1986—No major changes to the suspension, but the wheels and tires with the WS6 package will be upgraded to fifteen-inch designs. We have spotted test cars wearing Goodyear Eagle GTs in a 205/60R-15 size in front and a 215/60R-15 size in back. A Getrag-designed five-speed will be available with the V-6.

1987—This is the big year for a thorough overhaul of all suspension and brake equipment. The Chevette-based front axle will be trash-canned; in its place will go a clean-sheet design unique to the Fiero, which should remedy today's bumpy-road handling ills in one fell swoop. There will be longer control arms for more wheel travel, increased anti-dive geometry, a shorter scrub radius, and a far tighter turning circle.

A new electrohydraulic rack-and-pinion power-steering system will provide assist below 15 mph to help ease parking effort. Hydraulic pressure will come from a pump driven by its own electric motor instead of by the engine. An electronic circuit that senses road speed will switch off the assistance above 15 mph.

The rear suspension will also be redesigned at this time. The basic X-car struts will be saved, but the new layout will have two lateral links and one trailing link per side instead of the X-car's A-shaped control arms. This change will provide more anti-squat, greatly reduced impact harshness, and better deflection-steer characteristics.

The brake hardware will be revamped along with the suspension. Today's solid rotors will be upgraded to vented designs. Pontiac has experimented with anti-skid brakes in the 6000STE, but it's unclear at present whether such hardware might find its way into the Fiero.

Engine improvements are slated for not only the Pontiac-built Tech IV but also the V-6 supplied by Chevrolet: both should have new aluminum cylinder heads for the 1987 model year. Pontiac's racing department has demonstrated that its 300-horsepower, 2.7-liter, heavy-duty four-cylinder engine can be civilized for street use and still produce 190 horsepower—with pushrods. As a result, the prevailing attitudes lean more toward squeezing additional power out of existing designs than toward tooling up all-new engines. Nevertheless, Chevrolet's 2.8-liter V-6 is currently scheduled for a fairly ambitious improvement program: overhead camshafts. (By 1987, the distinction between Pontiac and Chevrolet engineering will have faded noticeably, because both divisions are now part of GM's new small-car group and all techni-

on Sunday morning for a hard run. The changes are all good as far as they go, and for that Pontiac deserves credit. But until the Fiero's chassis is up to the task, we suggest that you consider this car's call letters in a slightly different light. In this case, "GT" stands for "Good Touring," not "Grand."
—*Rich Ceppos*

cal resources will gradually be pooled.) In addition to more power, the Tech IV will be given balance shafts to improve idle and high-rpm shake characteristics.

1990—Eventually there will be an all-new Fiero. From today's vantage, the 1990 model year is the best guess as to when the new design will be unveiled. The mid-engine, two-seat configuration and the use of plastic body panels will certainly be saved, but the underlying steel structure will be reengineered to make the Fiero much lighter and a good deal less expensive to manufacture.

The aftermarket will of course fill in various voids in Pontiac's factory program. Turbo kits and T-top packages are already yours for the asking. GM's design staff is said to be cooperating with ASC on the ex-factory manufacture of a Fiero roadster. Fender kits will abound as soon as the fiberglass vendors learn how easy it is to graft parts onto Pontiac's substructure. Some firms have gone so far as to inquire about the possibility of buying the rolling chassis from Pontiac *sans* skin in the hope of adding their own bodywork. In other words, the Fiero may be the greatest boon to the kit-car industry since the VW Beetle.
—*Don Sherman*

Vehicle type: mid-engine, rear-wheel-drive, 2-passenger, 2-door coupe

Price as tested: $13,000 (estimated)

Options on test car: air conditioning, AM/FM-stereo radio/cassette, tilt steering column, intermittent wipers, sunroof, power windows, carpeted floor mats, rear spoiler.

Sound system: Delco AM/FM-stereo radio/cassette with graphic equalizer, 6 speakers, 7 watts per channel

ENGINE
Type .... V-6, iron block and heads
Bore x stroke .... 3.50 x 2.99 in, 89.0 x 76.0mm
Displacement .... 171 cu in, 2837cc
Compression ratio 8.5:1
Engine-control system .... Pontiac-Delco electronic
Emissions controls ..... 3-way catalytic converter, feedback fuel-air-ratio control, EGR
Valve gear .... pushrods, hydraulic lifters
Power (SAE net) .... 140 bhp @ 5200 rpm
Torque (SAE net) .... 170 lbs-ft @ 3600 rpm
Redline .... 6000 rpm

DRIVETRAIN
Transmission 4-speed
Final-drive ratio 3.65:1

Gear	Ratio	Mph/1000 rpm	Max. test speed
I	3.31	5.7	34 mph (6000 rpm)
II	1.95	10.0	60 mph (6000 rpm)
III	1.24	15.3	92 mph (6000 rpm)
IV	0.81	23.5	100 mph (4250 rpm)

DIMENSIONS AND CAPACITIES
Wheelbase .... 93.4 in
Track, F/R .... 57.8/58.7 in
Length .... 165.1 in
Width .... 68.9 in
Height .... 46.9 in
Ground clearance .... 5.4 in
Curb weight .... 2728 lbs
Weight distribution, F/R 43.5/56.5%
Fuel capacity .... 10.0 gal
Oil capacity .... 4.0 qt
Water capacity .... 13.7 qt

CHASSIS/BODY
Type .... unit construction with rubber-isolated powertrain cradle
Body material .... fiberglass-reinforced plastic

INTERIOR
SAE volume, front seat .... 51 cu ft
                    trunk space .... 6 cu ft
Front seats .... bucket
Recliner type .... ratchet
General comfort .... poor fair **good** excellent
Fore-and-aft support .... poor fair **good** excellent
Lateral support .... poor fair **good** excellent

SUSPENSION
F: .... ind, unequal-length control arms, coil springs, anti-sway bar
R: .... ind, MacPherson strut, coil springs

STEERING
Type .... rack-and-pinion
Turns lock-to-lock 3.0
Turning circle curb-to-curb .... 39.9 ft

BRAKES
F: .... 9.7 x 0.4-in disc
R: .... 9.7 x 0.5-in disc
Power assist .... vacuum

WHEELS AND TIRES
Wheel size .... 6.0 x 14 in
Wheel type .... cast aluminum
Tire make and size .... Goodyear Eagle GT, P215/60R-14
Test inflation pressures, F/R .... 30/30 psi

CAR AND DRIVER TEST RESULTS

ACCELERATION   Seconds
Zero to 30 mph 2.4
       40 mph 4.0
       50 mph 5.7
       60 mph 8.2
       70 mph 11.1
       80 mph 14.7
       90 mph 19.7
Top-gear passing time, 30–50 mph 9.6
                        50–70 mph 9.9
Standing ¼-mile .... 16.0 sec @ 85 mph
Top speed (manufacturer's rating) .... 119 mph

BRAKING
70–0 mph @ impending lockup .... 199 ft
Modulation .... poor **fair** good excellent
Fade .... **none** moderate heavy
Front-rear balance .... poor fair **good**

HANDLING
Roadholding, 216-ft-dia skidpad .... 0.81 g
Understeer .... minimal moderate **excessive**

FUEL ECONOMY
EPA city driving .... 22 mpg
EPA highway driving .... 26 mpg

INTERIOR SOUND LEVEL
Idle .... 55 dBA
Full-throttle acceleration .... 84 dBA
70-mph cruising .... 72 dBA
70-mph coasting .... 71 dBA

Pontiac's Fiero is here! The bad news is there's only one, to promote the use of plastic in cars. Mike McCarthy reports

PLASTIC IMPORT

TO LOOK at the Fiero is to *see* why it's a tearaway sales success in the USA. As Pontiac's (indeed America's) first mass-produced mid-engine two-seater, the Fiero looks the part: an attractively styled and properly packaged modern sporty car. From any point of view the Fiero has real eye appeal.

And driver appeal? The overall design suggests Pontiac has taken steps in the right direction. But that doesn't necessarily mean the development is far enough along for the Fiero's dynamics to live up to its styling. And that's something you can't tell just by looking, of course.

Thanks to Nylex we had the chance to do more than look, at an exclusive drive session at Oran Park, with the best part of an hour or so behind the wheel of Australia's one and only public Fiero. (Actually, GMH has one too, ostensibly as a styling study).

Plastics maker Nylex showed initiative by importing its Fiero as a promotional vehicle for display around the country to the Press, public and motor industry alike as a living example of the state of the art in plastic-body technology.

Although Nylex isn't connected in any way with the production of Fiero plastic panels and parts in the US, the corporation has a vested and natural interest in promoting plastics among local car makers and buyers.

While giving the innovative and perhaps trend-setting body its full due, our interest in the Fiero went beyond its style, materials and other individual areas. And for that hour or so at Oran Park we weren't interested in much besides the driving and related aspects of using the Fiero. It gives some rare insights to how the other (American) half motors in the '80s. Because of the short time factor and the newness of the unconverted, unregistered and unleaded Fiero (with only limited, specially imported low-lead petrol available), we couldn't pedal the Ponty as far and fast as we'd have liked, but managed enough laps at enough speeds to get a good idea what it's all about.

Even before opening the Fiero's door we had the obvious first impression: how good it looks. After manoeuvring the car from its parked position out onto the track, we had our first physical impression: how heavy it feels.

That impression manifests itself in several ways. At low speeds, for instance, the steering effort is surprisingly high for a car weighing about 1125 kg (not much more than an RX7), carrying only about 45

PHOTOGRAPHY: WARWICK KENT

Fiero feels tail heavy and steering and suspension are rubbery during changes of direction, for VW Beetle-like handling. Interior is comfortable, inviting, rear 'boot' tiny and front one non-existent

percent of the load on its front wheels, and with unassisted rack and pinion steering needing almost four turns to swing through a lazy 11.9 metre circle between kerbs.

We were also aware of slight but tangible tail-heaviness in the bends, particularly when threading quickly through the esses. During changes of direction the Fiero's steering and suspension become very rubbery, and there's some sense of disagreement between the front end and rear end. It's as though there's excess movement between the suspension and sub-frames, and between the sub-frames and chassis, as well as slight conflict between the front and rear suspension geometries, particularly in their respective roll and bump-steer angles. Combine that with a change in attitude from power-on understeer to power-off oversteer and you have a car lacking the fine balance which ought to be synonymous with a modern mid-engine sportster, as it is in the Fiat X1-9 for instance. Instead the Fiero handles and behaves more like a Volkswagen Beetle, or Porsche 911.

The only positive sides to this impression of heaviness are that the whole structure feels very tight and rides pretty well. The Fiero soaked up the worst of Oran Park's (pre-resurfacing) bumps with hardly a tremor through the body/chassis, and no loss of the supple yet secure ride comfort, which suggests the choice of springs and dampers is better than the suspensions' ill-suited rubbers and geometries.

The choice of engine and transmission doesn't attract many bouquets either. Borrowed from Pontiac's front-drive X series sedans, the transverse four is a relatively old overhead valve model with proven reliability, but it's heavy due to all-iron construction. It's known as the 'Iron Duke' in the US. Even though the Fiero version gets its own cylinder head and higher compression, the 2.5 litre engine can claim only 69 kW at 4000 rpm and 181 Nm at 2800 rpm. Circulating Oran Park without any fast company for reference, the Fiero felt adequately punchy. But US magazine tests reveal the Pontiac is about a second slower than the RX7 and Starion over the standing 400m, and measurably behind its peers for acceleration and in-the-gears flexibility.

The gears don't allow you to wring the best from the Fiero anyway. A four-speed manual is standard. The ratios are spread very wide, and the gearchange is one of the notchiest and slowest in memory. What it needs is a slick-shifting five-speed, but that's not yet available. From all accounts, the optional three-speed automatic is as exciting as watching paint dry.

What the X car drivetrain had going for it as the first choice for the Fiero was availability and economy. It must be remembered that the Fiero concept and design was sold to Pontiac management as a stylish, affordable, economical two-seater *commuter* car. Not a sports car. The long-toothed engine was relatively cheap to make and the factory had ample production capacity. Moreover the big four-banger could pull fairly tall gearing to provide the sort of fuel consumption numbers which would help justify the Fiero's existence. In the US, cars must meet prescribed fuel economy levels, not for individual models as such, but by average for the complete range of models. So you can still build a gas guzzler without incurring Government wrath and penalty if you also build an econocar which lifts the combined consumptions to the acceptable figure.

The Fiero plays its part in keeping Pontiac's fleet average in the black by earning official EPA ratings of 13 km/l (31 US mpg = 37 Imperial mpg) for the city cycle, and an impressive if doubtful 21 km/l (50 = 60 mpg) for the highway cycle. For comparative purposes against others of its class, the Fiero rates 11 km/l (26 = 31 mpg). It will be interesting to see how these figures change with the high-performance engine rumoured for 1985, either the J car (Camira) four-cylinder 1.8 litre turbo with 112 kW, or a 2.9 litre V6 turbo with 135 kW, both with five-speed transmission.

Although upgraded running gear and optional drivetrain are inevitable now the Fiero has settled in and proved itself a top seller (with a four months waiting list already, and first year's production set to exceed 90,000 units), significant changes to the overall package aren't likely. Nor needed. The cockpit is as comfortable as it is inviting, with excellent buckets separated by a deep centre tunnel which houses the too-small 39 litre tank. Driving position is excellent, thanks in part to the optional leather, tilt-angle wheel.

Directly ahead of the wheel is a boxy binnacle containing a battery of warning lights, water temperature and fuel gauges and an 85 mph (140 km/h) speedo opposite the tacho (with voltmeter). The engine's nature is illustrated by the warning sector from only 4500 rpm, with solid red beginning at just 5000 rpm. The instruments are well sited but surprisingly lack anti-glare lenses and so suffer many reflections.

Another initial surprise is the lack of a glovebox; just a simple pocket where you'd expect the box to be. There are small neat door pockets too, and a compact bin

which opens from the vertical console on the firewall between the seats. Although well appointed, the cockpit has almost severely simple styling. It's not unattractive and would, we imagine, help make for exceptionally easy right-hand-drive conversion. Nudge-nudge, wink-wink, hint-hint.

Apart from the lowly-scaled speedometer, the Fiero has several other noteworthy standard and optional features. Some, like the ignition key unlocking lever (a la Toyota's key release button), are fairly familiar. Others, like the starter disabler, take a bit of getting used to. This wonderful piece of fool-proofing prevents the starter operating unless the clutch pedal is down to the floor; same as having an automatic in Park or Neutral. Another unusual feature, and seemingly unnecessary complication, is that both sections of the lap/sash seat belts have separate retractor reels. The Fiero also has a metallic light orchestra which sounds off with assorted bells and buzzers should you dare trigger the system with diverse combinations of key in/door open/lights on/handbrake on. As an aid to optimising

fuel economy, a warning light flashes to suggest you change up at modest revs.

In the US the Fiero SE (the top of the two models available) lists for about $10,000. Even with the wealth of options Nylex ordered, the window sticker price was still less than $13,000. The extras included sunroof, Euro-design seats with suede side panels and sheepskin inserts, plus speakers in the headrests as well as in the facia, central door locking, electric windows, rear window demister, air conditioning, vanity mirror, leather-bound tilt steering wheel, heavy duty battery, P215/60HR14 tyres, and AM/FM seek and scan digital radio with cassette player and fixed mast antenna.

With that sort of keen pricing, added to that sort of smart styling, it's easy to understand why the Fiero has overrun its production estimates, even with that sort of so-so handling and lowly performance. The sales success has been crowned by many coveted design awards — among them three from the Reinforced Plastics/Composites Institute in categories of Design, Transportation and Innovation, and another two for "visual excellence" and "structural innovations" from the Industrial Design Society of America.

It follows that the Fiero has high marks and certainly high expectations to live up to. And after our drive we've no doubt that in spite of the existing shortfalls it really has the makings of a good thing. Its basics are mostly the right stuff already. But having made a fair fist of the concept, having gotten the car into production on time and on price, and having proved that the demand exists, Pontiac must now upgrade the Fiero's performance and dynamics to prevent the image being tarnished and to sustain the sales thrust when its novelty wears off.

When that happens the Fiero will meet the real test, with stiff competition from established favorites including the RX7 and Bertone X1-9 as well as yet unseen others which its success has helped inspire. Besides facing the likes of Toyota's new MR2 and, eventually, Ford's still-secret two-seater sportster, Pontiac will also be challenged from within by other GM econo-commuter sporties including a not-so-secret version from Buick and even the soft-top small Cadillac Callisto.

Will Pontiac respond? You bet. After all, Fiero means pride, and Pontiac has that and more at stake.

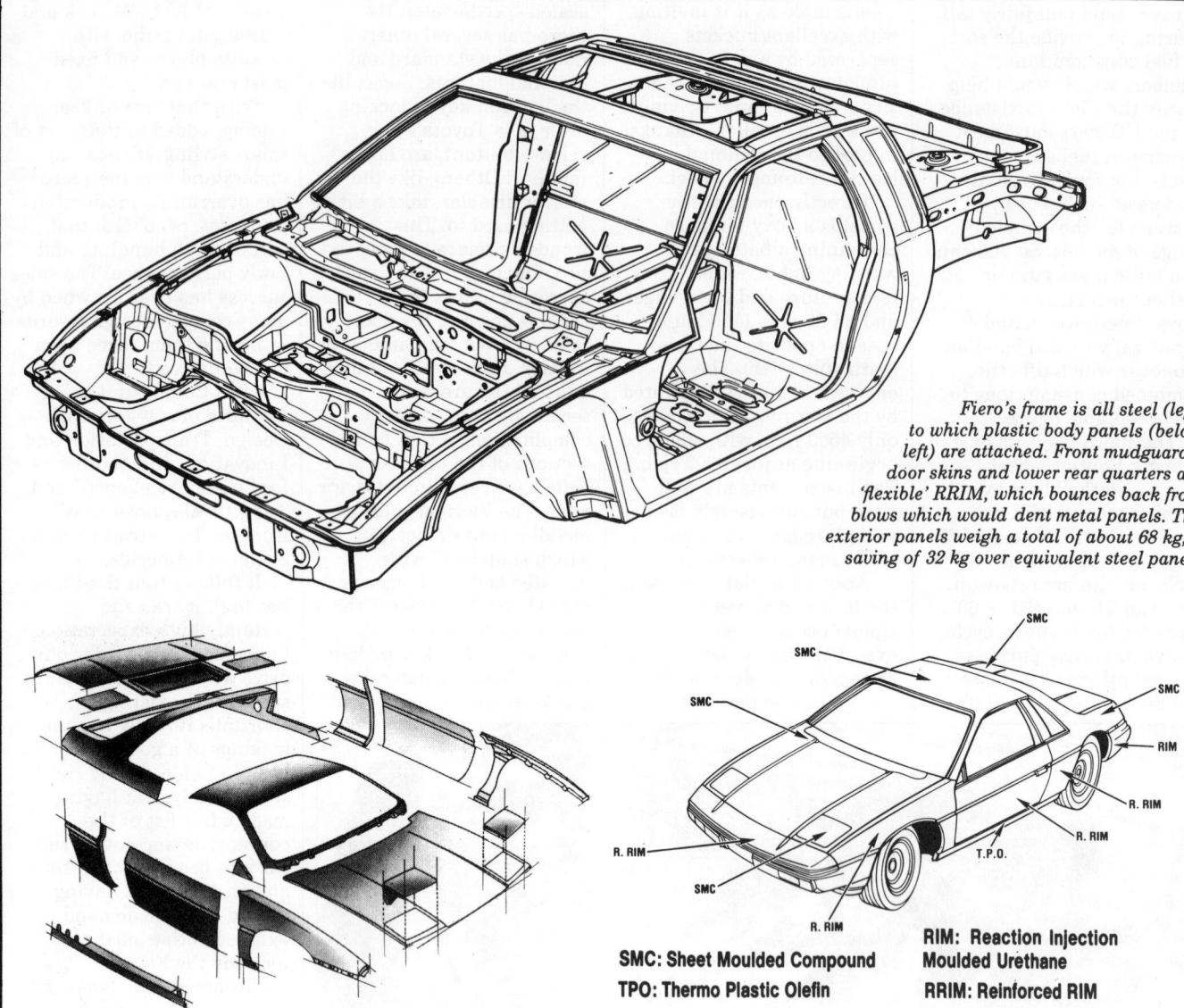

Fiero's frame is all steel (left) to which plastic body panels (below left) are attached. Front mudguards, door skins and lower rear quarters are 'flexible' RRIM, which bounces back from blows which would dent metal panels. The exterior panels weigh a total of about 68 kg, a saving of 32 kg over equivalent steel panels

SMC: Sheet Moulded Compound
TPO: Thermo Plastic Olefin
RIM: Reaction Injection Moulded Urethane
RRIM: Reinforced RIM

OBVIOUSLY THE Fiero is interesting if for no other reason than that it is new and different. But you'd be mistaken to consider it just a virtual showpiece of no real relevance to the local motoring scene. On the contrary, the fact that the Fiero is being shown by Nylex is very significant and may have far-reaching implications for Australia's motor industry. Much more than just a pretty face, the Nylex Fiero is here to parade its plastic.

The Fiero is not a plastic car, not in the way most cars are steel cars. But the Fiero has, and to some extent is, a plastic body. The mid-engine coupe is skinned with 16 major exterior panels. Six of them — the roof, headlight doors, bonnet lid, rear deck lid and upper rear quarter panels — are made of sheet moulding compound (SMC) for rigidity. The 'flexible' front mudguards, door skins and lower rear quarters are Reinforced Reaction Injection Moulded material (RRIM) while the side sill covers are thermoplastic olefin (TPO) and the bumper facias are Reaction Injection Moulded (RIM) material.

Altogether the exterior plastic parts weight about 68 kg, with the SMC panels accounting for two-thirds of the total, whereas equivalent steel panels would be more than 100 kg. Another 14 or so kg of reinforced plastics are used under the Fiero's skin, for the spare wheel well for instance.

Apart from light weight, the body panels boast excellent fit and finish. They are immune to corrosion of course, and also have tough resistance to damage from minor knocks and scrapes. They bounce back from blows that would deeply dent metal panels. And should the plastic skins be severely damaged, they are easily removed from the cage-like steel chassis. That feature facilitates after-market panel repair or replacement. It also points to another advantage in that relatively low-cost tooling means cheaper styling changes. It has been estimated that changes which would cost $100 to $150 million in tooling for steel panels could be as little as $20 million for the plastic Pontiac.

Take that concept to its absolute extreme and you could have two different cars, even two different makes, sharing the same basic chassis structure, even without the same engines and running gear, and each with its own completely different bolt-on plastic panels. Of course, things may never come to that, because makers' rivalries are too deeply entrenched. But having proved its practicality, the plastic-skin method obviously has a future, in Australia as well as Detroit if Nylex has anything to say about it. □

FLASHDANCE

PONTIAC HAD to work hard to convince General Motors management that a mid-engine two-seater had any chance of success in the US market, so the people at Pontiac must take great pleasure in its first year of production. Against what seemed like an optimistic prediction that 85,000 units could be sold in the first year, more than 104,000 Fieros were produced from January 1 through to November this year — and at that they are still so scarce at dealerships that customers continue to pay well above official prices for them.

Market success aside, we who have spent time with the original four-cylinder Fiero — myself and the *Motor* staff included — all concur on the basic likeability of the car as well as its excess weight, the blandness of its ancient pushrod engine, the need for five speeds and the inconvenience of its miniature fuel tank. Its handling, ride and wind noise earned less severe criticism. Right from the beginning, we all knew that better performance would eventually come in the form of the 2.8-litre Chevrolet V6, which is as much at home with the Fiero's X-car powertrain as the standard 2.5-litre Iron Duke four.

Now, going into the 1985 model year, the V6 is here and available in two guises: as an option on the upmarket SE version and as standard equipment on a new, still more upmarket Fiero GT. The GT is identifiable by a bulkier, aerodynamically cleaner front end, extended lower rear body panel and rocker-panel extensions — a package first seen on last spring's Indianapolis pace car and then offered optionally on four-cylinder Fieros. It makes the car look considerably heavier, lower and "meaner". A slight bulge in the engine cover, necessary to clear the V6, appears on all 1985 Fieros; a wing-type spoiler above the rear deck is optional. Against the basic Fiero's 0.377 Cd and 0.406 with wide tyres, the GT is claimed to register 0.350 with the wing.

Mechanically, the Fiero V6

Fiero GT: 2.8 litres of V6 power transform Pontiac's midship two-seater, but it still has warts

was utterly predictable. Its powerplant is the familiar 60-degree Chevy V6 first seen in front-drive GM X-cars back in 1979 and now used in the derivative A-cars as well as Chevrolet Camaro, Pontiac Firebird and (as reported last month) some J-cars such as the Cadillac Cimarron. In the Fiero it is the same new electronically port-injected version as in the Cimarron but treated to a dual exhaust system that lets it put out more power and torque than the Cimarron version: 140 bhp at 5200 rpm (up 11 bhp) and 170 lb ft at 3600 rpm (up 11 lb ft).

Also, and sadly, predictable was the absence of a five-speed gearbox. Paradoxically, the *four*-cylinder Fiero can now be had with an Isuzu five-speed, but GM doesn't yet have one to take the V6's torque. Expect one later, probably from Getrag. Taller (3.65:1 versus 4.10) final drive and first gear (3.31:1 vs 3.53) go with the V6, and detail changes to the gear linkage are claimed to improve its action.

Standard GT chassis fitment includes a suspension package that's optional on other Fieros (larger 23 mm front anti-roll bar, no rear one) and 14 × 6 alloy wheels wearing 215/60R 14 Goodyear Eagle GT tyres; brakes are the same 247 mm solid discs all round with servo assistance. Minor suspension changes apply to all 1985 Fieros: 5 mm lower mounting points for the "toe links" that help determine rear wheel geometry, claimed to reduce roll steer and thus geometry understeer, and about 13 mm more suspension travel up front.

Inside, the GT is just like the SE, which *Motor* staff drove,

except for revised seats, a tachometer reflecting the V6's greater rev capability (redline 6000 rpm) and 1985's across-the-board replacement of the voltmeter with an oil-pressure gauge.

As the photos show, my test car was the GT with spoiler. As I nosed it out on to a Southern California freeway into one of autumn's finest sunsets, I was captivated by the V6: butter-smooth, quiet and yet possessed of an almost exotic exhaust sound. Not at all peaky, it delivers generous low-speed torque but likes revs too; urge declines rapidly after 5500 rpm, but this is a long way from the doldrums that set in at 4000 rpm with the four.

In the test car this exemplary basic behaviour was marred by occasional stutters upon cracking open the throttle at less than 2000 rpm; perhaps related was a tendency to stall after a cold start and run shakily the first couple of miles. And the generous torque isn't sufficient to obviate the need for five speeds: though the on-paper ratios don't indicate it, there's a gaping hole between third and fourth, leaving one without a "right" gear for driving at 30-45 mph. Despite the claimed improvements, I found the gear shift linkage pretty much as before: a bit clunky but not bad for a mid-engine car, which you don't expect to shift as nicely as a Honda.

Whatever these details, the Fiero V6 does perform: I timed 0-60 mph in an exhilarating 8.4 seconds and wouldn't be surprised to see 125 on a long straight. I was never very critical of Fiero ride and handling. Like every midship car I've driven, it pitches over road undulations and goes into oversteer when you lift the throttle in hard cornering; I found the GT basically unchanged. An American magazine has reported 0.817 g cornering on the skidpad, slightly better than it recorded for the "four" with the same suspension and tyres despite about 150 lb more weight. The steering remains unassisted, somewhat heavy and not particularly quick, but road feel is adequate.

I was irritated enough by the 8.4-Imperial-gallon fuel tank with the four-cylinder engine; with the V6's 28-mpg (Imp.) fuel economy — itself a good value in view of the performance — it's scandalous. And there's not even a warning light. So I wasn't at all surprised when, after scrupulously filling up at 180 miles the first time around, I forgot and ran dry at 220 miles the next time. Lady Luck pointed me downhill to a filling station, but this is a fatal flaw. The engineers really must find a place for at least three more gallons somewhere.

Although the Fiero is better in this respect than most other US cars, it isn't strong on ergonomics. Reflections mar daytime instrument legibility; at night the main odometer is only half-illuminated, the radio's tone controls not at all. A lighted, visible control for the four-way hazard flasher would be infinitely preferable to the present one, hidden under the steering column. Longitudinal seat adjustment is too coarse; I was either too close to the pedals or too far away. As the staff noted, the boot aft of the engine is small; but my largest suitcase, a large one indeed, does fit into it.

The other Fiero flaw is — as with virtually every other American car, even in these days of quality *talk* — its workmanship. The plastic body panels are uneven and poorly painted; inside, various parts don't fit. Rough roads produced a cacophony of rattles from suspension and interior. This was a pre-production GT, but then all of its panels have been in production for some time.

This Fiero, though basically exciting, left me utterly frustrated. I love squat sports cars, love the mid-engine feel and found the V6 engine (except for the stuttering) ravishing. I could even live with the four-speed box. But not the tiny fuel tank, and not the lack of workmanship. Our American car industry keeps making progress, and yet never seems to get anything quite right.

Pontiac has not set prices on 1985 Fieros yet, but the GT is expected to start at around US$11,000 (£8500) and the test car with its air conditioning, stereo system, electric windows and door locks, cruise control and rear wing is expected to come to about US$13,000.

Owner Survey: Pontiac Fiero

by Bob Nagy

In the fall of 1983, Pontiac finally made good on its promise to market a low-cost, mass-produced, mid-engined 2-seater. Although the division was allowed to endow its radical Fiero with a rakish appearance and even threw in a genuine sporty-car, fiberglass-reinforced-plastic body, the General's overall gameplan specifically prohibited the newcomer from being even remotely construed as a Corvette challenger. Given these sizeable limitations, a number of critics, including several internal foes, expressed grave doubts regarding the first-year sales estimates of 85,000.

As it turned out, the gloom and doom-mongers were wrong in a big way. The Fiero hit the showrooms rolling and became a major automotive success story of 1984. Not only did the car exceed original expectations, the newest Pontiac came within a few hundred units of cracking the 100,000 mark. Given its status as an overnight sensation, we thought the Fiero also made an ideal candidate for an *MT* owner survey.

As one might expect, the Fiero's primary appeal was to younger singles and couples. Over half (51.6%) of the owners we polled had two or fewer members in the household. In 31.8% of the cases, the Fiero was the one and only car.

So what really prompted these folks to go out and take the plunge? It didn't take much searching to find we were dealing with a simple case of love at first sight. In this study in visual infatuation, no less than 82.7% of the buyers claimed that the Fiero's unique exterior styling was the major factor that most influenced their decision.

Cost was the second most frequently named factor in the buyer's hierarchy, with 22.1% stating that the Fiero's sub-$9000 base price was a key determinant. The average car in our survey sold for $11,658, less tax and title. But the range spanned over $6000. Lowball figures ran from $8400 for an Illinois owner, to the highest from a Michigan buyer who reported paying $15,080. Best prices apparently went to several GM employees who were able to take advantage of a long (and unspecified) deal through the company.

Despite the frequent incidence of pricing markups, owners we heard from voiced mostly positive feelings about dealer sales practices, with 67.4% ranking their respective outlets in the excellent or good ranges. Most frequent complaint in this area related to the long waiting period that often transpired between placing an order and taking delivery of the vehicle.

All of the Fieros in this survey were relatively early production models. All were fitted with the transversely mounted 2.5-liter four, the sole engine available at the time of introduction. The choice of transmissions was split 62.6/37.4% in favor of the 4-speed manual gearbox. The high percentage of 3-speed automatics and surprisingly frequent responses from female professional types indicated that, besides its nascent econosport following, a sizeable portion of Fieros actually were bought by people in the market for the latest thing in commuter cars.

Mileage considerations rated third on the list of major buypoints, and the Fiero appeared to live up to most owners' expectations. Fuel economy with both transmissions easily exceeded 20 mpg. Our sample reported averaging 22.6/28.8 city/highway mpg in autoshifted Fieros, and 24.2/30.3 mpg under similar conditions in cars fitted with the 4-speed. We also feel it our duty to advise you about a Catholic priest in Illinois who claims to be getting around 35 mpg in town and 48 mpg on the highway with his 4-speed Fiero. From what we can tell, either the padre really does have friends in extremely high places or he only drives to destinations that are downhill and downwind.

Over 9% of the buyers cited the Fiero's corrosion-free Enduraflex bodywork as another key factor in their purchase decision. The car's rustproof quality sparked particular interest in those who lived in areas where salt is used as part of the normal winter snow removal regimen.

Service did not turn out to be one of the Fiero's strong suits. More than half (56.4%) of the owners we heard from reported experiencing mechanical problems with their new Fieros. Amazingly, four out of every 10 (41.8%) survey respondents gave their local dealers fair or poor ratings on service-related matters. Much of this ire was the result of encountering individuals who were unable to diagnose and fix problems effectively. A sampling of representative comments: "The car has been in at least half a dozen times for the same heater and A/C troubles, and they're still not repaired." "The dealer replaced the throttle position sensor five times." "The engine has had a continuous miss since I bought the car a year ago." One owner actually was able to trade his original Fiero on a second car, but advised us that a recurring problem with engine surging has him looking to swap it again, but this time for some less troublesome vehicle.

The wonderful world of high technology was to blame for quite a few of the special headaches endured by the freshman Fiero. A whopping 30.3% of the owners who said they'd experienced troubles complained of chronic electrical problems. While some were related to wiring/fuse hassles and specific major component failures, the vast majority involved GM's notoriously precocious "check engine" light and other dash warning beacons, many of which were inclined to come on and remain on for no discernible reason. More than a few of the owners also complained about suffering frequent delays due to limited parts availability. But even with this acknowledged dealer service disenchantment, 83.3% of our survey respondents claimed they would buy another Fiero, and 84.7% allowed they would own another Pontiac product.

Despite some localized problem areas, the Fiero's basic construction and finish were judged well above average by owners, with 85.3% giving the car excellent or good marks. Those who felt otherwise cited a variety of problems with their Fieros, including paint imperfections and chipping problems, questionable fit of body panels, and various difficulties with the headlight activation system. However, one couldn't help but be struck by the sense of owner loyalty. Many who suffered through worst-case situations would still comment that it was probably just something wrong with their particular car.

Though some fairly substantial compromises left the Fiero's suspension well short of world class status and its powertrain ranks high average at best, owners still found much to praise in the car's overall capabilities. The Fiero's handling was rated excellent or good by 93% of the respondents, and two out of every three (62.5%) granted it their highest praise. Almost half (48.6%) also mentioned handling as one of their major specific likes. A few owners lauded the Fiero's rain/snow abilities, but most who resided in the harsher climes were a bit less complimentary. The consensus held that, despite its predictable dry-weather handling, the Fiero could be a bit of a handful under wet or icy conditions.

The owners also proved remarkably forgiving of the modest capabilities possessed by the Fiero's 92-hp 4-cylinder engine. Despite the lack of neck-snapping acceleration, 37.1% gave the TBI-fed Tech IV (nee: Iron Duke) excellent marks, with another 49.3% rating it good. The Fiero's 4-wheel disc brakes were also judged favorably, 87.7% of the owners evaluating the car's stopping power as excellent or good.

Although the supply-constrained sellers market prevented folks from being too picky about whether they would buy one of the original Fieros, owners did make it abundantly clear that a major powertrain upgrade was the central focus of their wish lists. A stronger engine was top priority of 51.6% of the owners. The vote was split fairly evenly among those who wanted more displacement and those who would settle for an increase in power regardless of how it was accomplished.

The second most frequent lament related to transmission and linkage ills that resulted in stiff and, in some cases, near impossible shifting. One unhappy California owner wrote: "I can't believe Pontiac engineers didn't experience the difficulty in shifting into 1st and reverse. And if they did, they should be ashamed for putting the car out on the market that way. I'm very unhappy and will probably trade my Fiero for something else." We heard frequent complaints about the lack of a proper 5-speed manual gearbox. And along with praise for the Fiero's overall maneuverability, quite a few owners bemoaned the lack of power steering.

Despite admitting that it is not perfect and far from the most trouble-free vehicle, the owners presented an overwhelmingly unified front in defense of the Fiero. The feelings of many were summed up by a Minnesota buyer who commented, "Right now, I can't think of a finer car for the money. I know about 10 other Fiero owners who are equally happy with their cars."

The votes were equally skewed toward the favorable when it came to assessing the Fiero's fun-to-drive quotient. Almost three quarters of the respondents gave it an excellent rating, while a mere 3.5% classified it in the fair/poor categories. A Michigan administrative assistant advised: "I put an average of 250 miles a week on my Fiero and haven't grown tired of it since the day I took delivery." A pilot from Maryland placed it into perspective. "I think my Fiero has lived up to what it was designed to be—a good looking, reasonably priced fun to drive and own car. It fills the gap (almost) left by the demise of the MGs and TRs of days gone by. I'll live with its faults, but I'm waiting for a turbo."

Several owners commented on how riding in the Fiero gave them a feeling of safety. Our favorite testimonial, straight from the believe-it-or-don't file, came from a female P.R. director in Florida who wrote to say: "Four months ago, my Fiero was almost destroyed by a 2-ton truck but I survived. I am comfortable knowing that this car is safe, the above incident being the second collision I have been in while driving my Fiero. The first occurred during my initial test drive . . . ." Okay, right.

Regardless of any perceived faults, the Fiero owner survey revealed a high degree of buyer satisfaction for the most part. Hardcore sports car enthusiasts came closest to feeling shortchanged by the package. Several buyers admit to viewing the Fiero as a stopgap en route to moving up to a Corvette or Porsche. However, with the introduction of the new high-performance GT model and several other additions to the option list, Pontiac has fully or partially addressed virtually all of the major weaknesses reported by our owner sampling. It seems likely that this further broadening of the already immensely popular vehicle line will only further enhance the Fiero's original success story.

VITAL STATISTICS:
Engine: 4-cylinder 100%
Transmission:
  Automatic 37.4%
  4-speed manual 62.6
Average mpg:

	City	Highway
Auto.	22.6	28.8
4-sp. man.	24.2	30.3

Average price $11,658
Total vehicle miles: 2,938,110
Average mileage test fleet: 10,309

PURCHASE CONSIDERATIONS:
Why did you buy a Fiero?
  Style 82.7%
  Price 22.1
  Economy/gas mileage 11.4
  Plastic construction 9.6
  Handling 8.8
Dealers' sales practices:
  Excellent 27.5%
  Good 39.9
  Fair 19.2
  Poor 13.4
Dealers' service practices:
  Excellent 28.1%
  Good 31.2
  Fair 18.1
  Poor 22.7
Would you buy a Pontiac product again?
  Yes 84.7%
  No 15.3
Would you buy a Fiero again?
  Yes 83.3%
  No 16.7
What other cars do you own?
  Chevrolet 30.2%
  Pontiac 21.7
  Ford 17.5
  Oldsmobile 14.8
  Cadillac 6.9
  Buick 6.3

PROBLEMS/ COMPLAINTS:
Mechanical problems:
  Yes 56.4%
  No 43.6
Types of mechanical problems:
  Electrical 30.3%
  Brakes 12.3
  Transmission 11.6
  Carburetor 8.4
  Shift 8.4
Specific complaints:
  Lack of power 14.8%
  Shifting 13.6
  Lack of luggage room 13.2
  No complaints 13.2
  Handling 7.4
  Workmanship 3.9
What changes would you like to see on the Fiero?
  Bigger engine 22.8%
  More power 17.2
  Turbo option 11.6
  Better shifting 9.4
  Transmission 7.9

PERFORMANCE/ CREATURE COMFORTS:
Performance rating:
  Excellent 37.1%
  Good 49.3
  Fair 8.6
  Poor 5.0
Fun-to-drive capabilities:
  Excellent 73.0%
  Good 23.5
  Fair 2.8
  Poor 0.7
Overall quality and workmanship:
  Excellent 46.7%
  Good 38.6
  Fair 8.4
  Poor 6.3
Specific likes:
  Style 69.2%
  Handling 48.6
  Comfort 11.6
  Economy/gas mileage 10.5
  Plastic construction 9.1
Braking:
  Excellent 45.8%
  Good 41.9
  Fair 8.5
  Poor 3.9
Handling:
  Excellent 62.5%
  Good 29.5
  Fair 6.3
  Poor 1.8
Seat comfort:
  Excellent 66.8%
  Good 28.6
  Fair 4.6
  Poor 0.0

MUSCLE MACHINE

When the Pontiac Fiero was launched, the company made it obvious there was to be a V6 version in the near future. The 2.5-litre, in-line 4-cylinder model was only to begin the line, a car for people more concerned with looks than performance. Now we finally have the Fiero GT with the V6 — and it was worth the wait.

The new drivetrain is tucked in sideways behind the cockpit, with the four replaced by Chevrolet's 2.8-litre, 60-degree V6. Though it only has an extra 0.3 litre, the larger engine produces 140bhp at 5200rpm and 170lb ft of torque against the four's 92bhp and 134lb ft. The difference in power in this 2740lb kerb weight car is enough to cut 0-60mph times from the high 10secs range to the mid-8secs. Top speed climbs from just over 100mph to the region of 125mph — and all at a minimal cost in fuel economy. (Too bad the fuel tank only holds 8.5gals.)

As welcome as the power, is the change in the demeanour of the Fiero when it gets the V6. Climb in, start the engine, and the general feeling is of a powerful car, not the timid impression left by the original Fiero. It doesn't hurt that this version has a nice rumbly sounding exhaust note. At 8.5secs to 60mph the Fiero GT still isn't a barnburner but, in low-emissions America, those numbers make it as quick as a BMW 533i or Mazda RX-7 GSL-SE, and half-a-second faster — and this is important — than Toyota's mid-engined MR2.

And this isn't a high-rpm, pause-for-the-power turbo powerplant, but an American-style engine with enough torque (relatively) to make the car move right now. You needn't be in exactly the right gear to get the power you want, just be within a gear either way. Unfortunately, there is only a choice of four gears, but there is the option of an automatic transmission.

With the V6 engine comes the soft, rounded nose that was first offered on the 4-cylinder Fieros marketed to announce the car's involvement as an Indy 500 pace car. There are extra rocker panels and a new lower panel at the back to allow for the car's dual exhausts. These pieces lower the drag co-efficient from the previous 0.40 (with the 14ins wheels) to 0.37. Add the optional rear wing and it drops to 0.35.

The suspension under the Fiero GT is not really new, having been an option on 4-cylinder models. Spring rates are higher and the shock absorber valving is firmer. Goodyear Eagle GT P215/60R-14 tyres are fitted on standard 14ins wheels. Brakes are still 9.7ins discs all around. Handling is firm and predictable, with the ride a little choppy, but not overly so.

The Fiero GT is a very pleasant, satisfying automobile, particularly if the fussy, doorstop styling of the MR2 (my opinion) isn't to your liking. On the other hand, the Japanese car can be had $1000-2000 less than the $13,000-13,500 asked for the Fiero GT. Toyota may have a legendary reputation for reliability, but Pontiac is no slouch either.

Incidentally, these are the only sub-$49,000 mid-engine automobiles of any consequence marketed in the US, unless you want to pay $10,000 for an an X1/9. Lotus's turbo Esprit is the $49,000 entrant, with Ferrari's 308 GTRi at $54,000 and the Mondial convertible going for $65,000. A Lamborghini Jalpa sells for about $60,000, while the Countach is priced over $100,000. A DeTomaso Pantera GT5 would set you back some $55,000. ∎

The GT has the optional uprated suspension package of the 4-cylinder model fitted as standard, which includes higher spring rates and firmer shock absorbers. Minor bodywork alterations drop the Cd factor from 0.40 to 0.37, and the optional rear wing drops it to 0.35

Motorsports on Parade

For fast-acting relief from the Fiero four-cylinder blues, say the secret words "Super Duty."

BY DON SHERMAN

• Out of the closet, sports fans! Motor racing has been declared clean, wholesome, and fit for factory involvement. So go ahead, let your pulse race to the beat of unmuffled exhaust, and allow your mind to rush with wild fantasies of the newest lightweight, high-powered, pure-competition exercises from the Motor City. Ford, Chevy, Dodge, Plymouth, Pontiac—all the old warriors are racing hot and heavy, so it's time to can the paranoia. And don't forget about Oldsmobile (drag racing), VW (Pro Solo, VW Cup, PRO Rallying, and Super Vee), Buick (CART and IMSA), AMC/Renault (Alliance Cup and Sports Renault), and Jeep (off-road), all elbowing their way in for a piece of the action. Domestic manufacturers are donning Nomex and strapping on helmets not so much to improve the breed as to keep from being trampled by the growing crowd of competitors.

Of course, nothing done the big-company way is ever simple. There are lofty executives to convince, middle managers to motivate, strategies to formulate, and longstanding policies to bend before a corporate race group can actually worry about screwing together a racer and signing up a hotshoe to pilot it around the track. In other words, politics are just as important as power-to-weight ratios in determining the final success of any big-brand racing effort. This is a phenomenon worth investigating, we felt, so we called on Pontiac for a look at its racing program during the off-season, when the heat of last summer's battle had cooled a bit.

Like all manufacturers who race, Pontiac does it to *sell more automobiles.* Promotion is the name of the game. Toward that end, Pontiac Motorsports has focused its attention tightly (but not exclusively) on two key products: the 2.5-liter Tech IV engine and the Fiero. If any combination needs help, this one does, so we can take comfort in knowing that a team of engineers is working diligently to make Fieros fast enough to win races.

And yes, Virginia, trickle-down from racing to the street does work, albeit at a much slower pace than most manufacturers would have you believe. You need only gaze over these pages to see that Pontiac has taken several significant steps toward pumping up its street machine with muscles developed at the track. The low and mean-looking Fiero is the engineering group's IMSA GTU road racer, which is kept around for developmental purposes. The taller one with the fancy paint job is Motorsports' own roadgoing project car. If you can contain yourself for a few more paragraphs, we'll soon fire up both of them for an editorial fling.

MOTORSPORTS FIEROS

But first, a bit more infrastructure. When we dialed Pontiac Motorsports, we reached John Callies, manager of Motorsports engineering. More a one-man band than an orchestra leader, Callies is the guy who coordinates the hard parts—the design, the development, and the procurement of every piece of hardware it takes to make a successful racer out of a Fiero. (Directly across the organizational chart, Ed McLean, manager of Motorsports on the sales side of Pontiac, worries about the more subtle aspects of turning racetrack success into showroom business.)

Born only three years ago, Pontiac's current racing program is like many great endeavors in that it was conceived in response to a rather desperate situation. A year before the Fiero went on sale, a number of Pontiac engineers were concerned that their new two-seater would bomb in the enthusiast press: we scribes were bound to be disappointed with the car's job-one performance. To help convince us (and thereby the public) that both the Fiero and Pontiac's four-cylinder engine had a future that would (or could) go way beyond 92 horsepower, John Callies and chassis engineer Terry Satchell proposed the creation of a legitimate in-house motorsports department—exactly the shot in the arm that the Fiero needed. Although Bob Dorn, Pontiac's chief engineer and true defender of the performance faith, was in the process of cleaning out his desk in preparation for a move to a new assignment, he nevertheless had the foresight to realize that Pontiac needed a racing program. In one of his final acts at the division, Dorn approved the Callies-Satchell plan, and Motorsports was off and running in a flash.

Callies, for one, hasn't stopped for a breather yet. During the first eleven months of Motorsports' existence (between Dorn's signature and the launch of the Fiero), the following was accomplished by an enthusiastic new team: the design and manufacture of one IMSA GTU racer (see following story); the creation of 34 new performance parts that would provide the foundation for a "Super Duty" four-cylinder engine, including a block, a cylinder head, and a crankshaft; and the publication, in cooperation with *Hot Rod* magazine, of a how-to handbook titled *Pontiac Performance Plus,* to let the world know how to fit the various parts together.

When the press showed up at the Silverado resort in northern California for the official unveiling of the Pontiac Fiero 2M4, they had more to feast their eyes on than a gorgeous but gutless production model. A Fiero-roadster prototype made the show, thanks to the design staff, along with a squeaky-clean, fresh-off-the-jackstands GTU racer to ooh and ah over. Mr. Callies looked a bit peaked but understandably proud.

The shiny racer, the inventory of competition parts, and the how-to handbook amounted to little more than the tip of the iceberg. The real mass sat quietly in Pontiac, Michigan: a huge engineering and manufacturing organization that cooperated with Callies' tiny group to create a racing Fiero in-house, even though all hands were busily trying to get the production model ready on schedule. Terry Satchell and several designers under him produced a set of blueprints that anyone may now buy and use to duplicate the racer's steel-tubing space-frame chassis and suspension. John Schinella and his Pontiac studio shaped the body panels around the racer's fat tires and ground-hugging dimensions to make it look the part on the track. Jill Vieira polished the aerodynamics in the GM wind tunnel. Tim Petersen toiled away at the Super Duty's block casting, putting back the meat that years of weight-saving efforts had systematically whittled away. Mr. Callies wielded a cattle prod when necessary, communicated with the aftermarket for the 1001 items that would be needed to turn the factory's core parts into a winning combination, and spent plenty of time explaining to journalists that, yes, indeed, this

was an aboveboard project at Pontiac.

The old Iron Duke (renamed Tech IV for the 1985 model year) may not seem like much of a motive force for a hard-charging racer, but consider the logic behind it. Pontiac builds only one engine these days, a four-cylinder, and the division was in effect the last to take a seat in the corporate game of musical chairs. Chevrolet has had the racing V-8 business all locked up for eons (except for Oldsmobile's 500-cubic-inch drag-strip mauler), and Chevy and Buick are wrestling over V-6 rights. With nowhere else to go, Pontiac quietly snapped up its own four-cylinder motor for "off highway" applications—and if the current trend toward smaller racing engines continues, this could turn out to have been a very shrewd move.

The Super Duty racing version of Pontiac's engine has only a few features in common with the stock powerplant. Bore centers, crank-to-cam spacing, and other important dimensions are essentially the same, making the Super Duty a "stock block" that can be manufactured on the same casting and machining lines that build the civilian engines. And yes, the Super Duty motor retains the one big handicap that distinguishes most American racing engines from their overseas competition: a pushrod valvetrain. As it turns out, though, this isn't much of a hardship, because virtually all sanctioning organizations give pushrod engines a weight-versus-displacement break when they race against rotaries or overhead-camshaft designs. In the greater scheme of things, all entries supposedly have the same chance to arrive first at the checkered flag.

Pushrods or no, John Callies does have the goods to run with the Mazda RX-7s, the Porsche 924 Turbos, and the Nissan 300ZXs in GTU. And his Super Duty can be built in several displacements—from 1.9 to 3.3 liters—making it eligible for a wide variety of NASCAR, NHRA, IMSA, dirt-oval, and even powerboat classes. Most of the development to date has gone into a 2.7-liter engine, and its output has been pumped up to a potent 300 horsepower at 7500 rpm. For political reasons, Callies is mum on the output of the new 3.0-liter four-banger that is defending Pontiac's honor in IMSA GTU this season.

For anyone who would like to race a Pontiac in general or a Fiero in particular, the process is simple in the extreme. Don't call Callies; he's a busy man. Instead, first buy the latest edition of the factory's race-car cookbook from Pontiac Performance Plus (P.O. Box 07130, Detroit, Michigan 48207) and read every word of it. Then, when you've saved the $45,000 or so it takes to assemble a complete race car (including a competitive four-cylinder engine, but no spares), follow the book's guidelines to the tee in ordering the right GM and aftermarket parts. (Callies' group goes so far as to include parts numbers for GM pieces and the phone numbers of the various companies that offer the right oil pans, valvetrain components, exhaust headers, etc.) Finally, screw it all together and John Callies will be there to greet you at the track with plenty of helpful tips. You should understand, though, that Pontiac's role is *support;* the racing itself is done by privateers, and private individuals and their sponsors pay the bills. Pontiac's investment is to make the technology and the basic competitive pieces available to everyone who would like to buy and race them. And don't for a minute swallow that old wives' tale that the factories actually turn a profit on the racing parts they sell to the public.

Perhaps you have no interest in racing a Fiero, but you wouldn't mind finding a way to bolt some life into that undernourished four-cylinder that powered your 2M4 home from the dealership. Help is available from the very same Pontiac Motorsports engineering department.

You start by buying the same *Performance Plus* book ($3.95), but think not of the tube-framed racer on our cover but of its brown-and-white sister ship. Thanks to the ever practical John Callies, a hot street Fiero is within your reach. It's his conviction that the four-cylinder in Super Duty trim has far more tuning potential than the new Fiero GT's Chevrolet-built V-6 engine, so there is indeed a tight kinship between the racer and the road car.

As you might imagine, 180 horsepower in a Fiero makes quite an entertaining sports car. Packing a 0-to-60 time of 6.3 seconds in its portfolio, the tuned two-seater is quite capable of eating Camaros, Mustangs, and 944s for breakfast, at least through the quarter-mile. The large-displacement four-banger (2.7 liters instead of the stock 2.5) is tractable around town, and we found no particular shake or vibration problem, even though Callies had eliminated the rubber isolators between the engine cradle and the body in an attempt to improve the rear suspension's behavior. A Hooker tri-Y header dumping into a Corvette muffler provides a potent-sounding yet entirely tolerable exhaust note, but we

MOTORSPORTS FIEROS

must be frank in admitting that we saw no sign of a catalyst to impede the eager flow of exhaust gases. At least half of the pages in the *Performance Plus* book advise that "Pontiac's Super Duty components are designed and manufactured for off-road use only," at the behest of the corporation's legal department, so let your clean-air conscience be your guide. The fully prepared Super Duty powerplant can be yours for about $2500, if you're willing to assemble the parts, or roughly $4000, if you'd prefer to have a shop build the engine.

A truly powerful engine in a Fiero is great news enough, but Pontiac's project car has several other interesting alterations that come right from the catalog. Diversified Glass Products in Pontiac, Michigan, sells the fattened fenders for both road and race cars, which you can bolt onto your machine for $2200 (parts only; painting costs more). Of course, you'll then need a meatier set of rolling stock to fill the wheel wells. Callies recommends Goodyear gatorbacks in the Corvette size for the rear and SVO Mustang rubber for the front. Center Line makes lovely modular alloy wheels with just the right dimensions for this application. This wheel-and-tire combo will cost you another $1100.

During our visit to the GM Desert Proving Grounds in Mesa, Arizona, we had ample opportunity to test a veritable wealth of chassis modifications above and beyond the fat-tire-and-wheel combination: vented disc brakes, electrically powered assists for the brakes and the steering, quicker steering ratios, firmer rear-suspension bushings, different anti-roll-bar sizes, experimental alignment settings, and a reinforced rear-cradle structure.

After a day or two of test-track and mountain-pass trials, we concluded that the Motorsports setup was indeed superior to the garden variety, though the Fiero's basic traits of heavy on-throttle understeer and awkward lift-throttle oversteer were still intact. Two alterations did, however, significantly improve handling: the quicker steering ratio that's practical with the new power-steering system and a set of firmer (by a factor of three!) rear-suspension control-arm bushings from the Citation X-11. The faster steering, which is scheduled for 1986 production, helped the Fiero feel nimble on its feet, and the tighter rear suspension tamed its lift-throttle oversteer.

Needless to say, we enjoyed the chance to play with this pair of feisty Fieros. It's heartening also to learn that a fast-acting group such as Pontiac Motorsports can exist within a huge, monolithic corporation. Future Pontiac Fieros—both on and off the racetrack—will surely benefit from the enthusiastic efforts of Mr. Callies and his capable crew. •

Vehicle type: mid-engine, rear-wheel-drive, 2-passenger, 2-door coupe

Price as tested: $19,000 (estimated)

Options on test car: Super Duty Stage III engine; Center Line wheels and Goodyear VR50 tires; fiberglass body panels, including GT nose, wider fenders, and rear spoiler.

ENGINE
Type .... 4-in-line, iron block and head
Bore x stroke .... 4.00 x 3.25 in, 101.6 x 82.6mm
Displacement .... 163 cu in, 2677cc
Compression ratio 12.5:1
Fuel system .... Rochester 1x1-bbl throttle-body fuel injection
Emissions controls .... none
Valve gear .... Crane camshaft, pushrods, roller lifters
Power (*C/D* estimate) .... 180 bhp @ 6000 rpm
Torque (*C/D* estimate) .... 170 lb-ft @ 5000 rpm
Redline .... 6000 rpm

DRIVETRAIN
Transmission 4-speed
Final-drive ratio 4.10:1

Gear	Ratio	Mph/1000 rpm	Max. test speed
I	3.53	5.2	31 mph (6000 rpm)
II	1.95	9.4	56 mph (6000 rpm)
III	1.24	14.7	85 mph (5800 rpm)
IV	0.81	22.5	131 mph (5800 rpm)

DIMENSIONS AND CAPACITIES
Wheelbase .... 93.4 in
Track, F/R .... 58.9/62.5 in
Length .... 165.1 in
Width .... 74.0 in
Height .... 46.9 in
Ground clearance .... 5.4 in
Curb weight .... 2756 lb
Weight distribution, F/R 43.5/56.5%
Fuel capacity .... 30.0 gal
Oil capacity .... 5.0 qt

CHASSIS/BODY
Type .... unit construction with a rubber-isolated powertrain cradle
Body material .... fiberglass-reinforced plastic

SUSPENSION
F: .... ind, unequal-length control arms, coil springs, anti-roll bar
R: .... ind, strut located by a control arm and 1 toe-control link, coil springs

STEERING
Type .... rack-and-pinion, electronically power-assisted
Turns lock-to-lock 2.8
Turning circle curb-to-curb .... 39.9 ft

BRAKES
F: .... 9.7 x 0.4-in disc
R: .... 9.7 x 0.5-in disc
Power assist .... electrohydraulic

WHEELS AND TIRES
Wheel size .... F: 8.0 x 16 in; R: 9.0 x 16 in
Wheel type .... cast aluminum
Tires .... Goodyear Eagle VR50, F: P225/50VR-16; R: P255/50VR-16
Test inflation pressures, F/R .... 26/26 psi

CAR AND DRIVER TEST RESULTS

ACCELERATION
	Seconds
Zero to 30 mph	2.0
40 mph	3.3
50 mph	4.7
60 mph	6.3
70 mph	8.5
80 mph	10.9
90 mph	13.7
100 mph	19.2
110 mph	25.7
Top-gear passing time, 30–50 mph	12.3
50–70 mph	9.7

Standing ¼-mile .... 14.7 sec @ 93 mph
Top speed .... 131 mph

BRAKING
70–0 mph @ impending lockup .... 195 ft
Modulation .... poor fair **good** excellent
Fade .... **none** moderate heavy
Front-rear balance .... poor **fair** good

HANDLING
Roadholding, 300-ft-dia skidpad .... 0.82 g
Understeer .... minimal **moderate** excessive

TRACK TEST

IMSA GTU Fiero

Hot-lapping the factory's developmental toy at Firebird Raceway and other venues.

BY CSABA CSERE

• In a world of 900-hp Grand Prix cars and 200-mph NASCAR stockers, an IMSA GTU car may not seem like a serious racing weapon at first glance. It looks all too stock, it has a small-displacement, production-based engine, and it couldn't possibly wrinkle pavement with its horsepower. But take a drive in one, as we did, and this impression quickly fades.

To get inside the GTU Fiero, you have to crawl through the window, sliding yourself carefully between the various tubes of the roll cage. You then squeeze into an all-enveloping, unpadded racing seat surrounded by stark painted metal, a scattering of ignition components, a fire bottle, and several metal-braided lines. Facing you is a fabricated panel containing a full complement of mechanical gauges and several no-nonsense toggle switches. The steering wheel and the shift lever are stock Fiero parts, but in every other respect the interior is pure race car.

Any remaining doubts about the seriousness of the GTU Fiero vanish when you start its engine. After you prime the fuel injection, it explodes into life with a violence that would do justice to a Top Fuel dragster. The short exhaust pipe that exits just behind the driver's door is the source of the commotion. John Callies, Pontiac Motorsports manager, explains that a rear-exiting pipe was used at first, but it cost 42 hp as it snaked through all the powertrain hardware. Now, even at idle, it seems that every one of those 42 uncorked horses is assaulting your ears.

Despite the racket, the GTU Fiero's Super Duty four-cylinder engine idles steadily at about 2000 rpm. And considering its rather large 2.7-liter displacement, it doesn't even vibrate too much. Blipping the throttle, however, instantly sends the revs soaring and plummeting through various vibration ranges, causing the entire car to buzz sympathetically and the instrument needles to quiver with anticipation.

Getting under way in the Fiero is easier than in most race cars because the stiff clutch is progressive, the engine runs cleanly at low rpm, and, for this test, it was fitted with widely spaced gear ratios. Unleashing the engine dispels this patina of civility, however, pinning you to the seat as the tach lunges toward its 8000-rpm redline. Quick shifts sustain the motor's voracious appetite for speed through second, third, and fourth gears with no noticeable slackening of acceleration.

Our test equipment verified these impressions by clocking a time from 0 to 60 mph of four seconds flat, to 100 mph in ten seconds flat, through the standing quarter-mile in 12.3 seconds at 112 mph, and to 120 mph in 15.8 seconds. And these times were achieved in a developmental car that was about 25 bhp down from the 300-bhp level of the latest no-holds-barred engines. Top speed was 161 mph at 8000 rpm with our test car's Daytona gearing.

Acceleration is strong in this car, not only in the forward direction, but along other axes as well. The suspension transmits even the slightest pavement imperfections straight to the driver, whose senses are in no way coddled by seat padding.

GTU FIERO

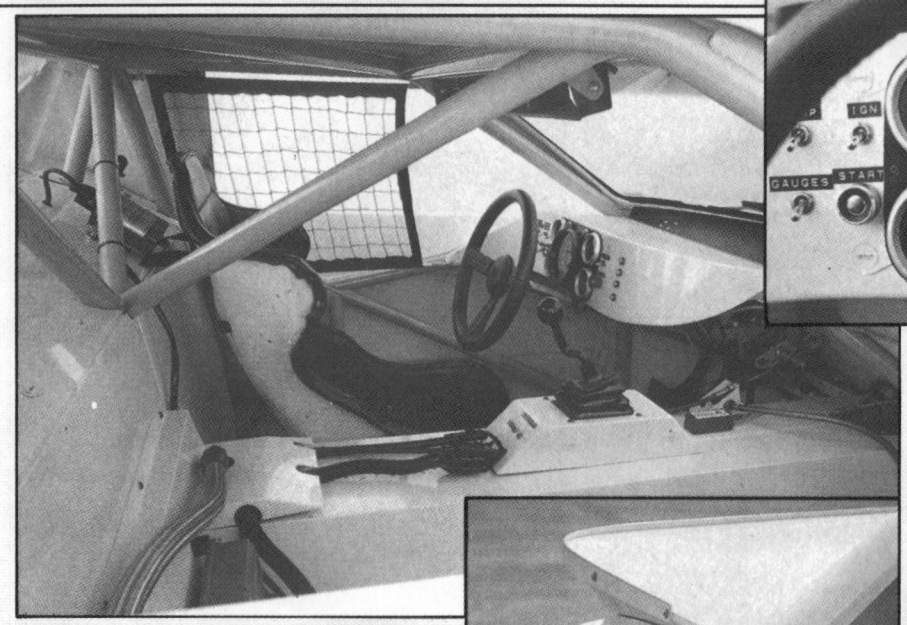

Even when you're deafened by the engine, the suspension messages are emphatic enough to keep you informed about each tire's activities.

The racing Fiero likes to accelerate laterally, too. Like many race cars, it has indifferent straight-line stability, but it turns into a bend very positively. It never seems to let go in the corners, either—we measured 1.16 gs on the skidpad—though one has to work up to using cornering speeds that would leave a street Fiero imbedded engine deep in a guardrail. The large tires and the fast steering ratio demand muscular inputs at the wheel, but the reward is excellent feedback and the ability to position the car precisely. Interestingly enough, the cornering balance of the GTU car is similar to a street Fiero's. Under power it understeers, while lifting off in a corner causes the tail to walk out. The race car steps far more deftly between the two modes, though, and it has plenty of thrust to induce power oversteer, particularly in low-to-medium-speed corners.

Drop-the-anchors deceleration is needed to arrest such potent forward and lateral acceleration on a racetrack, and the Fiero racer comes suitably equipped. With a curb weight of only 2050 pounds, a favorable weight distribution, and four large, ventilated disc brakes, it's a consummate stopper; although our test car suffered from premature lockup, caused by a rough rotor, we recorded a braking distance of 158 feet from 70 mph. Moreover, we detected no fade, and the pedal provided the excellent modulation that is typical of racing systems where no boosters are used.

Such a stunning transformation from stock seems incredible until you realize that the GTU Fiero is your basic silhouette racer. IMSA rules require that only a racer's external shape, basic layout, and engine family be shared with its road counterpart.

Consequently, the race Fiero is totally different under the skin. Instead of the stamped-steel structure of the street Fiero, the racer has a classic space frame with numerous triangulated tubes, ensuring maximum rigidity with minimum weight. The design was executed by Pontiac chassis designer Terry Satchell, who took advantage of Pontiac engineering's advanced CAD/CAM techniques.

Pontiac computer analysis also helped Satchell lay out the race car's suspension. Like the street car, the racer employs control arms in front, but the racer's are much stronger and have completely different geometry. In the rear, the standard strut suspension is supplanted by control arms with widely spaced pivots and a toe-control link. Special hub carriers are used at all four corners, along with Bilstein coil-over shock absorbers. Both ends of the car are fitted with adjustable anti-roll bars, and a few of the pickup points are adjustable as well. Steering is controlled by a Sweet Manufacturing rack-and-pinion mechanism. The twelve-inch vented rotors are from Stock Car Products, and Hurst Airheart makes the brake calipers.

To minimize weight-distribution changes during races, Pontiac engineers retained the Fiero's central fuel-tank location. The tunnel was widened, however, to accommodate a 29-gallon fuel cell.

The rear-mounted Super Duty engine seems close to stock at first glance, but most of it has in fact been heavily modified, redesigned, or otherwise overhauled. The block is a special casting with semisiamesed bores and extra iron in the deck surface, the main-bearing webs, and the pan rail.

John Callies, point man for Pontiac Motorsports engineering, operates from a clandestine base in the GM proving grounds at Mesa, Arizona.

The head has larger, freer-flowing ports, better cooling, and provision for stouter valvetrain components. A forged-steel crankshaft with full counterweighting spins inside the crankcase, and it can be machined to provide a variety of strokes from 2.60 to 4.125 inches. This crank design profited from the lubrication-and-stress-analysis expertise of General Motors R&D. According to Callies, it is bulletproof to 10,000 rpm with a 3.25-inch stroke, even with only two-bolt main-bearing caps. The crank is spun by JE forged pistons via connecting rods from a Chevrolet small-block.

Keeping the valvetrain together at elevated engine speeds has been more of a problem. The heads are fitted with 2.02-inch-diameter intake valves and 1.60-inch exhaust valves for good breathing, but these components are not light, even though they're made of titanium. They are actuated by roller rocker arms, special pushrods, and roller lifters—a lot of hardware to be jiggling around at 8000 rpm. Initially, very stiff valve springs were fitted to control these parts, but the results were broken rocker arms and excessive valve wear. These problems have been remedied by placing springs from a Ford flat-head engine between the roller lifters and the top of the block. These springs keep the lifters and part of the pushrod mass under control, allowing lighter valve springs. According to Callies, this solution is good to 9600 rpm.

Another knotty problem cropped up in the cam-drive gears. The crankshaft of this large four-cylinder engine may not break, but it does bend at high rpm. This phenomenon caused the early, helically cut cam-drive gears to break, even when the cam-gear material was upgraded from aluminum to cast iron to nodular iron. A change to straight-cut teeth eliminated the thrust forces and solved the problem.

Different fuel-injection systems have been tried in the search for power and reliability. Our test car was fitted with a Kinsler continuous-flow system with four port injectors, squirting through an EVM intake manifold. The same aluminum induction casting is also suitable for use with a four-barrel carburetor or throttle-body fuel injection. A GM-designed ignition system with an adjustable rev limiter and a racing distributor fires the mixture. The dry-sump lubrication requires two external drain-back lines from the head, because the powertrain assembly was tilted forward six-

GTU FIERO

teen degrees to raise the inner universal joints. Topping the engine is a lovely die-cast, polished-aluminum valve cover, which is thoughtfully fitted with an O-ring seal for easy servicing.

Power flows from the engine through a Quartermaster Industries dual-plate clutch (required for adequate torque capacity within the tight confines of the transaxle). A stock transaxle case has been used to date (a reinforced version is on the way), with a Weber straight-cut gearset to allow the selection of gear- and final-drive ratios. A stock cable-shifter assembly controls the gear selection, and 6000STE half-shafts distribute the power to the rear wheels.

Sixteen-inch Center Line wheels—ten inches wide in front, twelve in the rear—exploit the latest in Goodyear racing rubber. Fiberglass panels from Diversified Glass Products cover these tires and the rest of the hardware. This bodywork was developed with input from both General Motors aerodynamicists and Pontiac stylists to make the racing Fiero as sleek and stunning as possible.

Considering that it was an all-new car, the GTU Fiero fared surprisingly well last year. Sponsored by Dole and driven by Clay Young, the factory-supported Fiero was fast right out of the box, never qualified lower than sixth, and ran as high as second or third in nearly every race. Unfortunately, the inevitable teething problems, usually associated with the valvetrain, forced Young to DNF in his first four races.

The Dole Fiero's first checkered flag came at Charlotte, where it finished a commendable third. This race was a real heartbreaker, though: the Fiero had been leading late in the race, with a two-lap cushion, when a driver's error knocked it out of contention. In the next four races, the team accumulated several seconds and thirds, then won a big victory at Michigan International Speedway in front of Pontiac brass. That win was a breakthrough: the first ever for an American car in GTU. To prove that it was no fluke, Clay Young drove to victory circle at the next race, at Watkins Glen.

The Fiero's numerous DNFs limited it to seventh place in the final standings, but it had clearly demonstrated its speediness all season long. For 1985, Young has a new sponsor, Entech Engineering, and other Fieros will likely take to the track as well.

John Callies and Pontiac hope to see many more Fieros out there. Toward this end, the hardware, the suppliers, and the technology are all ready and waiting. The use of proprietary and production-based parts has kept the price down to about $45,000 for a complete car, which is about one-third the cost of the other top GTU contenders. The relatively affordable entry fee says a lot for factory involvement: this Fiero is most assuredly the cheapest competitive GT racer around. ●

Vehicle type: mid-engine, rear-wheel-drive, 1-passenger GTU race car

Price as tested: $36,000

ENGINE
Type .... 4-in-line, iron block and head
Bore x stroke .... 4.00 x 3.25 in, 101.6 x 82.6mm
Displacement .... 163 cu in, 2677cc
Compression ratio 12.5:1
Fuel system ... Pontiac/Kinsler continuous-flow mechanical fuel injection
Valve gear ..... Ultradyne camshaft, pushrods, roller lifters
Power (C/D estimate) .... 275 bhp @ 7500 rpm
Torque (C/D estimate) .... 250 lb-ft @ 6500 rpm
Redline .... 8000 rpm

DRIVETRAIN
Transmission 4-speed
Final-drive ratio .... 3.66:1, spool drive

Gear	Ratio	Mph/1000 rpm	Max. test speed
I	3.54	5.5	44 mph (8000 rpm)
II	2.11	9.2	74 mph (8000 rpm)
III	1.36	14.3	114 mph (8000 rpm)
IV	0.97	20.1	161 mph (8000 rpm)

DIMENSIONS AND CAPACITIES
Wheelbase .... 93.4 in
Track, F/R .... 56.0/63.5 in
Length .... 168.0 in
Width .... 76.9 in
Height .... 45.5 in
Ground clearance .... 3.4 in
Curb weight .... 2050 lb
Weight distribution, F/R 41.6/58.4%
Fuel capacity .... 29.0 gal
Oil capacity .... 8.0 qt

CHASSIS/BODY
Type .... steel-tubing space frame
Body material .... fiberglass-reinforced plastic

SUSPENSION
F: .... ind, unequal-length control arms, coil springs, anti-roll bar
R: .... ind, unequal-length control arms, 1 lateral toe-control link, coil springs, anti-roll bar

STEERING
Type .... rack-and-pinion
Turns lock-to-lock 2.0

BRAKES
F: .... Hurst Airheart, 12.0 x 0.8-in vented disc
R: .... Hurst Airheart, 12.0 x 0.8-in vented disc
Power assist .... none

WHEELS AND TIRES
Wheel size .... F: 10.0 x 16 in; R: 12.0 x 16 in
Wheel type .... Center Line modular aluminum
Tires .... Goodyear Eagle, F: 22.0 x 10.5-16; R: 25.5 x 12.5-16
Test inflation pressures, F/R .... 18/18 psi

CAR AND DRIVER TEST RESULTS

ACCELERATION — Seconds
Zero to 30 mph 1.4
      40 mph 2.1
      50 mph 3.1
      60 mph 4.0
      70 mph 5.0
      80 mph 6.5
      90 mph 8.2
    100 mph 10.0
    110 mph 12.0
    120 mph 15.8
Standing ¼-mile .... 12.3 sec @ 112 mph
Top speed .... 161 mph

BRAKING
70–0 mph @ impending lockup .... 158 ft
Modulation .... poor fair good **excellent**
Fade .... **none** moderate heavy
Front-rear balance .... poor **fair** good

HANDLING
Roadholding, 300-ft-dia skidpad .... 1.16 g
Understeer .... **minimal** moderate excessive

FUEL ECONOMY
Typical racing .... undisclosed

Driving Impression:
PONTIAC FIERO GT
Ferrari beater or Italian poser?

Last August, we described the previous edition of the Fiero GT as "Pontiac's version of the Dino 246 GT." For 1986, the appellation seems particularly apt—from sloping nose to flying buttress the new Pontiac 2-seater could fit into a Pininfarina styling catalog as easily as Marcello Mastroianni in a Federico Fellini film. But does it *rappresentare*—pardon, perform—like Mastroianni?

Depends on how you look at it. If you go back to our February 1974 comparision test of five high performance 2-seaters and down the columns labeled Dino 246GTS, well, Enzo may have grounds to sue for patent infringement. Note:

COMPARISON

	1986 Pontiac Fiero GT	1974 Ferrari Dino 246 GTS
Layout	mid-engine, 2-seater	mid-engine, 2-seater
Curb weight, lb	2860	2910
Weight dist, f/r, %	43/57	43/57
Length, in.	165.4	165.1
Wheelbase	93.4	92.1
Width	68.5	68.9
Engine	transverse, 2.8-liter V-6	transverse, 2.4-liter V-6

Performance? Our 1986 Fiero GT could clip the Dino's wings to 60 mph by 0.3 seconds (7.7 to 8.0) and better it to the quarter mile by 0.5 sec (15.7 to 16.2). Only at decidedly illegal speeds in the States can the Ferrari pull away. Still, what goes up (speed) must come down, and braking from those velocities spells another Pontiac thumbs-up. From 60 mph, the Fiero hunches to a halt in 166 ft, the Dino, 20 ft longer; stops from 80 mph double the Pontiac advantage to 40 ft (283 to 323 ft). But surely the Ferrari is the handler? Nope, through our slalom the Fiero snakes around the cones 8.5 mph quicker (54.9 versus, gads, 63.4 mph).

Then what we have here is a latter-day Dino-killer at a Pontiac price? Depends on how you look at it.

If you look under the Fiero GT's aggressive new skin, you'll find some familiar hardware—not just *déjà vu* for 1985 Fiero owners, but also for registration-holders of Chevy Chevettes and Citations. And there's the rub.

As lore has it, Pontiac originally peddled the Fiero to GM's brass as an economy commuter. Don't worry, they comforted the execs; this would be no high-ticket sports car. Suspension duties would be handled by the Chevettes' front double A-arms; the Fiero's hindquarters would be carried by X-body MacPherson struts tricked into being a rear suspension by bolting their steering rods to the chassis. GM bought the story.

And as a commuter car, we have no strong complaint. But as a sensitive sports car, we're less impressed. The original Fiero's high-school-yearbook good looks have blossomed into the stuff of *Playboy* centerfolds. Last year's abrupt ending B-pillars now sweep gracefully to the stern. The taillight band is now wider and taller, suggesting an even more exaggerated wedge shape that began with the 1984 (original) Fiero GT's cowcatcher sloped nose. Even the tires have grown up to 15 inches (from 14s) and have differential widths, 205-mm front, 215-mm rear (previously 215s at both ends). The 1986 Fiero GT is from every angle a serious-looking sports car; and it should deliver the goods, not just the groceries.

But doesn't it outperform the legendary Dino? In cold fact, yes; in subjective subtlety, no. On a smooth skidpad, a suspension does little more than keep the tires from scuffing the wheel wells; but in the real world, potholes expose the Fiero's components for what they are. True, the GT's spring and shock rates have been massaged for their latest assignment, but you can only squeeze so much water out of a rock. Tire technology has come a long way since our 1974 Dino 246 GTS test, and the Fiero GT capitalizes on this.

Under the hood, the Fiero GT is unchanged, which is not a bad thing as the 2837-cc V-6 simultaneously delivers good power (140 bhp), better torque (170 lb-ft), a healthy guttural snarl and a reasonable 22.5 mpg under our staff's heavy right feet. Still, this is only a good sports-car engine, not a great one. While brisk off the line, the ohv V-6 goes into oxygen debt well before its 6000-rpm redline, which is just where the Dino would come alive and sing on up to 7800 rpm. The transaxle, another 1985 carryover item, remains a remote-shifting 4-speeder and pointedly out of place in any modern car, least of all one with this Pontiac's pretensions. Further, its reputation has been sullied around these halls by the lever's tendency to randomly slip into reverse instead of the desired and more socially acceptable 1st cog moving away from rest. (To be fair, our 1974 Dino test also noted ". . . a problem common to most mid-engine cars; less than satisfactory gear linkage . . . the gated shifter required quite deliberate motions . . . " However, we are quoting a dozen years in the past tense here.) Also carried over is the steering, which—despite skinnier front rubber that might have abated the Fiero GT's absence of power assist—remains slow, heavy, and less communicative than we'd like.

Our Fiero GT had a base price of $12,695, up almost $1000 over last year's GT, and was trimmed with such amenities as air conditioning (good), central door locking (useful), electric mirrors and window lifts (ditto), rear wing (silly, blocks rear outward vision), a pop-up sunroof (mandatory) and a fine sound system, all of which added $1878 to the base figure (totaling $14,573 less tax, prep and dealer profit). Still, not bad for a 2-seater in this class with style like this, particularly if you can overlook the shifter's antics.

ROAD TEST

Pontiac Fiero GT

Looks aren't everything.

• We're all suckers for a pretty face. Members of NOW and knee-jerk liberals notwithstanding, that statement is as true today as when it was first uttered. Whether you're man, woman, or other, looks count.

For evidence we enter Exhibit A, one jet-black Pontiac Fiero GT. The Fiero was cute from day one, and it's gotten better looking every year. In 1984 it was treated to a nose job for its role as Indy 500 pace car. In 1985 it began pumping iron when a lusty 2.8-liter V-6 was implanted in the engine bay. In the middle of last year the pace-car body was mated with the V-6, and the Fiero GT was born.

Nineteen eighty-six is the year of the rear-end lift. This spring, the GT will reappear (it's been off the market since the beginning of the 1986 model run), and it will be dressed to kill. Run your eyes over the all-new plastic aft of the doors and you'll know that the design department did the right thing.

The new GT looks like a Honda CRX raised by a pack of Ferraris. The new shape is a single swoop from bumper to soft molded bumper that's sleek enough to fool the eye. The spec sheet says that the Fiero is a little fireplug, but the image burning into your retinas registers "exoticar." The drag coefficient has been lowered a point, to 0.34 (with the optional rear wing), so the new architecture represents some functional improvement as well. Yes, America, this car's got a body that just won't quit.

The tail end, however, is about all that Pontiac is changing this year in its effort to entice enthusiasts to drop more than fourteen grand for the top-of-the-line Fiero. The GT is once again saddled with the same chassis hardware we found less than perfect in the past. The steering is difficult, and the handling is so-so—and the promised fixes have failed to materialize for yet another year.

There is one basic explanation for this less-than-happy state of affairs: money. The Fiero was conceived as a cheap-to-produce automobile. Its front suspension comes from the lowly Chevette, and its midship engine and rear suspension are from the business end of the late X-car line—and there's precious little pressure to change any of these pieces. The Fiero factory can pump out a maximum of about 100,000 cars per annum, and the dealers easily sell them all. GM's number crunchers see no reason to okay millions for improvements that won't result in sales gains.

"We're trying to move the GT upscale," explains Fiero marketing manager William Heugh, a trace of frustration creeping into his voice, "but we've really split the Fiero line in two." About 50 percent of all Fieros are sold to women, says Heugh, "and frankly, they don't really care about handling"—at least not in the enthusiast sense. What's more, some 40 percent of all Fieros are actually base models, which sticker out well below the ten-grand mark.

Pontiac is loath to make major mechanical changes to the Fiero line that will raise the base price significantly. Dig into GM's financial workings and you'll find that every one of its car lines has a return-on-investment target that must be met. Pumping high-dollar improvements into the Fiero that don't produce extra profits is a no-no, or at least a very tough uphill battle. So forget the romantic, visionary notions currently operating at Ford, where building great cars is as important as raking in big profits. At GM, at Pontiac, and in the Fiero marketing group, the car guys would do more and move faster, but the accountants won't let them. It's a simple matter of cold, hard business decisions—and hold the passion.

The changes will come, our sources claim, but more slowly than anyone first anticipated. The five-speed, Getrag-designed gearbox originally planned for this model has been held up by quality problems. It might be in place for the 1987 run. A completely new suspension system, including sorely needed power steering, will be along in 1988, five full years after this car debuted—even though the engineers were admitting the need for improvements as the first production cars rolled off of the line.

But what of the new, sleeker 1986½ GT? There are a couple of mechanical changes worth noting. A close look at the Fiero's footwear reveals that the Goodyear Eagle GT tires are now sized differently front and rear. Previously, Fiero GTs jogged down the pike on 215/60R-14 tires. The

latest version is fitted with smaller-section 205/60HR-15s up front and 215/60HR-15s in the rear. "The switch to a fifteen-inch diameter is mostly a styling consideration," product-engineering manager Jim Lyons admits candidly, "but a tail-heavy car needs more rubber in the back."

Besides new sneakers, the suspension was treated to a thorough recalibration. The rear springs were stiffened to compensate for the tire-size differential, and the shock-absorber valving was reworked to reduce porpoising on rough roads.

The rest of the Fiero GT is virtually as you know it. In the case of the interior trimmings, this is no bad thing. The cockpit is every bit as inviting as the come-hither exterior shape. Visually, there is quite a lot going on inside the GT, but it all hangs together. The heavyweight woven cloth upholstery and the low-nap carpet suggest European tastefulness. The dash sculpturing is artful, and it's tied in gracefully with the between-the-seatbacks glove box. The seats seem shaped for action, and the steering wheel is as right as romance. The standard battery of gauges are of the analog persuasion and are attractively backlighted.

Even the engine is a sight for sore eyes. The 140-hp sideways six is topped off with luscious lipstick-red valve covers and a matching intake plenum. It's the kind of detailing you'd expect in a Ferrari or a Japanese boy racer. If ever a car looked hot to trot, it's this Fiero.

To drive the GT, however, is to know precisely how Pontiac spent its money—and here is where the story changes dra-

FIERO GT

matically. The new GT's shortcomings are virtually the same ones we carped about when we tested the original (November 1984). Despite the new tires and suspension mods, the feel from the left seat is all too familiar. The steering is not only heavy but as numb as a doorknob. Part of the reason is the tight steering damper required to help reduce the system's inherent kickback over bumps. The steering is so artificially stiff that you actually have to help it unwind after easing around a 90-degree corner in town.

You hard chargers will notice that the GT doesn't feel particularly happy when you use it as a sports car is intended to be used. When you hustle, the chassis gets loose in the knees and throws you off stride. Lifting off the throttle abruptly in the middle of a corner is unsettling, and if you're walking the tightrope of tire adhesion, get ready for a snap of the tail. There's nothing about the Fiero's handling that we'd call dangerous, but there's nothing inspiring, either.

The difference between the Fiero and its arch rival, the Toyota MR2, is the difference between an ax and a scalpel. The MR2 is light, agile, accurate, and effortless in a way that makes even toddling around in downtown traffic enjoyable. The Fiero GT, by comparison, is ponderous and reluctant.

The necessary big fix, of course, is new suspension and steering equipment, and both, we're assured, are in the pipeline. But from the start, the heat really hasn't been turned up as high as it should have been. We can understand such straight business decisions as well as the next magazine. It's just unfortunate when a company decides to spend its money engineering something like a light-up rear nameplate, rather than honing a sub-par clutch linkage, making the instruments easier to read, or working up a rear wing that doesn't block so much of your view.

There are other problems with the GT that no amount of money can cure. The front wheelhouses funnel your legs into a tight tunnel filled with pedals; there's no place to rest your left leg comfortably. (The MR2, by the way, has sedanlike legroom.) The relationship of the steering wheel, the seat, and the shifter is less than optimal: too tight around the thighs and too high under the right elbow. And this little two-seater weighs almost 2800 pounds because of its plastic-over-steel

FIERO GT

Vehicle type: mid-engine, rear-wheel-drive, 2-passenger, 2-door coupe

Price as tested: $14,800 (estimated)

Options on test car: air conditioning, rear spoiler, AM/FM-stereo radio/cassette with subwoofer, cruise control, rear defroster, power locks

Standard accessories: power windows, tilt steering

Sound system: Delco/GM AM/FM-stereo radio/cassette, 5 speakers

ENGINE
Type .... V-6, iron block and heads
Bore x stroke .... 3.50 x 2.99 in, 89.0 x 76.0mm
Displacement .... 171 cu in, 2837cc
Compression ratio 8.4:1
Engine-control system .... Pontiac-Delco electronic
Emissions controls ..... 3-way catalytic converter, feedback fuel-air-ratio control, EGR
Valve gear .... pushrods, hydraulic lifters
Power (SAE net) .... 140 bhp @ 5200 rpm
Torque (SAE net) .... 170 lb-ft @ 3600 rpm
Redline .... 6000 rpm

DRIVETRAIN
Transmission 4-speed
Final-drive ratio 3.65:1

Gear	Ratio	Mph/1000 rpm	Max. test speed
I	3.31	6.0	36 mph (6000 rpm)
II	1.95	10.1	61 mph (6000 rpm)
III	1.24	16.0	96 mph (6000 rpm)
IV	0.81	24.4	123 mph (5050 rpm)

DIMENSIONS AND CAPACITIES
Wheelbase .... 93.4 in
Track, F/R .... 57.8/58.7 in
Length .... 165.1 in
Width .... 69.0 in
Height .... 46.9 in
Ground clearance .... 5.4 in
Curb weight .... 2778 lb
Weight distribution, F/R 42.4/57.6%
Fuel capacity .... 10.0 gal
Oil capacity .... 4.0 qt
Water capacity .... 13.7 qt

CHASSIS/BODY
Type .... unit construction with rubber-isolated powertrain cradle
Body material .... fiberglass-reinforced plastic

INTERIOR
SAE volume, front seat .... 51 cu ft
           trunk space .... 6 cu ft
Front seats .... bucket
Seat adjustments .... fore and aft, seatback angle
General comfort .... poor fair **good** excellent
Fore-and-aft support ...... poor fair **good** excellent
Lateral support .... poor fair **good** excellent

SUSPENSION
F: .... ind, unequal-length control arms, coil springs, anti-roll bar
R: .... ind, strut located by a control arm, coil springs, anti-roll bar

STEERING
Type .... rack-and-pinion
Turns lock-to-lock 3.1
Turning circle curb-to-curb .... 39.9 ft

BRAKES
F: .... 9.7 x 0.4-in disc
R: .... 9.7 x 0.5-in disc
Power assist .... vacuum

WHEELS AND TIRES
Wheel size .... 6.0 x 15 in
Wheel type .... cast aluminum
Tires .... Goodyear Eagle GT, F: P205/60HR-15; R: P215/60HR-15
Test inflation pressures, F/R .... 30/30 psi

CAR AND DRIVER TEST RESULTS

ACCELERATION — Seconds
Zero to 30 mph 2.2
        40 mph 3.8
        50 mph 5.4
        60 mph 7.5
        70 mph 10.8
        80 mph 14.0
        90 mph 18.5
       100 mph 26.4
       110 mph 37.9
Top-gear passing time, 30–50 mph 9.6
                      50–70 mph 9.6
Standing ¼-mile .... 15.9 sec @ 85 mph
Top speed .... 123 mph

BRAKING
70–0 mph @ impending lockup .... 200 ft
Modulation .... poor fair **good** excellent
Fade .... **none** moderate heavy
Front-rear balance .... poor fair **good**

HANDLING
Roadholding, 300-ft-dia skidpad .... 0.80 g
Understeer .... minimal **moderate** excessive

COAST-DOWN MEASUREMENTS
Road horsepower @ 30 mph .... 5 hp
                 50 mph .... 14 hp
                 70 mph .... 29 hp

FUEL ECONOMY
EPA city driving .... 19 mpg
EPA highway driving .... 27 mpg
C/D observed fuel economy .... 16 mpg

INTERIOR SOUND LEVEL
Idle .... 57 dBA
Full-throttle acceleration .... 80 dBA
70-mph cruising .... 74 dBA
70-mph coasting .... 74 dBA

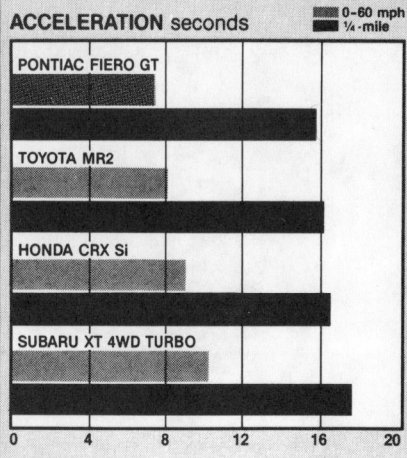

CURRENT BASE PRICE dollars x 1000
- HONDA CRX Si
- TOYOTA MR2
- PONTIAC FIERO GT (estimated)
- SUBARU XT 4WD TURBO

ACCELERATION seconds (0–60 mph / ¼-mile)
- PONTIAC FIERO GT
- TOYOTA MR2
- HONDA CRX Si
- SUBARU XT 4WD TURBO

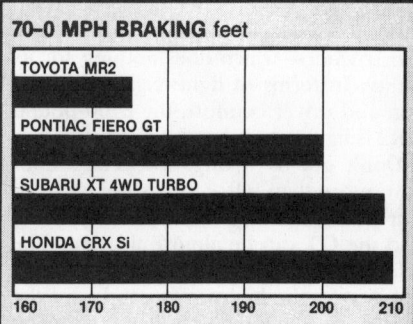

70-0 MPH BRAKING feet
- TOYOTA MR2
- PONTIAC FIERO GT
- SUBARU XT 4WD TURBO
- HONDA CRX Si

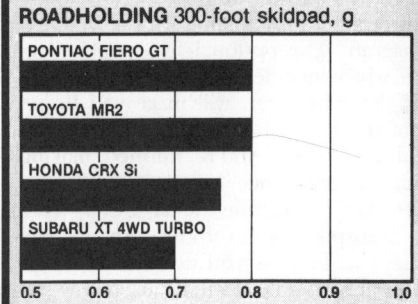

ROADHOLDING 300-foot skidpad, g
- PONTIAC FIERO GT
- TOYOTA MR2
- HONDA CRX Si
- SUBARU XT 4WD TURBO

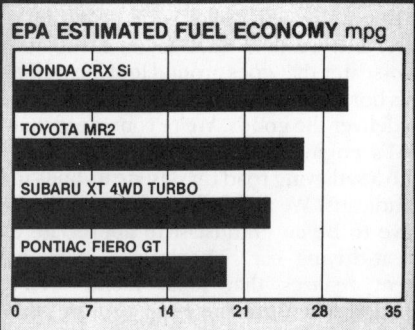

EPA ESTIMATED FUEL ECONOMY mpg
- HONDA CRX Si
- TOYOTA MR2
- SUBARU XT 4WD TURBO
- PONTIAC FIERO GT

FIERO GT

construction—which does nothing for its agility. In terms of lightweight construction and driver comfort, the 2400-pound MR2 is light-years ahead.

Don't get us wrong. The Fiero does have more than a few things going for it. Throttle back to an easy cruise and you'll find the GT can be almost pleasant. The ride is surprisingly fluid, the directional stability on the highway is good, and the wind noise is low. The 2.8-liter, fuel-injected six is a strong-running, free-breathing powerplant with a sound track fit for a Maserati. The optional five-speaker stereo, which includes a separate gain control for the subwoofer, will make you forget your troubles. And the plastic body won't rust out before you're finished making monthly payments. In other words, the Fiero GT can handle the day-to-day work of transportation without driving you crazy—as long as you don't ask it to be something it isn't. It will do just fine in polite society.

But we're not polite society. We love cars, and we think that any mid-engined two-seater that goes around looking as if it was born on an autostrada ought to be able to deliver the goods. We're convinced that GM's engineers can whip the Fiero GT into a satisfying road car despite its built-in handicaps. We also believe that you don't have to be an enthusiast to appreciate a great-driving car. The sooner management realizes that looks alone aren't enough to ensure the Fiero's future, the happier we'll all be. —*Rich Ceppos*

COUNTERPOINT

• I'd like to think Pontiac is only now recovering from the scalding I gave our last Fiero GT, but judging by the latest version, thick hide only grows denser.

Pontiac has twice presumed that an expensive face lift (actually, this time a fanny lift) could correct the wishy-washy muck-up of a good, sporty idea. Against all logic, the bean counters had sucked the guts out of the original Fiero until its handsome shell held no beans at all. Even so, the meek commuter model gave hope to those who believed in the idea of a mid-engined sports car. But when the halfhearted hot-rod GT finally came along, it brought us to a boil for all the wrong reasons.

The latest GT is better, but I am only lukewarm. Its engine still isn't ripe for the part. Its four-speed is still a gear short. Its suspension is better, but still out of phase. Its steering still gives no feel and no help whatever in centering the wheel.

Pontiac has blown its money on lifts of face and fanny, but the Fiero had a nice body to begin with. What it needs is a heart lift. —*Larry Griffin*

Is this GM's version of Chinese water torture, or what? Every few months, Pontiac trickles a drop or two of good news and perhaps a piece of hardware to suggest that there really is hope for the Fiero. Then there are delays and sideways shuffles, and in the meantime, another irresistible Japanese toy pops into the market.

So I've stopped hoping for a truly feisty Fiero and have essentially resigned myself to the notion that, with GM calling the shots, we'd better be thankful for what we've got. In the case of this '86½ Fiero GT, that's a handsome (please forget the rear airfoil), quick, somewhat entertaining excuse to leave the mother-in-law at home. The Fiero is not going to get the mechanical help it needs to be truly wonderful until GM is good and ready, because the dealers are already selling all the cars the assembly plant can produce.

That's frustrating, but on the bright side, the Fiero has taught the industry one lesson: fun cars—even if the fun is largely visual, as in this case—will outsell boring cars every time. I consider this a prerequisite to the lesson that GM hasn't yet learned: in this business, good enough will never again be good enough. —*Don Sherman*

The new Fiero GT makes a nice-enough first impression. It looks wonderful, has a cozy interior, and is plenty quick. But to serious car enthusiasts, the Fiero is a rolling example of unfulfilled potential.

Five years ago, when we first heard about the Fiero, we were ecstatic. The prospect of an American-built, mid-engined, two-seat coupe with four-wheel disc brakes, all-independent suspension, and a fuel-injected V-6 was more than we dared hope for in the dark days of fuel economy *über alles*. We had visions of a reasonably priced Ferrari knockoff with excellent handling, great stopping, and a sweet five-speed.

Instead, in its third year of production, the Fiero is still a patchwork of miscellaneous GM parts. The car's handling discourages probing its limits, the brakes are disappointing, the steering combines the heavy effort of a manual with the numb feel of an old power unit, and the gearbox has only four speeds. Although sales are good, this Fiero is fast becoming a non-car to enthusiasts. —*Csaba Csere*

PREVIEW

PONTIAC FIERO GT

America's mid-engined coupe learns some worldly lessons.

BY JOHN STEIN

Ann Arbor—Pontiac has gleaned a few things from the Germans and the Italians, and the division is putting this information to good use. For starters, the Fiero has finally received its long-awaited Getrag/Muncie five-speed. And Pontiac engineers recently indicated that another of their objectives is to make the coupe's steering and handling qualities mimic those of a Ferrari 308, which General Motors has acquired (among other cars) for comparison purposes.

Throughout its young life, the mid-engined Fiero has been under steady but apparently unhurried development. Even so, the car has helped to maintain an element of hope for the performance-car buyer who wishes to support the home team.

The P-car, despite its tricky space frame and plastic body, started life in 1984 as a rather ordinary performer—four cylinders and 92 bhp—with T-car (Chevette) and X-car (Citation) mechanicals. In 1985 it received the 2.8-liter, 60-degree V-6 engine and GT supplements, which helped the Fiero stand up a little better against the likes of Mazda's RX-7.

Now there are four Fieros from which to choose: the base Fiero Coupe and Sport Coupe, and the upwardly mobile SE and GT, equipped with the rounded nose adopted from 1984's Indianapolis 500 Fiero Pace Car. The revamped GT, with its longer, semifastback rear end, was introduced in mid-1986.

This season's big Fiero news is

PHOTOGRAPHY BY ROGER HART

the Getrag-designed, GM-developed, and Muncie-built MG282 gearbox, which replaces the Muncie FX125 four-speed in the V-6. (GM's Isuzu-supplied five-speed, which has insufficient torque capability to manage the V-6, is still used in the four-cylinder Fieros.)

One of the primary reasons for developing a new transmission was to improve the Fiero's "shiftability," a favorite term of Pontiac's powertrain engineers. In its old four-speed form, the V-6 Fiero's shifting feel and function fell somewhere between the Toyota MR2's and the 308's. The five-speed edges close to the Toyota's magic touch.

Working the Fiero's evenly spaced primary ratios and its taller overdrive fifth is a pleasant experience.

The lever pressure required between gears is refreshingly light, and it's possible to nudge the selector quietly from gear to gear with a single digit. The only significant resistance is from the springs that center the lever in its middle shift gate.

Although the new gearbox was sorely needed, Pontiac's market research shows that the Fiero's pushrod V-6 has been one of the car's best-loved features. The engine's iron cylinder heads have been retained for another year, though most other applications of the 2.8 V-6 now include the use of aluminum heads. The moderate 8.5:1 compression ratio permits a relatively large amount of ignition advance to produce maximum power on regular unleaded gas. As an added advantage, temperatures are lowered in the exhaust system and in the engine bay.

The Fiero's multiport, fuel-injected engine is unchanged for 1987, but its output is now rated at 135 bhp at 4500 rpm (versus last year's 140 bhp at 5200 revs); the car still offers 165 pounds-feet of torque at 3600 rpm. Peak horsepower is recorded from the lower point on the rpm band strictly to help the Pontiac squeak under pass-by noise standards.

Even on cold mornings, the V-6 fires immediately and then settles down to a 1500-rpm fast idle. We always took pleasure in booting the throttle and hearing the engine's terrific ripsaw note, delivered by a tubular exhaust manifold, the first of its kind for GM's 2.8-liter six. A stainless steel muffler and exhaust plumbing and a quartet of megaphone outlets complete the system. The V-6 does a more than acceptable job in inspiring the 2761-pound coupe. It's redlined at 6000 rpm, and would willingly surge beyond that speed, but an automatic fuel limiter cuts in at 6200 revs.

The front suspension design, borrowed from the T-car, consists of unequal-length A-arms with coil springs, shocks, and an anti-roll bar; the rear layout, purloined from the X-car, is composed of double-pivot lower control arms, MacPherson struts with progressive springs, and lateral tie rods that help to determine rear wheel geometry. Pontiac's WS6 high-performance suspension components—including special control arms and pivot bushings, stiffer springs, and new shocks with more rebound damping—are tuned exclusively for the GT.

Fifteen-by-seven-inch BBS-type wheels are used all around, but following exoticar practice, the front and rear tires are sized differently; the Fiero GT uses 205/60R front and 215/60R rear Goodyear Eagle GTs. Nonvented, 9.7-inch disc brakes are at work in all four corners. Under normal conditions they are virtually impervious to fade, and they modulate well, making threshold braking an easy task.

Quick-ratio rack-and-pinion steering transfers an accurate feel to the fourteen-inch wheel. Despite the large turning radius (37.4 feet) imposed by the GT's limited front wheel angle, nimble handling is one of the Fiero's best and most noticeable characteristics.

The responsive steering proved fabulous while we blasted around town, but the quickness turned quirky when we encountered highway irregularities, especially when pressing the Fiero faster than 75 mph. Then the coupe forgot its willingness to follow a steady course over the bumps—a result, we suspect, of a change in steering angle through the course of the front wheels' travel.

Because of its sport suspension,

FIERO GT

the Fiero's ride is less compliant than that of the base car or even the luxury sport SE, which has the "middle" Y99 suspension. Our Fiero was delightful to drive on smooth surfaces, but when we encountered the occasional obstacle course of broken pavement, potholes, or speed bumps, the front end made a resounding crash and directed a harsh jolt to the driver. The rear suspension does a better job, especially over the worst obstacles or at high speeds.

There will be little regret when Pontiac installs the Fiero's long-overdue new suspension system in 1988. The plan is to eliminate "ride steer" and the resulting front-end

hunting by correcting the Fiero's geometry. This, along with soft springing and firm damping, should dramatically improve the Fiero's overall behavior.

The generous contact patches provided by 205/60 front tires probably don't help the hunting and darting, but the coupe's roadholding does profit from all that rubber. The Fiero sticks magnificently. It's hard to imagine running out of traction when cornering in anything near a law-abiding manner.

The Fiero's dent-resistant plastic body panels bolt onto a space frame, making it possible to rework the car's external character with minimal production lag or expense. According to John Schinella, Pontiac chief designer and father of the Fiero shape, the GT's recently updated rear end provides the aerodynamic benefits of a true fastback, without the engine air-management problems that surface with such a design. Pontiac points out that the revamped rear end also accounts for a slight increase in downforce at the rear wheels. The drag factor is approximately the same as for the short-tailed '85 GT.

With a body that stands just an

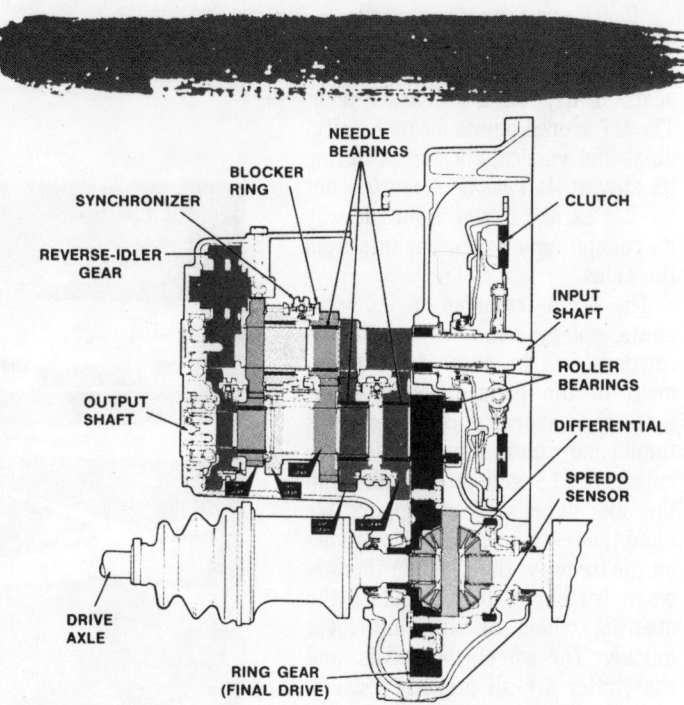

THE GETRAG/MUNCIE AFFAIR

Scouring the planet in search of the perfect shift.

Early in 1982, Pontiac engineers went shopping for a five-speed gearbox design to serve the upcoming Fiero V-6 and virtually all other 2.8-liter, transverse-engined General Motors cars. They ended up in Ludwigsburg, near Stuttgart, West Germany, at the doorstep of Getrag Getriebe- und Zahnradfabrik GmbH, a company with more than fifty years of experience designing and producing transmissions for companies such as BMW, Daimler-Benz, Ford, Jaguar, Opel, and Porsche.

Getrag designed a compact five-speed unit and, in conjunction with GM engineers, developed and refined the transmission over the following years. Key directives included the fifth gear ratio, a high torque capacity, improved shift quality, quiet operation, and consistently high production standards.

Specific MG282 (Muncie/Getrag identification number 282) elements include a low-inertia clutch, roller and ball bearings that replace tapered rollers on the input and output shafts, larger synchronizers, three shift-fork rails instead of a single rail, shift forks with more rail contact area, and Teflon coatings on critical surfaces. A final machining step, performed after the hard-finishing process, helps to reduce operating noise.

The final stages of development and production coordination of the MG282 took longer than normal. Since the transmission was destined to play such an important role for several General Motors car divisions, the company sought to introduce it as a perfect state-of-the-art product, free of bugs right from the start.

Detroit Diesel Allison builds the MG282 in Muncie, Indiana, home of the famed Muncie four-speed transmissions from decades past. The manufacturing plant there was completely revitalized with new technology prior to production startup; this equipment allows certain tolerances to be held to within a third of those for prior designs.

Design engineers at General Motors believe the MG282 has emerged at the highest quality level, but they are still keenly interested in any service problems that might occur. If an owner experiences difficulties with a gearbox that cannot be readily corrected, the unit will purportedly be exchanged outright with an individually tested replacement. —JS

inch shy of four feet tall, the Fiero has to carry its scooped-out bucket seats nearly on the chassis floor. The GT scored points for its longitudinal and vertical roominess during its stay at *Automobile Magazine*, but the car earned demerits for the way its cockpit squeezes occupants from the sides.

The cabin impinges on its occupants, not by means of overall narrowness, but because of the placement of the padded center elbow rest—the cavernous central chassis tunnel surrounds the Fiero's newly enlarged, 11.9-gallon fuel tank—and the door panel's elbow support. We liked the rests just fine while driving on the freeway; they were in the way when we began to manipulate the steering wheel or the shift lever quickly. The wheel, the pedals, and the shifter are all properly located, and only the disruptive elbow supports impede comfortable use of the controls.

A single steering-column stalk operates the turn signals, the wipers, the cruise control, and the headlight beams. It manages all those functions pretty well, but we found its stiffness, as well as the plastic-against-plastic creaking sound it made, rather bothersome.

We enjoyed the Fiero's sound system. Our car's optional Delco UT4 stereo had a built-in equalizer and a low-range control to dial up the boost to subwoofers in the kick panels. The highs can be spurred seemingly beyond hearing range, and the lows are so low that they positively vibrate your thorax.

Fiero drivers must remember to travel light, and to carry their gear in small parcels. The GT offers a modicum of storage in four interior pockets and in an oven-hot tray beneath the rear deck lid. The only way to keep valuables out of sight without their ending up like so much roasted poultry is to tuck them beneath the hood, on top of the spare tire.

Pontiac has done a good—if gradual—job with the Fiero's changes over the past few years. The latest, the Getrag/Muncie gearbox, is a significant improvement. For now, the two-seater must make its way through life with its Citation/Chevette-derived suspension, but we're happily anticipating a new setup. With this addition in another year, the Fiero may finally realize its worldly potential.

PONTIAC FIERO GT

GENERAL:
Mid-engine, rear-wheel-drive coupe
2-passenger, 2-door plastic body
Base price/price as tested $13,489/$15,609

ENGINE:
OHV V-6, iron block and heads
Bore x stroke 3.50 x 2.99 in (88.9 x 75.9mm)
Displacement 173 cu in (2828cc)
Compression ratio 8.5:1
Fuel system Rochester multiport fuel injection
Power SAE net 135 bhp @ 4500 rpm
Torque SAE net 165 lb-ft @ 3600 rpm
Redline 6000 rpm

DRIVETRAIN:
5-speed manual transmission
Gear ratios (I) 3.50 (II) 2.05 (III) 1.38 (IV) 0.94 (V) 0.72
Final-drive ratio 3.61:1

MEASUREMENTS:
Wheelbase 93.4 in
Length 164.9 in
Width 68.9 in
Height 46.9 in
Curb weight 2761 lb
Weight distribution front/rear 43/57%
Fuel capacity 11.9 gal

SUSPENSION:
Independent front, with upper and lower A-arms, coil springs, anti-roll bar
Independent rear, with MacPherson struts, lower control arms, coil springs

STEERING:
Rack-and-pinion

BRAKES:
9.7-in discs front
9.7-in discs rear

WHEELS and TIRES:
15 x 7.0-in cast-aluminum wheels
205/60R-15 front, 215/60R-15 rear Goodyear Eagle GT tires

PERFORMANCE (manufacturer's data):
0–60 mph in 8.5 sec
Standing ¼-mile in 17.0 sec @ 80 mph
Top speed 120 mph
EPA city driving 18 mpg

ROAD & TRACK ROAD TEST

PONTIAC FIERO GT

Exotic good looks, V-6 power and—at last—5th gear

PHOTOS BY JOHN LAMM

IT'S TOO BAD the word *convertible* has already been taken up in the description of cars with fold-down tops because, in another sense, it would be almost the perfect word to describe the Pontiac Fiero. With its steel underbody, replaceable plastic skin panels and various drivetrain options, you might say the Fiero is the compleat convertible; it can be made into just about anything from a vanilla-plain commuter to a hard-charging sports car, so long as the basic layout is left as a mid-engine 2-seater. When Pontiac engineers designed the Fiero, they left the door open for some pretty substantial changes in its look and character. And a good thing, too.

When the first Fiero came out four years ago, most people agreed that it was an innovative design and that it had won the poor-man's Dino styling contest, hands down, with Toyota's MR2 and the Fiat/Bertone X1/9. It was a clean, integrated-looking car with interesting technical and production features, and Pontiac was credited for its resourcefulness in producing the car at all.

But: There was also a sense that the Fiero had been put into production without the full set of drivetrain options its racy looks demanded. For one thing, the only engine was GM's low-revving Iron Duke, an adequate but not terribly exciting 2.5-liter 4-cylinder unit. Furthermore, it was mated to a clunky 4-speed transmission in an era when everyone else in the world (i.e., Europe and Japan) had been producing good 5-speed gearboxes for about 10 years, and the car itself was surprisingly heavy. Praises were mingled with groans for what might have been.

Then a GT version came along last year with even racier, more aerodynamic body panels snapped into place and a 2.8-liter V-6 engine, but still with a 4-speed transmission. More praise, fewer groans.

And now, for 1987, Pontiac has at last produced the Fiero we would like to have seen that first year. The new Fiero GT has the good-looking aero body with snarky nose, flying buttress roofline, the 135-bhp

V-6 and—at last—a Getrag 5-speed transmission, not to mention Pontiac's WS6 sport suspension package, wide alloy wheels and wide Goodyear Eagle GT tires. The too-small 10.0-gal. fuel tank has also been replaced by a more livable 12.0-gal. tank. All of the choice pieces have finally dropped into place on one car.

The base 2.5-liter Fiero coupe and an upscale SE model with firmer suspension are still available, but the GT, at the top of the line, is likely to be of the greatest interest to those who like their winding roads to slip by quickly. The features available in the GT have not only changed the look and feel of the Fiero, but also transformed it into an entirely different animal from that first 4-banger commuter car. It has, in effect, been converted.

So what is it like to drive the new fully realized Fiero GT? To find out, we commuted back and forth to work and ran errands for a few weeks, then took it for a weekend of hard driving on straight desert roads and the endless fast switchbacks of the Angeles Crest Highway.

First of all, it would be fair to say that the Fiero GT is almost a car with two personalities. Mid-engine cars tend to be something of a compromise when it comes to luggage space, ingress and egress and outward vision, and the Fiero driver feels that compromise in day-to-day driving around town. The front trunk is filled mostly with spare tire, radiator and brake paraphernalia, leaving just enough space for a small piece of soft, malleable luggage. The rear trunk, behind the engine, is deep but not very long, good for maybe two medium-slim suitcases. In other words, this is not the car for hauling rakes, shovels and bags of fertilizer on the weekend; a front-engine hatchback configuration offers much more hauling flexibility. (It's worth mentioning, however, that the Fiero rear trunk is well insulated from engine heat; none of our luggage melted or even felt warm after a long climb.)

You also sit low in the Fiero, befitting its sports-car character, and the high back deck gives a sense of restricted rear vision common to mid-engine cars. Steering is lighter than it used to be, but still somewhat heavy in slow maneuvering, despite Pontiac's installing narrower tires on the front end, and the Getrag-designed, GM-built 5-speed transmission is good, but still doesn't quite have that light snick-snick quality of, say, the Toyota MR2 transmission. Add to that the loudest and most irritating set of seatbelt/headlight/parking brake buzzers this side of an air-raid siren, and you have a car that is not as pleasant as it could be for the dray service of daily driving. Like the 246 Dino Ferrari, the Fiero GT feels like a car that wants to get out of town.

And it goes very nicely when it gets there. Pass that last city limits sign on your way up the Angeles Crest Highway, shift

up through 3rd and 4th gears and the Fiero GT really starts to come alive. The steering that was a little heavy suddenly becomes effortless and accurate, giving excellent feedback and feel for traction through the steering wheel. As speed builds and you start throwing the car into corners, you discover that those big Goodyear Eagle GTs provide almost endless stick, and you have to be going incredibly fast to make them break loose into mild understeer, and they have to be tossed hard into oversteer. In other words, the car is beautifully balanced and almost refuses to do anything but go where you point it. In its tenacious stick and ability to go very fast over a mountain road with a minimum of driver effort, the Fiero GT feels more like a smaller, tighter Corvette than a direct competitor to any of the imported 2-seaters. It feels solid, strong, fast and a little bigger than it looks.

Sound is part of that impression. The engine, played through the Fiero's dual "twin-trumpet" exhaust system, sounds more like a small-block V-8 than a 2.8-liter V-6, and its excellent midrange torque furthers the sensation. Tall gearing takes advantage of that torque and adds to the big-engine feel, though the Fiero GT does use a shorter axle ratio than the standard SE version with 5-speed: 3.61:1 versus 3.35:1. Even so, 5th is very much an overdrive/cruising gear, and even 4th is quite relaxed at highway speeds. On a winding road, you can simply leave the Fiero in 3rd gear and drive it almost like a car with an automatic transmission because 3rd will provide good throttle response and quick acceleration all the way from 50 mph up to about 90 mph without going over redline.

That flexibility and the car's superb handling and steering make the Fiero a true, exhilarating pleasure to drive on roads where sports cars are meant to be driven. Relaxed gearing and surprisingly good ride, especially for a car with so little roll and sway in corners, make it an equally good highway cruiser for long trips. Only a few minor rattles and a bit of tire rumble transmitted through the chassis intrude on your serenity, and our particular test car had a small wind leak somewhere

around the molding in the driver's door.

The interior is a mixed bag—comfortable seats, nice materials in attractive shades of gray, with an occasional finish flaw. The vinyl handbrake cover, for instance, had a sharp edge that cut one driver's hand, and the setscrew loosened on the rearview mirror bracket, allowing the mirror to fall off and land in the driver's lap while he was adjusting it. The analog instruments are easy to read, though the center-mounted voltmeter and oil-pressure gauge look like afterthoughts on an otherwise clean, integrated dash panel. The radio is of the million-small-button type, a school of design whose doors we all hope will soon close.

There may still be a few of the small details to be refined, but Pontiac has done its job on the important things. What more can you ask of a real sports car than you get from the Fiero GT? It looks racy and exotic, sticks to the road like glue, sounds good and gets you from one side of the mountains to the other quicker than all but a few cars on earth—for $13,489.

—*Peter Egan*

Base price	$13,489
Price as tested	$15,449

Price as tested includes: power door locks ($145), front floor mats ($24), air cond ($775), power sport mirrors ($79), visor vanity mirror ($7), cruise control ($775), Calif. emissions ($99), heavy-duty battery ($26), speaker system ($150), AM/FM stereo/cassette ($160)

GENERAL DATA

Curb weight, lb	2710
Length, in.	165.1
Suspension, f/r	unequal-length A-arms/Chapman struts, lower A-arms
Brake system, f/r	9.7-in. discs/9.7-in. discs
Wheels	cast alloy, 15 x 7
Tires	P205/60R-15f, P215/60R-15r
Steering type	rack & pinion
Engine type	ohv V-6
Displacement, cc	2837
Bhp @ rpm, SAE net	135 @ 4900
Torque @ rpm, lb-ft	160 @ 3900
Transmission	5-sp manual

PERFORMANCE

Acceleration
Time to distance, sec:

0–1320 ft (¼ mi)	16.0
Speed at end of ¼ mi, mph	86.5

Time to speed, sec:

0–30 mph	2.3
0–60 mph	7.7
0–80 mph	13.6

Braking
Minimum stopping distances, ft:

From 60 mph	165
From 80 mph	276
Control in panic stop	very good

Handling

Lateral accel, 100-ft radius, g	0.83
Speed thru 700-ft slalom, mph	61.5

Interior noise

Maximum, 1st gear	77
Constant 70 mph	76
Fuel economy, mpg	19.5

REVIEW

SPORTS CARS FOR

Honda Civic CRX Si, Pontiac Fiero GT, Toyota MR2:
In search of brilliance among two-seat coupes.

BY JOHN STEIN

THE REAL WORLD

Lancaster, California—A good sports car does not have to be priced like a corporate jet, nor does it have to be too high-strung for easy daily use. That is the consensus of this staff after spending time with the Honda Civic CRX Si, the Pontiac Fiero GT, and the Toyota MR2. Of course, lower-priced sports cars are somewhat nonexclusive; but, although you may not be the only guy at a traffic light in one of these two-seaters, there are about a million other reasons to love them. All three cars are wonderful, each in its own way.

You don't have to make any excuses for the way the coupes work. Although they are heavily oriented toward performance, these cars are also well equipped for more than just shamelessly zipping from one place to another. They all serve perfectly well in the day-to-day driving cycle.

PHOTOGRAPHY BY ROBIN RIGGS

The Honda, Pontiac, and Toyota in question are also relatively inexpensive (in base form, they average around $12,000). It helps to put their cost into perspective if you consider that their prices, added together, still total less than that of a Porsche 911 Carrera. In addition to being practical and fun, the CRX Si, Fiero GT, and MR2 are clearly good values.

To best compare a group of cars, a

The wonder of a CRX: light weight, a 91-bhp four, and a big cabin.

SPORTS CARS

driving trip is always in order. (We'd opt for a road trip for many less important reasons, anyway.) After quite some time shuttling participants through Los Angeles traffic, our crew (including Jean Lindamood, Kevin Smith, your scribe, John Phillips III, Trant Jarman, and photographer Robin Riggs, driving a panting Dodge Raider camera car) headed up California 33 to begin a back-road driving loop.

Snaky Highway 33 ("wiggle-wiggle," as Jarman calls it) runs out through the coastal mountain town of Ojai, then branches toward Frazier Park on Interstate 5's famous "grapevine" grade. This first part of our four-day driving schedule had nearly everything you could ask for in motorized recreation, including alpine passes, hairpin turns, fast sweepers—and sparse traffic. It guaranteed us time enough to think about the similarities and the differences of these cars.

The three coupes come from different design camps, but they still manage to mix well. The front-wheel-drive Honda CRX may be properly defined as an economy car (it's based on the five-passenger Civic), but with the Si's high-output engine, a shorter wheelbase, a sloping roof, and no back seat, its character is quite different. Blessed with low weight (1978 pounds) and excellent handling, the CRX Si is absolutely convinced that it is a sports car.

Fiero devotees are quick to embrace the mid-engined P-car's unique engineering approach: a rigid steel space frame, with dent- and rust-proof plastic body panels. In addition to that exclusive chassis, the car incorporates suspension pieces originally adopted from the Chevette and the Citation, and a V-6 it shares with other GM divisions. The Fiero GT is rolling testimony to the workability of using existing bits to thriftily create a unique vehicle.

Considering that its pedigree includes ordinary GM components, the Fiero is really a pretty good package. But when corralled with its trim Japanese competitors, the shapely GT seems to be something of an odd duck, a fraction too large and a few hundred pounds too heavy. Over the course of long-term ownership, however, the punching-bag sturdiness of the 2712-pound Fiero could prove to be a real asset.

By comparison, the mid-engined Toyota MR2 (at 2389 pounds, not drastically lighter than the Pontiac) is closer to an ideal size. The MR2 is a truly well-balanced car, with spirited handling and marvelous control function. Toyota is the only one of the three carmakers that does not offer its two-seater in multiple power and trim levels. If you want a fancier MR2, you simply load it with options. This year, the buyer's choices have been expanded slightly by the addition of a new T-bar roof.

Despite careful packaging of accouterments, the engines and chassis are what really make the character of each car. Honda relies on a 1.5-liter hot rod version of its twelve-

Formula for a Fiero: big-car steering feel, a lusty 135-bhp V-6, and fat, sticky Goodyears.

SPORTS CARS

valve, overhead camshaft four (also found in the Civic Si) to produce 91 bhp at 5500 rpm. Components that differentiate the Si include an 8.7:1 compression ratio, larger exhaust valves, and multiport fuel injection. No question, the CRX Si's power is a great improvement over the standard CRX's 76 bhp. But if its role is to be a sports car, the CRX could do with ten or fifteen more horses.

Pontiac's 2.8-liter six uses an iron block and two pushrod-operated overhead valves per cylinder, and its high-flow iron heads and multiport fuel injection help it deliver 135 bhp at 4500 rpm. Oddly, the Fiero seems almost to fall short in its power output, because solid low-end and midrange strengths nearly overshadow the top-end charge. Given the Fiero GT's generous displacement, Pontiac engineers might consider pushing some of the impressive midrange power higher in the rev range, for more driving thrill between corners.

The Toyota MR2 has a 1.6-liter, 112-bhp (at 6600 rpm) aluminum four whose layout is closest to racing's engineering status quo—double camshafts and four valves per cylinder. In specific output, the free-breathing engine makes 70.6 bhp per liter, four percent more than the CRX Si and nearly half again as much power per liter as the Pontiac. (Remember the old saw "There's no substitute for cubic inches"? Volumetric efficiency comes close.)

Where the ratio of power to weight —a more critical element in the

CONTINUED ON PAGE 85

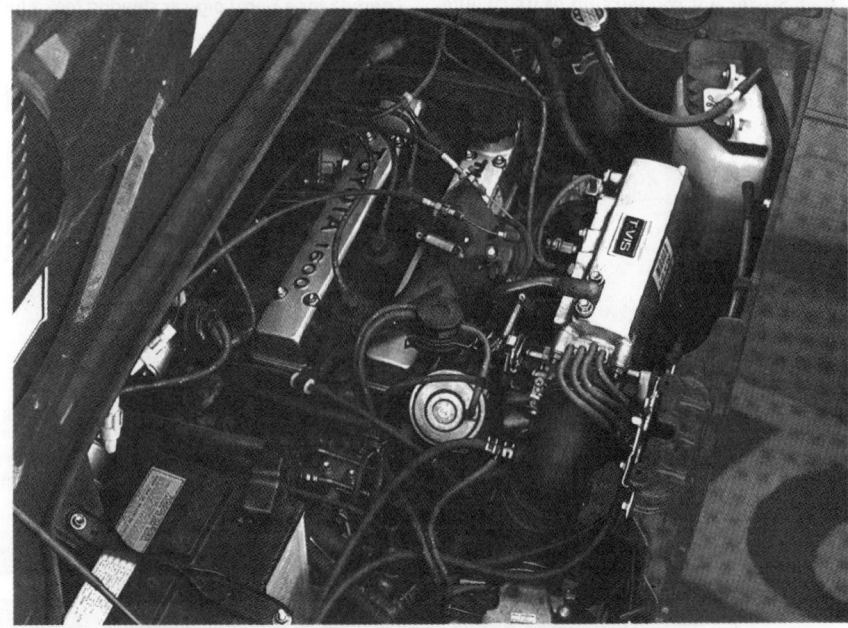

Just-right ergonomics and a hard-working 112-bhp DOHC four help shape the marvelous MR2.

REACTIONS

Some people might expect me to disqualify myself from passing judgment on these three two-seaters. After all, I did go out and buy a shiny black CRX Si when the Smith household landed in Michigan last year and needed good transportation.

On the other hand, what more honest ballot can I cast than one torn from my own checkbook?

As our Mr. Stein points out, the CRX, MR2, and Fiero are genuine sports cars, and reasonably priced ones at that. Now, I'm all for affordable fun, of course, but realistically, I think the great virtue of these automobiles is their broad-ranging talent. Few of us can count on room in the family budget for lots of different vehicles of narrowly defined purpose. So it is the practical enthusiast's dream come true to be able to own—with just one purchase, one insurance premium, and one garage space—an economical runabout that makes perfect, practical sense in daily use, *and* a responsive, refined sportster that delivers lots of genuine driving pleasure.

How do these little gems stack up against one another in my estimation? I like them all, but to be frank, I only *love* two of them. I've never been able to muster much enthusiasm for the Fiero. Maybe I'm still disappointed about what it might have been. And maybe the chassis upgrades on the drawing board will help change my feelings toward it. But for something with its snug accommodations and sporting mechanical layout, it sure does a fine impersonation of a big car. It tries to please everyone and ends up thrilling no one.

You know how I feel about the Honda CRX. Particularly in its spirited Si form, the combination of fun and practicality is impossible to beat. It offers stretch-out roominess and lots of cargo space, plus economical running and all the reliability of a half-inch bolt. And there are few cars I'd rather drive for the sheer, lighthearted fun of it.

But one of those, I must admit, is the two-place Toyota. Ever since Lotus pieced together its quirky little Renault-powered Europa in 1966, I've pondered what major manufacturers could do with their best front-drive powertrains *behind* the seats. At no great cost except in useful payload space, we'd have smooth, refined, and civilized rear-drive sports cars that could hardly help being snappy and great fun to pitch about. Well, Pontiac took a gallant run at that target, but Toyota nailed it at dead center.

Yes, the brilliant mid-engined MR2 sits on my short list of favorite cars, cost no object. Take purchase price and running expenses into account, and it stands alone as the delight-per-dollar champion.

So why do I own a CRX? Because even the healthiest golden retrievers have to be hauled in to see the vet now and then.
—Kevin Smith

The Fiero GT is an exercise in exercise. To go fast, you can expect to wrestle the over-heavy steering, stomp the brakes, mash the accelerator to aim the nose, grope furiously for gears in a process akin to putting on a Playtex rubber glove in the dark, and generally work up a marathon-quality sweat. Simply put, the Fiero needs to lose 400 pounds. The big V-6, of course, is a boon, launching the car in tire-smoking spurts, with Ferrari-esque sounds emanating from Pontiac's quartet of megaphone pipes. But the V-6 *itself* is heavy, and the Fiero was in need only of a diet, not a rocket booster that would blast it four seconds sooner to the Weight Watchers meetings. So what do you get for $15,449? Stunningly handsome styling and tailbone-tingling acceleration, in a car that is happier on Sunset Strip than on Mulholland Drive.

In stark contrast, the Toyota MR2 is nubile, svelte, and lean—the epitome of grace. Anybody, including my aging Aunt May, can plant Mister Two's front tires within inches of a fast-approaching apex. Miss the mark? No sweat; pick another. Sure, there are times you'd like another fifteen or twenty horsepower, mostly for on-ramp work. And there are periods when the motor's resonant boom forces you, in sheer annoyance, to search for KROQ-FM to mask the din. But on all other counts, the MR2 was the only car from which every driver emerged looking as if he'd just played a Robin Williams tape. Now, if only the Fiero's styling could be grafted to the MR2's chassis, automotive nirvana would be at hand. Its gaudy exterior gewgaws notwithstanding, the Toyota earns heartfelt respect. We should drop the Mister nickname and start calling it Sir.

As for the Honda, all of us have been dead wrong in expecting fwd econocars to be inherently boxy, weak-legged, tinny torque-steerers. The CRX is some piece of clever engineering. It's light enough to be tossed from side to side with minimal disruption of balance. It has the turning circle of a Schwinn. The steering is lighter than Grandma's dollar pancakes, never demanding more than a flick. (Why should it? The car weighs only 1978 pounds.) The clutch is, in smoothness, the equal of anything BMW has yet devised. And the handling is so supremely forgiving that we never did get the rear end to snap or the nose to plow until we forced the issue with impossibly rude capers. Under the CRX's silver metallic bodywork lurk many of the attributes that made old MGs, Triumphs, and Healeys such shamelessly entertaining contraptions. Of course, the Honda is enormously more reliable.

Dollar for dollar, which car has my vote? The Honda CRX Si, hands down. —John Phillips III

HANDLING DYNAMICS: THE "WUMPS" AND "YUMPS" TELL THE TALE

As an engineer, when you are developing or testing suspensions, you have graphic test and design data available that show exact geometry behavior through the total wheel travel. Without this precise information, it is a little difficult to judge exactly what you are feeling. Knowing that the Fiero had some suspension pieces that originated with the Chevette and the Citation, I expected the car to suffer over high-speed, high-amplitude deflections, such as one particular 70-mph curve we saw with a "wump" in the middle. Quite surprisingly, this latest version of the car could be trusted, despite some uncalled-for wiggling.

I suspect the front geometry is supplying camber change that doesn't quite match roll angle. This will cause the front of the car to "nibble," or hunt about. These unwanted wiggles are generally further exaggerated by the addition of a good sports tire and wheel, which the Fiero GT has. The larger and stiffer contact patch creates tensions that upset the clean, intended line of travel.

There was a section of mountain road that aggravated the suspension behavior a little more: winding, quite smooth, but with many gradient changes. The continuous second- or third-gear corners never gave the car a chance to stabilize or "settle in." Until I had thought things through and adapted my driving style, the Fiero was upset. I could not establish any rhythm or smoothness.

If a car has some quirky transient behavior (quite minor in this case), it is advisable to quell the tendency to chuck it about and concentrate instead on smooth technique. That lets the suspension move with as little violence as possible.

Once I had the hang of the Fiero, I really enjoyed making it behave so I could take advantage of its good V-6 torque and new gearbox. It has come a long way, and I look forward to the next development stage. It would be nice if that could include a major reduction in weight.

The MR2 is wonderful on the demanding sections. I cannot bring to mind another small sports car that has solved the compromise of ride behavior and high-speed handling quite so well. The spring rate and damping choices are nearly at passenger-car levels, yet when attacking the mountain sections, the car's behavior is superb. With something this good, one tends to be left with technical nitpicking or personal tuning. I would add roll stiffness at the rear, I think, to make the car a little more neutral, particularly during corner entry, and I would like it to be flatter everywhere. The car asks to be steered with power, and I would prefer more.

The very best car of the bunch on the undulating blacktop with "yumps" was the CRX Si. Its predictable behavior is helped immensely because the car is so light. Here is proof positive you can build an economy car that really performs. A detailed inspection is an object lesson in simplicity, efficiency, clean structure, and weight saving.

This little car nearly makes front-wheel drive the sporting equal of a well-balanced rear-driven device. Nearly—but not quite. I suppose, in every car that you really admire, there always seems to be an interesting technical mystery. In this case, it is the CRX's rear suspension. The method of articulation to arrive at "nearly independent" wheel behavior (trailing arms and a beam axle, with a pivot on the right side) is very clever. But does it really work? I think I feel unwanted wiggles, but I'm not sure. In a car this basically sound, I suspect I don't understand it properly—yet.

—Trant Jarman

CONTINUED FROM PAGE 82

performance scheme—is concerned, the big-engined Fiero GT is a nick ahead of the MR2 and the CRX Si, with 20.1 pounds per horsepower. The Toyota engine moves 21.3 pounds with each horsepower, and the Honda pushes 21.7. The slight advantage enjoyed by the Pontiac is roughly equivalent to the smaller cars' each toting a 150-pound passenger.

Naturally, other factors, including gear ratios, driveline power losses, and aerodynamics, also affect a car's performance. But the power figures—and our own observations—paint a solid performance portrait of these coupes: the Fiero out-accelerates both Japanese competitors, the same way the MR2 generally leaves the diminutive CRX in its wake.

But in competitive L.A. traffic, each car always had ample power to take us where we wanted to be, *whenever* we wanted to be there. Partly because all three vehicles have great exhaust notes, we frequently exercised our option to spurt some length ahead of traffic.

When motoring on the freeway or on an open road, the Pontiac worked to best advantage. Its relatively strong torque output (165 pounds-feet at 3600 rpm) far outguns what the smaller engines produce (93 pounds-feet at 4500 for the Honda, and 97 pounds-feet at 4800 rpm for the Toyota). As a result, the Fiero can climb grades or punch around slower traffic without needing a downshift, and low-rpm, fifth-gear cruising is a peaceful experience.

This is not to imply that the imports are without gumption. But obtaining the right reaction from them can take a slap at the gear lever and a solid imprint of your sneaker on the throttle pedal. Top speed is an even 120 miles per hour for both the Pontiac and the Toyota, and 115 mph for the Honda.

We were scarcely midway through our first afternoon of driving when the Pontiac's twenty-mpg thirst forced us to retreat to Ojai for fueling. Part of the blame for our early stop goes to the car's 11.9-gallon fuel tank (still small, even though the cell has been newly enlarged by 1.7 gallons) that mounts inside the central chassis tunnel. Mileages for the other cars proved higher in exactly five-mpg increments: the MR2 averaged 25 mpg; the CRX Si used a gallon of unleaded every 30 miles.

With such good fuel economy, touring range is a problem only for the Pontiac, whose limit is about 240 miles. That can really cramp your style if you're into exploring. The slightly thriftier Toyota can go 270 miles on its 10.8-gallon supply, but the stingy Honda can run nearly 360 miles between 11.9-gallon fill-ups.

After early morning photography in the desert, and a romp around the 2.5-mile Willow Springs International Raceway road course, we headed

SPORTS CARS

out a circular mountain road beginning north of Tehachapi, one that Phillips announced reminded him of nothing more than a gigantic Nürburgring. The California " 'Ring" slithers around the top of Harper Peak, a bit south of Lake Isabella, and its turns are coiled, ropelike, for much of its forty-mile length.

On this road, power counted for a lot, but not for everything. We found our enjoyment of the cars was based more on good handling than on good power characteristics. When we drove the muscular Fiero back to back with the Toyota and with the Honda, we felt that the Pontiac represented a double-edged sword. It was quite capable in the corners and very rewarding to drive quickly, but to do so was also a lot of work.

Trant Jarman compares driving the Fiero with driving a loose and ornery Grand National stock car. The analogy is extreme, but it does point out the Pontiac's biggest single fault: the Fiero feels and steers like a big car, rather than like the compact and nimble sports car it is supposed to be. Weight is a major factor in this phenomenon, but other contributors are the Fiero's larger tires (205/60R-15 front, 215/60R-15 rear Goodyear Eagle GTs), its heavyish controls, and its cockpit ergonomics.

To drive the Fiero well, it helps to remember a concept that driving instructor Bertil Roos points out in his SlideCar training. You must, first and foremost, be concerned with smoothly directing the car's *mass*. By driving rhythmically, you'll be able to diminish sudden weight transfer and its sometimes startling effects, and you'll also derive more pleasure from the whole experience.

Weight does have its advantages. The husky Fiero, with its extra insulation, its torquey engine, and its tall overall gearing, makes the best long-distance carriage. Only the car's storage capacity and its limited fuel range detract from its usefulness.

By virtue of its smaller dimensions, lighter weight, superior seating, control operation, and outward visibility, the MR2 is highly enjoyable to throw into corners, especially at the adhesion limits of its tires (185/60R-14 Bridgestone Potenza RE88s). The Toyota can make carom shots from apex to apex with gratifying quickness (albeit with significant body roll), or tie corners together in smooth arcs.

Trip Notes

Essex House Hotel & Racquet Club, Lancaster—Autographed air force spy photographs, tiny coffee percolators in rooms. Jacuzzi closed because "some perverts got in it."

The Pub (at Essex House)—"The Most Relaxing Lounge in the Valley." Entertainment by Alexander Longrifle (carries cassette tapes in Igloo cooler). Complimentary Ritz crackers and bite-size Kraft singles.

Murata Restaurant, Lancaster—Private Japanese dining room, comely pink-sweatered waitress. The best food in Lancaster (and the only sushi in the area). Sapporo draft beer, snails fresh from the garden, green tea ice cream.

Tres Hermanos, Mojave—"Mexican-American Dining," pancake-makeup waitresses. Steak and eggs for $3.49, hockey puck biscuits, and gruesome mountain climbing stories in which hikers eat their dead.

J.E.'s Old Firehouse, Palmdale—Cheese Bullits, Fire Engine Skins, and beefy ribs "Cooked to Perfection." Well, nice try. Lighted digital advertising in dining room, model train running along walls, miniature biplanes used as ceiling fans.

ARCO AM/PM, Lancaster—Coin-operated, drive-through car wash and vacuum cleaners (five minutes for fifty cents). Tokens and quarters only. A clean place. Good work.

R&J's Place, Beverly Hills—This is the spot. Sawdust on the floor, quarter-mile-long salad bar, caviar-filled potato skins. Pretty people aching to be seen, and waitresses who can tell a good joke.

Sheraton Plaza La Reina Hotel, near Los Angeles International Airport—Bucks-up valet parking, full-race breakfast buffet, dirty movies in the privacy of your own room.

A light flick of the wheel is all that's necessary to guide the MR2, even through a set of sharp esses or switchback turns such as those on our " 'Ring" road. But the Toyota's willingness to react to driver input also means that when you make a mistake, so does the car. A jerky technique will be immediately reflected in the car's behavior.

Toyota made minute adjustments to the steering geometry this year to reduce steering effort, but we think the MR2 already steered lightly enough. The coupe has received another little refinement in the form of a new mounting point and method of attachment for the rear suspension's lateral links, a fix the company indicates minimizes wheel deflection during hard cornering.

Although the Honda handles quite differently from the Toyota, it was almost as captivating on the mountain loop. It is a classic example of a predictable front-wheel-drive chassis. The CRX doesn't require a lot of busywork to drive—only simple executions. However, some additional wheel effort is required to overcome the stronger self-centering tendency of the front-wheel drive, and this is most noticeable when you wish to run quickly down a series of turns.

As Lotus helped to demonstrate with its featherweight Elite nearly thirty years ago, a carmaker can accomplish a great deal for handling by making a commitment to light weight. Even though it lacks the power of the Fiero or the MR2, the Honda can keep up nicely—thanks in part to its careful diet.

With a gathering of speed, the Honda's clawlike grip—provided by 185/60R-14 Yokohama AX-323s—gradually diminishes in understeer. But this loss of traction is not the least bit alarming. Gently pulling back from the throttle pedal restores traction and tightens the turning radius.

More goes into the making of a good sports car than merely the right amount of power and precise handling. Another important element is how agreeable the car is to control, whether in morning traffic or during recreational flogging. The controls' placement and smoothness to operate, the amount of arm and elbow room, even the position of window pillars and the amount of glass area are critical.

HONDA CIVIC CRX Si

GENERAL:
Front-engine, front-wheel-drive coupe
2-passenger, 2-door steel body
Base price/price as tested $9395/$10,709

MAJOR EQUIPMENT:
Air conditioning $599
Sunroof standard
AM/FM/cassette $539
Leather interior not available
Cruise control not available

ENGINE:
12-valve SOHC 4-in-line, aluminum block and head
Bore x stroke 2.91 x 3.41 in (74.0 x 86.5mm)
Displacement 91 cu in (1488cc)
Compression ratio 8.7:1
Fuel system electronic multiport injection
Power SAE net 91 bhp @ 5500 rpm
Torque SAE net 93 lb-ft @ 4500 rpm
Redline 6500 rpm

DRIVETRAIN:
5-speed manual transmission
Gear ratios (I) 2.92 (II) 1.76 (III) 1.19 (IV) 0.87 (V) 0.71
Final-drive ratio 4.40:1

MEASUREMENTS:
Wheelbase 86.6 in
Track front/rear 55.1/55.7 in
Length 147.8 in
Width 64.0 in
Height 50.8 in
Curb weight 1978 lb
Weight distribution front/rear 60/40%
Fuel capacity 11.9 gal

SUSPENSION:
Independent front, with MacPherson struts, lower control arms, torsion bars, anti-roll bar
Semi-independent rear, with beam axle, trailing arms, Panhard rod, coil springs, anti-roll bar

STEERING:
Rack-and-pinion

BRAKES:
7.5-in vented discs front
7.1-in drums rear

WHEELS and TIRES:
14 x 5.0-in cast aluminum wheels
185/60R-14 Yokohama AX-323 tires

PERFORMANCE (manufacturer's data):
0–60 mph in 8.7 sec
Standing ¼-mile in 16.7 sec @ 82 mph
Top speed 115 mph
EPA city driving 30 mpg

MAINTENANCE:
Headlamp unit $82.78
Front quarter-panel $144.48
Brake pads front wheels $25.85
Air filter $5.35
Oil filter $3.95
Recommended oil change interval 7500 miles

	EXCELLENT	GOOD	FAIR	POOR
ENGINE				
power		•		
response		•		
smoothness		•		
DRIVETRAIN				
shift action		•		
power delivery		•		
STEERING				
effort		•		
response				•
feel		•		
RIDE				
general comfort		•		
roll control		•		
pitch control		•		
HANDLING				
directional stability				•
predictability				•
maneuverability				•
BRAKES				
response		•		
modulation		•		
effectiveness		•		
GENERAL				
ergonomics				•
instrumentation		•		
roominess		•		
seating comfort		•		
fit and finish		•		
storage space		•		
OVERALL				
dollar value				•
fun to drive				•

SPORTS CARS

PONTIAC FIERO GT

GENERAL:
Mid-engine, rear-wheel-drive coupe
2-passenger, 2-door plastic body
Base price/price as tested $13,489/$15,449

MAJOR EQUIPMENT:
Air conditioning $775
Sunroof not available
AM/FM/cassette $310
Leather interior not available
Cruise control $175

ENGINE:
OHV V-6, iron block and heads
Bore x stroke 3.50 x 2.99 in (88.9 x 75.9mm)
Displacement 173 cu in (2828cc)
Compression ratio 8.5:1
Fuel system electronic multiport injection
Power SAE net 135 bhp @ 4500 rpm
Torque SAE net 165 lb-ft @ 3600 rpm
Redline 6000 rpm

DRIVETRAIN:
5-speed manual transmission
Gear ratios (I) 3.50 (II) 2.05 (III) 1.38 (IV) 0.94 (V) 0.72
Final-drive ratio 3.61:1

MEASUREMENTS:
Wheelbase 93.4 in
Track front/rear 57.8/58.7 in
Length 164.9 in
Width 68.9 in
Height 46.9 in
Curb weight 2712 lb
Weight distribution front/rear 43/57%
Fuel capacity 11.9 gal

SUSPENSION:
Independent front, with upper and lower A-arms, coil springs, anti-roll bar
Independent rear, with MacPherson struts, lower control arms, coil springs

STEERING:
Rack-and-pinion

BRAKES:
9.7-in discs front
9.7-in discs rear

WHEELS and TIRES:
15 x 7.0-in cast aluminum wheels
205/60R-15 front, 215/60R-15 rear Goodyear Eagle GT tires

PERFORMANCE (manufacturer's data):
0–60 mph in 8.5 sec
Standing ¼-mile in 17.0 sec @ 80 mph
Top speed 120 mph
EPA city driving 18 mpg

MAINTENANCE:
Headlamp unit $36.25
Front quarter-panel $101.00
Brake pads front wheels $54.17
Air filter $21.47
Oil filter $8.03
Recommended oil change interval 7500 miles

	EXCELLENT	GOOD	FAIR	POOR
ENGINE				
power				●
response				●
smoothness				●
DRIVETRAIN				
shift action		●		
power delivery				●
STEERING				
effort		●		
response		●		
feel		●		
RIDE				
general comfort			●	
roll control			●	
pitch control			●	
HANDLING				
directional stability			●	
predictability		●		
maneuverability		●		
BRAKES				
response			●	
modulation			●	
effectiveness			●	
GENERAL				
ergonomics		●		
instrumentation			●	
roominess		●		
seating comfort			●	
fit and finish			●	
storage space		●		
OVERALL				
dollar value		●		
fun to drive				●

Where ergonomics is concerned, the Toyota is everything the Pontiac should have been, but did not quite achieve. Despite its small cabin size, the MR2 scores big in a pair of important areas: one, all of the controls—clutch, shifter, and steering—are well placed, and they have the correct throw lengths and a good feel; and, two, there is ample room to operate without feeling cramped. As in a formula racer, the MR2's shift movements are short, crisp, and light. This quality is a prime example of how Toyota has given the two-seater such a tight, cohesive feel.

The MR2's cockpit also affords a good view. But a feeling of real spaciousness arrived with the introduction of the T-bar roof. Its pair of glass panes may be removed and stored inside the car, one behind each seat; the new roof's weight (about forty pounds) doesn't hurt much, and the overhead windows add an airy feel to the interior. Toyota reports no structural remedies to counteract the loss of roof panel area, but a new strut connects the front shock towers. Similar gussets also serve in other '87 Toyotas.

In contrast, the Fiero's tight interior layout and more limited outward visibility detract from the real-world needs of observing the roadway and the surrounding traffic. We felt cramped by the Fiero's offset footwell, by the high shifter location, and by a large central tunnel. But there are positive things about the cabin. The Pontiac offers the most relaxed environment: its V-6 is mechanically quiet, and neither engine vibration nor excessive exhaust noise—the note is absolutely *perfect*—diminish the driver's enthusiasm over a long trip. Unfortunately, that's more than can be said for the Toyota, whose cabin fills with the drone of the twin-cam engine.

This year, the Fiero's shift quality has taken a welcome leap ahead with the addition of its new five-speed Getrag/Muncie gearbox (see "The Getrag/Muncie Affair," *Automobile Magazine*, December '86). The shifting is precise, with one exception: in our review car, we had recurring trouble selecting fourth gear on the downshift from fifth.

Honda has done a masterful job with space utilization in the tiny CRX. It has more interior volume, the company claims, than a Nissan 300ZX. With its tidy front-wheel-drive packaging and its rear cargo area (accessible by hatchback), the CRX appears to have endless interior space, although it is shorter and narrower than either of the other two cars reviewed here. A powered sunroof slides rearward *above* the roof, allowing for maximum headroom.

The Honda's shifting is exceptional, even if it does have a little bit more of a rubbery feeling than does the Toyota. Its impeccable handling is complemented by tight, smooth controls and by excellent visibility. On the open road, a moderate engine buzzing intrudes above 4000 rpm. But that's about the only highway fault the Honda possesses. Even at 75 mph, the lightweight CRX is stable and composed.

Near the end of our Harper Peak loop, as we stood at the top of one of the many wooded passes that overlook the road, we were smitten with just how versatile these little coupes are. We used the CRX, the Fiero, and the MR2 in a different way each day, and the cars faced up well to the challenges.

We love the Fiero GT for its creative concept, its engine, its looks, and its relaxed highway demeanor. With the suspension upgrades expected in 1988, the car should handle and ride better. It remains to be seen whether Pontiac will address ergonomic needs. For now, the Fiero, burdened by its big-car soul, asks too much of its driver to permit an entirely pleasant day's drive.

We love the CRX Si because it is quick and light and friendly, and because its impossibly small structure could swallow an entire Texas horizon and still have room for a half-dozen pieces of baggage. It really is an ideal work/play car. We would love it still more if it were a little faster, if its engine were a little quieter at high revs, and if it were as fun as the MR2 to hurl around corners.

The Toyota suffers from a couple of compromises of its own, namely, limited storage capacity and too much engine din. But these are largely part and parcel of the mid-engine design that makes the MR2 so good. The car drives—no, romps —so gracefully that you can't imagine why other sports cars aren't as much fun. Above all else, the Toyota promises, and delivers, immense driver satisfaction.

That's why we love the MR2 the best.

TOYOTA MR2

GENERAL:
Mid-engine, rear-wheel-drive coupe
2-passenger, 2-door steel body
Base price/price as tested $13,738/$16,103

MAJOR EQUIPMENT:
Air conditioning $795
Sunroof $355
AM/FM/cassette $400
Leather interior $760
Cruise control $220

ENGINE:
16-valve DOHC 4-in-line, aluminum block and head
Bore x stroke 3.19 x 3.03 in (81.0 x 77.0mm)
Displacement 97 cu in (1587cc)
Compression ratio 9.4:1
Fuel system electronic multiport injection
Power SAE net 112 bhp @ 6600 rpm
Torque SAE net 97 lb-ft @ 4800 rpm
Redline 7500 rpm

DRIVETRAIN:
5-speed manual transmission
Gear ratios (I) 3.16 (II) 1.91 (III) 1.31 (IV) 0.97 (V) 0.82
Final-drive ratio 4.31:1

MEASUREMENTS:
Wheelbase 91.3 in
Track front/rear 56.7/56.7 in
Length 155.5 in
Width 65.6 in
Height 48.6 in
Curb weight 2389 lb
Weight distribution front/rear 44/56%
Fuel capacity 10.8 gal

SUSPENSION:
Independent front, with MacPherson struts, coil springs, anti-roll bar
Independent rear, with MacPherson struts, dual links, coil springs

STEERING:
Rack-and-pinion

BRAKES:
10.2-in vented discs front
10.3-in discs rear

WHEELS and TIRES:
14 x 5.5-in cast aluminum wheels
185/60R-14 Bridgestone Potenza RE88 tires

PERFORMANCE (manufacturer's data):
0–60 mph in 8.0 sec
Standing ¼-mile in 16.2 sec
Top speed 120 mph
EPA city driving 26 mpg

MAINTENANCE:
Headlamp unit $21.44
Front quarter-panel $147.29
Brake pads front wheels $13.76
Air filter $5.44
Oil filter $4.57
Recommended oil change interval 10,000 miles

	EXCELLENT	GOOD	FAIR	POOR
ENGINE				
power			●	
response				●
smoothness		●		
DRIVETRAIN				
shift action				●
power delivery			●	
STEERING				
effort			●	
response				●
feel				●
RIDE				
general comfort			●	
roll control			●	
pitch control			●	
HANDLING				
directional stability			●	
predictability				●
maneuverability				●
BRAKES				
response			●	
modulation			●	
effectiveness				●
GENERAL				
ergonomics				●
instrumentation				●
roominess		●		
seating comfort			●	
fit and finish			●	
storage space		●		
OVERALL				
dollar value			●	
fun to drive				●

FIERO AT LAST

Revised suspension means that Pontiac's mid engined sports car can now bear its name with pride; it's a sports car at last, as Phil Berg explains.

The Pontiac Fiero has at last made up its mind. After $30 million (£18 million) of suspension and chassis development, the 'utility commuter' car that looked like a sports car is now aimed down a new road for '88. Now it *is* a sports car.

Three versions of the new 1988 Fiero are available, and all are equally improved. The coupe is a base model powered by a 2.5-litre four — this year with welcome balance shafts. The Formula is a coupe lookalike with a 2.8-litre V6 that puts out 135bhp and moves the car to 60mph in about eight seconds. The Formula also has a rear anti-roll bar, stiffer springs, larger wheels and tyres, and shocks to match the springs. In fact, it gets everything you find underneath the fastback-bodied GT, except the Formula gets all-weather tyres where the GT uses summer rubber.

The new suspension hardware, on top of other recent improvements such as the V6 engine and five-speed transaxle, transforms the Fiero. In fact, we think Pontiac should have changed the name of the car to reflect just how differently it drives.

What changes the Fiero is new double A-arm front suspension and trailing arm rear end. The suspensions were *not* borrowed from one of GM's front-drivers — as '87 and earlier models had been.

The new Fiero maintains its good grip when you set these suspensions in motion, but leaves its former bad habits behind. The steering wheel kick-back you used to get over bumps

Fiero GT V6: *ride and handling have been absolutely transformed*

has been reduced to low modern levels by the use of shorter front axle spindles. These are held by twin A-arms, both considerably longer than the Chevette-style on previous models. These pieces allow some anti-dive geometry (Pontiac says the old Fiero was set up the opposite way), which cuts down front-back pitching motion. The new suspension also has more travel, smoothing the car's ride and helping its wheels stay on the ground over ruts and railroad tracks.

An advantage of the shorter front spindles is less scrub radius, which translates directly to easier steering. Pontiac has developed an electric motor-powered hydraulic steering assist, but had second thoughts about its necessity on the new Fiero with its

Nearly £20 million *has been spent on the Fiero and spent where it matters*

much-improved manual steering. It finally settled on offering the power assist as an option. We'd recommend it for two reasons: It is speed variable, offering full assist up to 10mph and then gradually decreasing assist to only 10 per cent at 50mph. Also, it has a tremendous capacity to soak up lateral shocks. It retains nearly as much road feel as a manual steering Fiero.

The new rear end is MacPherson strut, but very different from the backwards-mounted Cavalier front-end design holding up older Fieros. Instead, two lateral arms hold each rear wheel straight and trailing arms guide the struts up and down. Mazda uses this arrangement on its 626.

On the road you can drive a new Fiero without the clenched-fist grip on the wheel you needed on older Fieros. On glass-smooth roads, all you notice is a quieter ride. But on any other surface the difference between the old and new is astonishing. Bumps get soaked up without upsetting the car, the steering is linear and accepts small corrections easily. That could never be said of the old car.

When hard pressed, however, the new Fiero's front end will skip wide on bumpy corners. It also feels vague when turning into a corner, but once you're in it gets more confident. In total, zipping over challenging roads is more rewarding. It is a new feel as well, for *any* General Motors product, including even the Corvette.

The new Fiero rides flat and steady, too. It gives you a floaty sensation, though not one you'd feel would diminish control, and the annoying hopping and bouncing of the old car are all but gone.

While you're concentrating on the suspension, you will likely overlook that the engine is not transmitting much stress to the rest of the car. An hydraulic engine mounting system is responsible for this, and it rids the Fiero of shakes and clatters that made the old model a torture chamber at times.

Overall, then, the new Fiero has made quantum leaps in driveability. But several problems still exist. One deficiency is its small fuel tank. A 2.8-litre Fiero will go about 22 miles, we've found, on a US gallon of fuel, and with only 11.6 gallons of fuel on board you can't be choosy about which petrol stations you pass by.

Other complaints we have are the pedals — clutch, brake *and* accelerator. They are heavy and have long travel. GM has an easier-working throttle linkage for the 2.8-litre engine, but only Pontiac's 6000 and new Grand Prix get the fix in 1988.

You can treat the clumsy pedals and the car's lack of range as character traits and still be happy in a Fiero. But one question remains on our minds: Why didn't Pontiac make the Fiero this good from the start?

"When we realised how good the (1988) car turned out, everybody wished we had done it in 1984," says Sam Slaughter, Fiero marketing specialist. The new Fiero suspension, we are told, was on the drawing boards at Pontiac since before the Fiero was introduced as an '84 model. Funding, however, was slow in coming, according to Slaughter. "We were on a shoestring budget and were just trying to get the car out."

The Fiero began its development history at a bad time. Memories of 1979's petrol crisis were lingering during the initial design of the car in the early 1980s. During an economic slump, many car makers tell us, the sporty market is the first to suffer. Frills drop in popularity; utility has more demand. Positioning the Fiero as a utilitarian car seemed wise.

In addition, when the Fiero was introduced there was no MR2. No Honda CRX. The Nissan Pulsar was ugly. And almost 100,000 people thought the Fiero was pretty enough.

Last, Pontiac was only beginning to assert its current strong image as GM's sporty car division. Its direction as a whole was not as focused as it is today.

Today, competition with the small sporty car market has become fierce. The two-seater market has dropped 25 per cent in size, according to Pontiac, and there is a battery of different makes competing. Fiero sales have been especially hard hit; they're off 50 per cent from 1984.

Now GM is thinking differently about the Fiero. Pontiac is serious about its image as a proletarian Porsche. It has a chance to compete with invaders such as the MR2, Pulsar, CRX and other two-seaters. In fact, says Slaughter, the Fiero will have a price advantage over cars like Honda's Prelude and Nissan's 300ZX —both two-seaters.

During the past four years we've had various talks with Pontiac about future Fieros. From listening to engineers we've gathered that the car has nearly limitless potential. There is no limit to the amount of power a mid-engine can handle, one of the Fiero's original development engineers told us. Also, the huge wheel wells can be made to surround the largest tyres available today. And now that the car is headed in a sporting direction, it has its best chance at becoming one of the performance stars of GM, and likely the country. ■

FIERO FORMULA vs MR2 SUPERCHARGED

Both cars are improved, but how much?

PHOTOS BY RON PERRY

COMPARISON R&T ROAD TEST

Two 2-seat, mid-engine sports cars. The configuration is acknowledged as the way to go for all-out enthusiastic driving, and both of our test cars have established more than respectable credentials. The older of the two, the Pontiac Fiero, is now entering its fifth year of production; the Toyota MR2 is one year newer.

The Fiero started out as a relatively tame 4-cylinder "commuter" with an awkward 4-speed gearbox and has since offered the buyer a substantial list of options: V-6 engine, 5-speed Muncie/Getrag gearbox, and GT body with a new nose and an extended roofline. But the original suspension, derived from the lowly Chevrolet Chevette in front and the front-drive halfshafts (and thus the wide track) of the Citation for the rear, has been a compromise all along. It has cried out for significant improvement.

The Toyota MR2, if lacking truly inspiring styling, has been essentially right from the beginning. A 16-valver all along, its 1587-cc 4-cylinder, 112-bhp engine has made the MR2 a lively performer from day one, while the usual add-on aerodynamic aids have since provided a more aggressive-looking but still chunky exterior. Now, with a supercharger, it moves up a class, in performance if not in accommodations or trim, and takes a hefty jump in price.

Both mid-engine 2-seaters are significantly improved. How much? We put →

one each of these 1988 models through their paces, head to head, side by side and back to back, in a quick but intensive comparison test and called upon one each of the older versions to see what has been achieved, and how. After track testing for the absolute numbers, four staff members, alternating as pilots and co-pilots, took them on the road for energetic real-world driving. Here's what we learned:

Pontiac Fiero Formula

BECAUSE WE'VE always felt that the original coupe styling of the Fiero was fresh and appealing, it's good to see the 2.8-liter V-6/Getrag 5-speed package in its midst. The weight saving compared to the GT version is scarcely 50 lb, but we'll take (away) what we can get (out).

The styling is improved by the smoother ends introduced on the Coupe last year; the tail has the full-width wing you either like or don't like, while the flanks are quite garishly emblazoned with the FORMULA label. Hey, guys, not necessary; we could already see it coming, especially in its yellow paint. The interior is still bright and attractive in the way Pontiac does so well.

The V-6/5-speed drivetrain made the GT a vast improvement over the original car. A properly balanced 60-degree V-6, the 135-bhp engine is smooth, sounds great and has good torque, although it runs out of urge at about 5000 rpm. The gearbox is a bit balky until warm and somewhat vague in use; reverse and 5th are particular bothers. But the gearing is right, and when you're used to the gate, you can put the engine to good use. In other words, essentially the same as in the 1987 GT. With one big difference:

> *The Fiero has cried out for significant improvement.*

When the power gets to the wheels, the wheels do a whole lot better job with it.

With its wide stance and big footprint, the car always had plenty of grip; Pontiac has redesigned the Fiero WS6 suspension with the expressed purpose of improving steering effort and ride. In front: elimination of the steering damper assembly, shorter spindle length, smaller scrub radius, reduction in kingpin angle, longer upper and lower A-arms, and a larger (28- vs 22-mm) anti-roll bar. In back: new subframe with different suspension attachment points, 3-link design allowing adjustment of each component, reduced impact harshness, lower spring rates, and the inclusion of a 22-mm anti-roll bar on the Formula and GT (i.e., V-6) models.

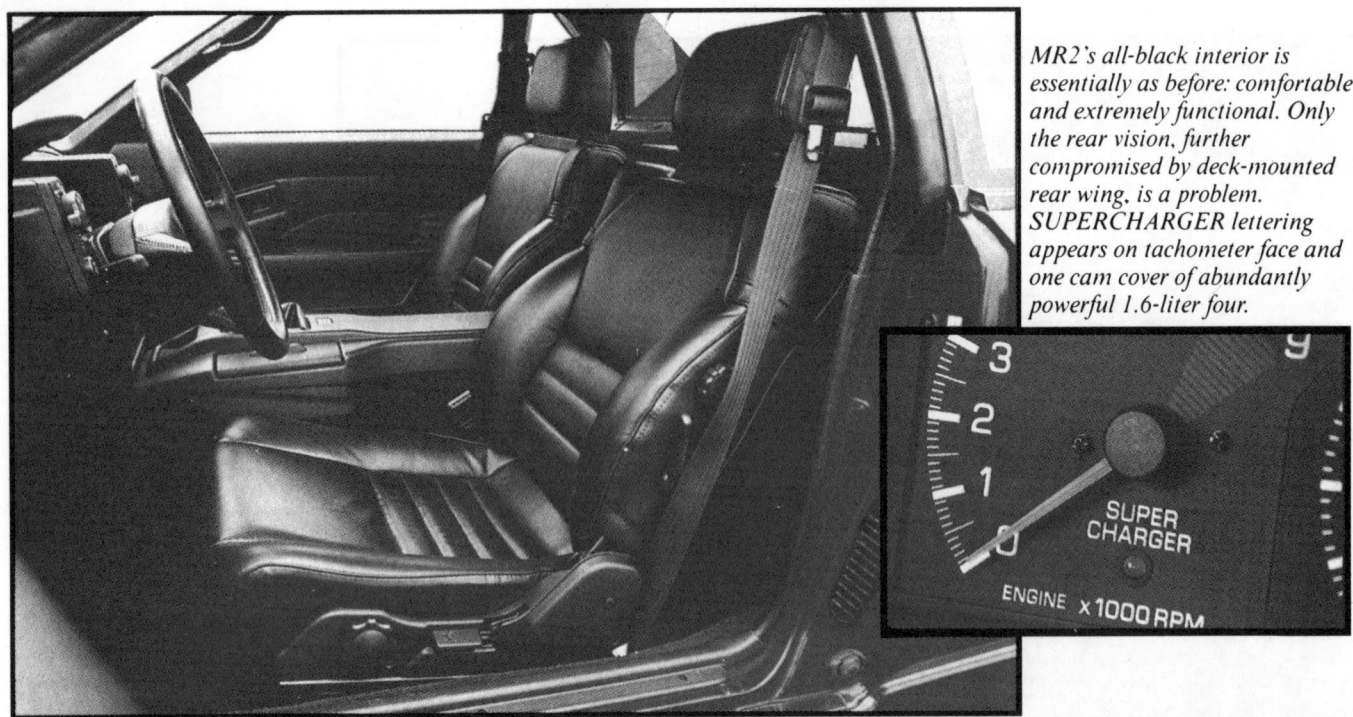

MR2's all-black interior is essentially as before: comfortable and extremely functional. Only the rear vision, further compromised by deck-mounted rear wing, is a problem. SUPERCHARGER lettering appears on tachometer face and one cam cover of abundantly powerful 1.6-liter four.

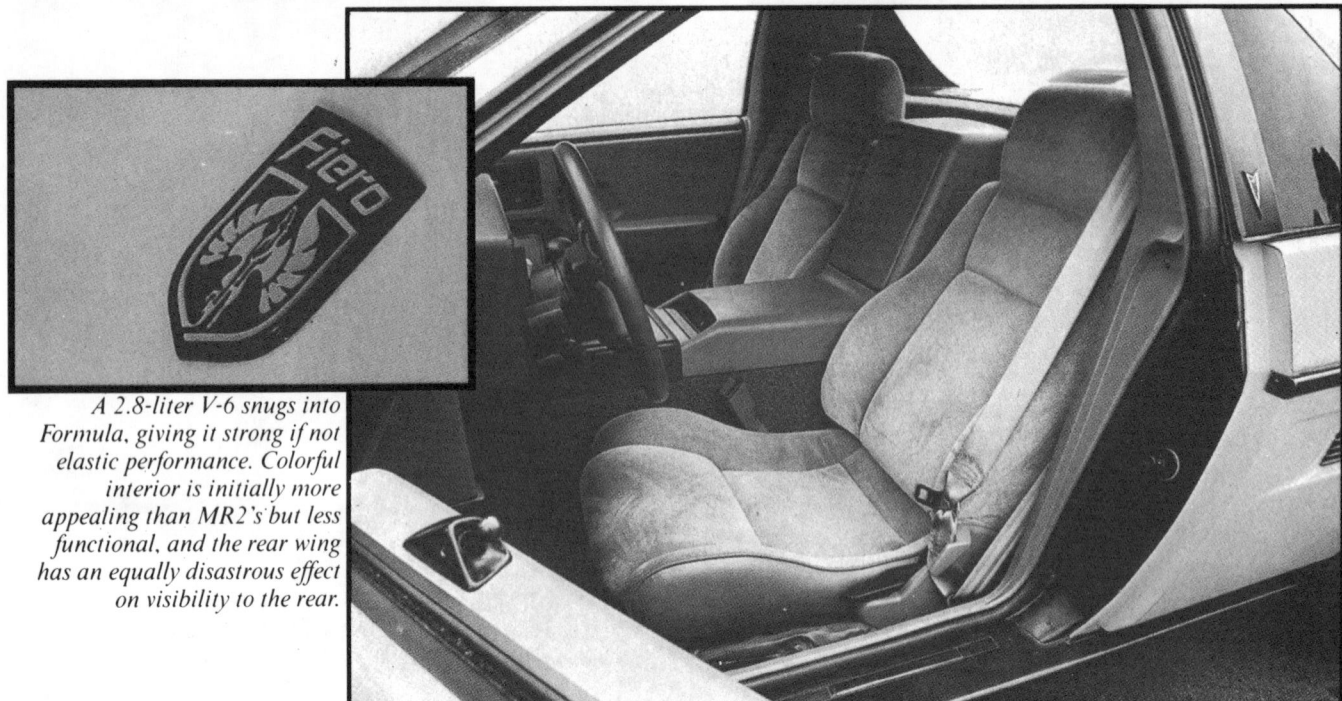

A 2.8-liter V-6 snugs into Formula, giving it strong if not elastic performance. Colorful interior is initially more appealing than MR2's but less functional, and the rear wing has an equally disastrous effect on visibility to the rear.

Does all this work better? Definitely yes. How much better? It's a noticeable improvement over the 1987 Fiero but still with a way to go, especially when compared with the nimble MR2. The Fiero remains a wide, heavy car with slow steering, not very subtle and not responsive to the light touch. Manhandle it and you'll get results. Much of the older design's numb feel is gone, there is more road feel and the car turns in better, though retaining a basic understeer. But it still has the annoying bump steer (maybe we can call it "bump wander" now), and undulating road surfaces produce so much suspension movement that it is hard to place the car accurately. Whether this is excessive front-end sensitivity or misaligned rear suspension, the driver must make constant corrections on all but the smoothest roads. On an ideal surface the Fiero has lots of grip, hanging in there better than the MR2. The ride is improved, especially in reducing the shocks that were transmitted so jarringly through the structure before.

The brakes do a good job—balanced, progressive and easy to modulate. The stopping distances, longer than the MR2's, are easily explained by the Fiero's greater weight. The fuel consumption, 17.2 mpg for the nearly 1000 miles of mostly hard driving we put on it, is acceptable and quite close to the MR2's 21.1 mpg when engine displacement, weight and frontal area are considered.

In all-around driving the 1988 Fiero is more pleasant than before. With its good gearing and improved ride, it's a fine cruiser, though still too wide and with outward vision too poor for confident in-town play. While the exterior is not up to the MR2's finish and the cargo and engine compartments are crudely finished, our drivers found the interior very attractive, but not as functional as the MR2's. Three of the four found the Fiero's driving position too low.

Toyota MR2 Supercharged

THE MR2 doesn't look much different for 1988. There is a better-shaped air dam in front, more nicely formed taillights with integrated license lamps, the engine lid is slightly higher to accommodate the intercooler and our test car had a T-top with removable (but lockable) glass panels and snap-in shades. The Supercharger lettering was discreet, especially in comparison with the Formula's pronouncement; in any case, the new supercharged model could go by you slowly and you probably wouldn't notice much difference.

Except that it wouldn't go by you slowly. The MR2's supercharger, despite being based on an ages-old method

> *The MR2 seems like a leap forward in technology.*

of adding horsepower, adds so much of it so well that it seems like a leap forward in technology. The 16-valve 1.6-liter four was already such a high-revver, and geared for strong acceleration all the way up through 5th, that all we could ask for was lower-end muscle. And a turbo would only make it fiercer at the top. Toyota's answer is a Roots-type blower, with an air-to-air intercooler, that boosts the output by 29 percent, from the 1987 MR2's 112 bhp to a whopping 145 (the 1988 unsupercharged engine is now up to 115 bhp). We're talking 90 bhp/liter, 1.5 bhp/cu in., here. Even better, the torque is improved 44 percent, up from 97 lb-ft at 4800 to 140 at 4000.

On the road, you'll *feel* what's been done. This is one truly super engine. It's smooth, flexible, instantaneous in re-

GENERAL DATA

	Pontiac Fiero Formula	Toyota MR2 Supercharged
Price		
Base price, est.	$11,000	$17,500
Price as tested, est[1]	$13,000	$17,500
General		
Curb weight, lb	2775	2620
Test weight	2935	2780
Weight dist (with driver), f/r, %	43/57	43/57
Wheelbase, in.	93.4	91.3
Track, f/r	59.7/60.4	56.7/56.7
Length	163.1	155.5
Width	68.9	65.6
Height	46.9	48.6
Fuel capacity, U.S. gal.	11.9	10.8
Engine & Drivetrain		
Engine type	ohv 2-valve V-6	supercharged dohc 4-valve inline-4
Bore x stroke, mm	89.0 x 76.0	81.0 x 77.0
Displacement, cc	2837	1587
Compression ratio	8.5:1	8.0:1
Bhp @ rpm, SAE net	135 @ 4500	145 @ 6400
Torque @ rpm, lb-ft	165 @ 3600	140 @ 4000
Fuel delivery	elect. port inj	elect. port inj
Transmission	5-sp M	5-sp M
Gear ratios, :1	3.50/2.05/1.38/0.94/0.72	3.32/1.91/1.26/0.92/0.73
Final drive ratio, :1	3.61	4.29
Chassis & Body		
Layout	mid engine/rear drive	mid engine/rear drive
Body/frame	fiberglass panels/pressed steel	unit steel
Steering type	rack & pinion	rack & pinion
Brake system, f/r	9.4-in. vented discs/ 9.4-in. vented discs	9.6-in. vented discs/ 9.4-in. discs
Suspension, f/r	upper & lower A-arms, coil springs over tube shocks, anti-roll bar/Chapman struts, lower trailing links, lower lateral links, lower lateral toe links, coil springs over tube shocks, anti-roll bar	MacPherson struts, lateral links, compliance struts, coil springs over tube shocks, anti-roll bar/Chapman struts, lateral links, trailing arms, toe links, coil springs over tube shocks
Accommodations		
Seating capacity	2	2
Head room, in.	36.5	35.5
Leg room (max)	43.5	43.0
Seat width	2 x 18.5	2 x 19.0
Seat travel	8.0	7.0
Seat recline angle, deg	30	30
Trunk space, cu ft	5.9	7.8

[1]Price as tested includes, for the Pontiac Fiero Formula, air cond, AM/FM stereo/cassette, elect. window lifts, cruise control; for the Toyota MR2 Supercharged, air cond, T-roof with removable glass panels, AM/FM stereo/cassette, elect. window lifts, elect. adj mirrors, central locking, cruise control.

sponse and progressive all the way. To eliminate a constant drag on the engine, there is an electromagnetic clutch and air-bypass system that disengages the supercharger when not in demand. A little green light—for go—tells you when it *is* engaged. As if you couldn't tell!

In a little car like the MR2 the results are marvelous. It humbles an engine almost twice its size without any fuss whatsoever. Is the turbo suddenly passé as a means of packing real charge into a combustion chamber? With a slight qualification regarding fuel efficiency, Toyota seems to be measuring the "old" exhaust-driven system for a coffin.

The supercharged MR2 is *fast*. You don't wait for acceleration and you never seem to run out of it. The MR2

> *Now, with a supercharger, the MR2 moves up a class.*

reaches 60 mph in 7.0 seconds, a full second before the Fiero, and never looks back, passing 100 mph before the sweep second hand touches 20. The shifter works well, with good ratios, but it may not hold up under all this power. Our long-term MR2's gearbox is getting a bit notchy at 30,000 miles, and we did beat

the supercharged car's box in fast shifting, so a little care is advised for the owner who wants it to live. In a car that gains speed so well, it's good that the brakes work, and they really do, bringing the car up smartly, with full control, in very short distances.

But with this superb engine, the chassis is displaying some shortcomings and in fact did not produce as good skidpad and slalom results as the long-term car. On the road the handling is neutral until near the limit, then it pushes, but if you get off the throttle it becomes suddenly tail-happy, almost in Porsche 911 fashion. Because of the excellent road feel and precise steering, this can be dealt with by an alert driver. In any case, it's probably time to give this instant super-

PERFORMANCE

	Pontiac Fiero Formula	Toyota MR2 Supercharged
Acceleration:		
Time to distance, sec:		
0–100 ft	2.9	2.9
0–500 ft	8.5	8.2
0–900 ft	12.4	11.9
0–1320 ft	16.0	15.3
Speed at end of ¼ mi, mph	85.5	90.5
Time to speed, sec:		
0–30 mph	2.3	2.1
0–40 mph	3.8	3.6
0–50 mph	5.5	5.0
0–60 mph	8.0	7.0
0–70 mph	10.4	9.2
0–80 mph	13.7	11.7
0–90 mph	18.1	15.1
0–100 mph	24.2	19.7
Estimated top speed, mph	125	135
Trip fuel economy, mpg	17.2	21.1
Brakes:		
Stopping distance, ft, from:		
60 mph	160	151
80 mph	268	258
Control	good	very good
Overall brake rating	good	very good
Handling:		
Lateral acceleration, g	0.83	0.80
Slalom speed, mph	63.9	64.0
Interior noise, dBA:		
Idle in neutral	52	47
Maximum, 1st gear	83	85
Constant 30 mph	64	64
50 mph	71	68
70 mph	74	na

CALCULATED DATA

	Pontiac Fiero Formula	Toyota MR2 Supercharged
Lb/bhp (test weight)	21.7	19.2
Bhp/liter	47.6	91.4
Engine rpm @ 60 mph in 5th	2100	3030
R&T steering index[1]	1.17	1.01

[1]Lower numbers indicate greater steering responsiveness. Defined as steering turns (lock to lock) times turning circle (curb to curb) divided by 100.

car some further chassis tuning.

In regular use, the supercharged car has the many virtues and few failings of the previous model. The exterior, cargo and engine compartments, and interior are all very well finished, much better than the Fiero's. While the styling of the interior is no more exciting than the outside, its function is excellent in every way except outward vision, particularly to the rear; as with the Fiero, an already existing blindspot from the pillars is enlarged by the decktop rear wing. But the MR2 is a narrower, more nimble handler, so this problem is less intimidating.

Only available to us for a short time and driven hard for the 750 miles we were able to pack in it, the supercharged MR2 did not return the fuel mileage we

> **When the power gets to the Fiero's wheels, they do a whole lot better job.**

have come to expect from the type. In fairness, a long highway cruise, with the supercharger not in play, would probably yield closer to 30 mpg.

And the winner is...

TALK ABOUT David and Goliath. In this battle the little Samurai hacks

In track testing, the MR2 was a handful at the limit and did not generate quite the lateral acceleration of the very stable Fiero; on the road, the situation was reversed, the MR2 being far more nimble and responsive.

away at the giant without pity, swinging a sharp, swift sword. The MR2 is so much faster that the Fiero just can't keep up, falling even farther behind on long grades. Despite the Formula's slightly better grip at the limit, the MR2 has such superior steering and road feel that the average driver can go much quicker, with confidence. Add its superiority in braking and fuel mileage, and the MR2 dominates in performance. In our ratings, the Fiero didn't win a single driving category.

The drivers were divided on the esthetics of the two coupes; half of them finding the Fiero's appeal greater, half preferring the MR2's practical look. The Fiero got the styling nod on points. But in assembly quality and finish, the MR2 was again a clear winner.

All four drivers preferred the MR2 overall, even with price as a factor. Considering the $4500 higher tag for the MR2, that's really saying something. What it says is: When you buy a driver's car with performance in mind, paying quite a bit less for a lot less is no bargain. But nobody was talking bargain; the MR2 at an astronomical $17,500 and the Fiero at $13,000 are high-performance cars that just happen to have two seats. Runabouts they're not.

CUMULATIVE RATINGS— SUBJECTIVE EVALUATIONS

	Pontiac Fiero Formula	Toyota MR2 Supercharged	Comments
Performance:			
Engine	7.2	9.2	Toyota's is state of a new art
Gearbox	6.5	7.8	Neither terrific, MR2 easier
Steering	6.2	8.2	Fiero vague, MR2 precise
Brakes	7.0	9.0	Both good; lighter stops shorter
Ride	7.8	8.5	Best aspect of Fiero, still 2nd
Handling	6.8	8.2	Balance and confidence over grip
Body structure	7.0	8.5	Toyota tighter and quieter
Average	6.9	8.5	
Comfort/Controls:			
Driving position	6.2	8.8	MR2 better for all but largest
Controls	7.0	8.2	Toyota's direct function wins
Instrumentation	7.2	8.5	Fiero handsome, MR2 complete
Outward vision	6.2	7.5	Both poor; Fiero's seating low
Quietness	7.5	8.8	MR2 superb for such hard worker
Heat/vent/air cond	7.5	7.5	Both equally effective
Luggage space & loading	5.8	7.0	Both modest; MR2 more usable
Average	6.8	8.0	
Design/Styling:			
Exterior styling	7.5	7.2	Best Fiero feature, only victory
Exterior finish	6.8	8.8	MR2 surfaces, detailing superior
Interior styling	7.8	8.0	Fiero handsome, but MR2 for detail
Interior finish	7.8	8.2	MR2, but Fiero excellent inside
Average	7.5	8.1	
Overall Averages	7.0	8.2	
Staff Members' Preferences:[1]			
Price-independent	4	8	
Price-dependent	4	8	

[1] Four staff members' preferences: 1st choice = 2 points; 2nd choice = 1 point.

NEWS FROM PONTIAC

Public Relations Department · Pontiac Motor Division · General Motors Corporation · Pontiac, MI 48053

FOR RELEASE   August 5, 1987

1988 PONTIAC FIERO

In 1984 when the Fiero was introduced, Pontiac created a new market for sporty two-seat automobiles with Fiero's mid-engine design, rust-free Enduraflex body panels, state-of-the-art spaceframe construction, 4-wheel power disc brakes and 4-wheel independent suspension. The market acceptance in this new segment was immediate -- with nearly 100,000 units sold in the first model year, and a total of 300,000 sold through the 1987 model year.

Since its introduction, the Fiero has evolved from its sporty two-seat "commuter" heritage into a contemporary road car that offers the ultimate in sporty driving. The addition of a 5-speed transmission, V-6 engine and fastback GT, combined with refinements in steering, clutch, brakes, suspension and powertrain, present a car line with a completely new personality.

For 1988, Fiero, the number one volume mid-sporty two seater in the USA, is relaunched with an all-new fully independent suspension that gives it the smooth, firm ride, crisp handling and nimble maneuverability that will set the pace in the highly competitive two-seat car market. The new suspension makes the Fiero more agile around town with a much lighter steering effort and a smoother ride that handles road irregularities effortlessly.

Add the exciting suspension to its already distinctive styling, introduce a new high performance edition on the Coupe, and Fiero becomes the complete road car that Pontiac driving enthusiasts have come to expect.

FIERO GT

An exciting new monochromatic exterior paint treatment and upgraded interior appointments make the aggressive Fiero GT a winning combination of sophisticated looks and world-class performance.

The GT's striking monochromatic exterior color scheme is available in black, white, bright red and silver metallic, with new bright yellow available mid-year. Black or gold diamond-spoke cast aluminum wheels with new Eagle GT + 4 all-season tires (P205/60R15-front; P215/60R15-rear) are part of the WS6 suspension package which complements the completely redesigned suspension system on 1988 Fieros. The GT, with Pontiac's WS6 Performance suspension package standard, has excellent cornering and handling capabilities that make it a leader in the mid-sport segment.

The standard powerful 2.8L MFI V-6 engine coupled with the GM Muncie/Getrag 5-speed transaxle gives the 135 horsepower vehicle a 0-60 mph time of about 8.0 seconds.

Inside, the standard GT interior has been upgraded to a luxurious Metrix cloth and a new camel trim color is introduced. Two optional seats are available: one with an inflatable lumbar support and another in "soft" leather.

FIERO FORMULA

New for 1988 is an exciting option on the Fiero Coupe: the Formula. Topping the list of standard features in the Formula option package is the improved, spirited 2.8L MFI V-6 engine (see POWERTRAIN section).

In addition to a standard GM Muncie/Getrag 5-speed transaxle, the Formula gets the WS6 suspension package which includes special front and rear shock absorbers, special springs, 15-inch black diamond-spoke aluminum wheels with Goodyear Eagle GT + 4 all-season tires (P205/60R15 - front; P215/60R15 - rear), 28 mm rear stabilizer bar, special bushings, and special front and rear control arms. A rear spoiler and Formula graphics complete the package.

FIERO COUPE

The affordable, distinctively-styled, fuel-efficient sporty Fiero Coupe is a driver's delight with its responsive handling and roadability afforded by the all-new suspension system for 1988. The much-lighter parking and around-town steering effort make Fiero Coupe even more fun to drive today.

The standard 2.5L EFI/TBI 4-cylinder engine incorporates balance shafts for smoother operation. Fuel economy is estimated to be 25 mpg city, 35 mpg highway. The revised four-wheel disc brake system assures improved brake feel.

The popular high-tech turbo cast aluminum wheels are now standard on the Fiero Coupe.

Inside, the Fiero Coupe has upgraded Pallex cloth trim and an AM/FM stereo sound system standard.

###

COMPARISON TEST

The Gee Force

Three budget-priced sports cars that deliver high g-loads and loads of gee-whizzes.

• Is there anyone in the audience who hasn't at least once imagined himself the proud owner of a sports car? Please raise your hand so we can make you an appointment for a complete regrooving.

The rest of you can relax. Recent studies by a team of *Car and Driver* researchers confirm that well-adjusted, responsible adults purchase two-seaters for the same three sound reasons they always have: (1) fun, (2) fun, and (3) fun.

Sports cars are the party animals of the automotive world. They love sunny days. They invite meandering through the countryside. They urge you to hack through traffic like a motorized Rambo. They're perfect for intimate two-up travel to romantic destinations. If sports cars could speak, they would never stop pleading, "C'mon, let's drive off into the sunset." As a fashion statement, a sports car is bold. What other kind of vehicle would you slip into when you're feeling frisky and in the mood to get noticed?

Unfortunately, most sports cars have grown up—in size and in price. The large-caliber two-seaters, a group that includes the RX-7 Turbo, the 300ZX Turbo, and the Corvette, carry prices that start at twenty grand and rise faster than the Alps. If your emotional self is ready to write the check, but your practical self keeps nagging, "How do you plan to pay the rent, gas breath?" you have our sympathies. Sports-car fever is tough to shake.

But maybe you won't have to shake it. Maybe there's a better way. Maybe what you need is some help from the Gee Force. The trio of inexpensive commandos we've enlisted here—the Honda CRX Si, the Pontiac Fiero Formula, and the Toyota MR2—battle boredom and annihilate apathy every mile of the way.

All three combatants pack potent combinations of sophistication, refinement, true grit, and efficiency. Their technical specifications take dead aim at Ferrari. Their engine compartments carry enough performance firepower to impress Dirty Harry. Their prices, which range from $11,499 to $15,468, make them tremendous values. Whether you're talking about delivering high g-loads or evoking gee-whiz responses, these three two-seaters are *the* force among inexpensive sports cars. The Gee Force.

Selecting these hard-as-nails heroes from the ranks of potential recruits was simple. There are but five cheap two-place automobiles on the American market. The two washouts, the Ford Escort EXP and the Bertone (known as the Fiat X1/9 in its younger days), are too old and too battle-scarred to be considered front-line soldiers in today's sports-car wars.

The members of the Gee Force wear familiar name badges, but this year they're brandishing more fresh ammunition than the Sandinistas. Honda has remade the CRX for 1988; nary a nut or a bolt from the old model remains. The Fiero may look much the same, but under its plastic skin it's been thoroughly reengineered; the Formula model, new this year, combines the most aggressive Fiero pieces in a low-cost package for serious drivers. Only the MR2 remains largely unchanged.

The Gee Force may be inexpensive, but it does not lack for combat-ready equipment. A quick recon turns up two midship-mounted engines, two four-valve-per-cylinder heads, one all-alloy powerplant, three fully independent suspension systems, and two sets of four-wheel disc brakes. All three cars are equipped with five-speeds, full instrumentation, 60-series tires, and alloy wheels.

When the troops are this tough, picking a winner requires something more than a polite discussion of the facts. A forced march is what's called for. We settled on an automotive triathlon: our normal battery of performance tests; a vigorous two-day, 400-mile road drive; and a handful of laps at a road-racing circuit.

To make sure the road workout was challenging, we borrowed a test route from the gentlemen of the Corvette development group. Their shakedown loop is a 30-mile country-road circuit located just north of the GM proving grounds in Milford, Michigan. We made friends with each car during a day of slicing and dicing the back roads. Several rain-and-snow squalls, and the tricky conditions that ensued, gave us further insights into each contestant's constitution.

Next we trekked west to Grand Rapids, Michigan, for a morning session at Grattan Raceway. The 1.85-mile Grattan course is a delightful combination of twists, turns, and drop-offs that favors agility rather than raw power. Several timed laps by techmeister Csaba Csere revealed what each car is capable of in the heat of battle.

Test-track numbers and road-course lap times, however, form only a small part of the total picture. The racetrack and the test track fill gaps in our knowledge, but they are not the real world. The four *C/D* editors charged with bringing home the facts based their conclusions primarily on how the three cars performed in the environment of double yellow lines, stop signs, and left-lane bandits. The road, with all of its variables and vagaries, is always the ultimate test.

You'll find our opinions expressed in numerical form in the Editors' Ratings chart. Each editor rated each car in eleven categories on a 1-to-5 scale (5 being best). The number in each box is the sum total of points earned. The Overall Rating scores were tallied in the same fashion; they are not averages of the other scores.

Before we reveal the finishing order, we have one last good-news flash to deliver: there are no losers in this test. All three sportsters are engaging, exciting, and easily capable of supplying the minimum daily adult requirement of fun. Any one of them will relieve your sports-car fever without transferring the pain to your hip pocket. Gee Force, indeed.

And now, the official results:

Pontiac Fiero Formula
Third Place

Have we got a surprise for you. The

GEE FORCE

new Fiero Formula looks exactly like the flat-footed Pontiac two-seater that has been disappointing us for years—and it did finish last in this test. But don't laugh up your sleeve (or write us a nasty letter) just yet: the same old body is home to a brand-new soul. The Fiero elicited oohs and ahs from all four editors. "This thing is really improved," rejoiced Larry Griffin, and he speaks for all of us.

The Fiero acts like a different car now, because that's what it is. The new suspension Pontiac has been promising us since its debut has finally arrived, and it transforms the Fiero Formula into an agile, confident road-eater. Up front, the ancient pieces inherited from the Chevette have given way to longer control arms. The X-car hand-me-downs that held up the back end have been superseded at each wheel by a strut located by a trailing link and two lateral links. The anti-roll bars are thicker at both ends. And all four corners now wear vented brake discs instead of solid ones.

The Fiero's structure has also been upgraded. A massive new front subframe, a revised rear subframe, and a host of small changes enhance the chassis's rigidity. You can feel the improvements every time you bound over a bump or thump across railroad tracks. The plastic body panels no longer slap against each other when the road jabs at you. The new Fiero feels as solid as Mount Rushmore.

In fact, not much fazes this car anymore. It's a pleasure to hurry it down a two-lane. The clocks reveal that it knows how to sprint, too. It was the quickest car in this test from 0 to 60 mph (7.9 seconds) and through the quarter-mile (16.1 seconds at 82 mph), and it had the highest top speed (123 mph). It also posted the best finishes on the skidpad, through the slalom, and on the road course. No, this is not the truculent Fiero of old.

To build yourself a high-value Fiero like our red test car, all you need to do is check the "Formula" box on the order form. The package includes the 135-hp, 2.8-liter V-6, the WS6 suspension (the most aggressive calibration), a five-speed transaxle, 60-series Goodyear Eagle GT+4 tires on lacy alloy wheels, full instrumentation, and a rear wing. Sprinkle with A/C, a tilt wheel, a rear defogger, a stereo, and power windows and you've still spent only $13,021.

That's what we call a first-rate return on investment. As improved as the Fiero is, though, it still needs work. The Formula lags behind its two Japanese competitors in both ergonomics and comfort. Steering it is still a Nautilus workout. The front wheelhouses intrude so far into the passenger cell that you can't stretch your left leg. The shifter is a bit notchy. The gauges point at your navel. These failings aren't serious, but they conspire to skim off some of the fun.

There is no denying, though, that the Fiero has been reborn. It's now almost everything it should have been right from the start. A new power-steering system, due before year's end, promises to correct its worst fault. It's a shame that it's taken half a decade to get the Fiero right, but Pontiac and America finally have a budget-priced sports car to be proud of. Well done.

Toyota MR2
Second Place

The Toyota MR2 is proof that the numbers don't always add up. The MR2's test-track results would make it the last-place finisher. On the other hand, it won more categories on the Editors' Ratings ballot than either of its foes. That makes it the winner, no? No. But it fell short of first place by just one point.

The photo finish should tell you how much we like Mister Two. It's almost everything a sports car should be: as light on its feet as Baryshnikov, as easy to operate as a Bic, and as much fun as your best drinking buddy. And, of course, it has the added advantage of being a Toyota: nothing short of a low-yield nuclear device will knock it out of service.

Not much about the MR2 has changed for 1988. The sixteen-valve, 1.6-liter four that lies crossways aft of the cabin has been squeezed for three more horsepower, up to 115. The other major revision comes under the heading of marketing: Toyota has been struggling to keep the MR2's price down, so the standard-equipment list is shorter than it used to be. Our test car was heavily loaded, however, with alloy wheels, a pop-up sunroof, air, leather wrappings for the steering wheel and the shift knob, power locks, power windows, cruise, and more. It stickered for $15,468—significantly more than the competition. Then again, you could easily knock off about a grand worth of gingerbread without cramping the MR2's gung-ho personality.

What strikes us about this car is how

Vital Statistics

	price, base/as tested	engine	SAE net power/torque	transmission/ gear ratios:1/ axle ratio:1	curb weight, lb
HONDA CRX Si	$10,195/$11,499	4-in-line, 97 cu in (1590cc), aluminum block and head, Honda electronic engine-control system with port fuel injection	105 bhp @ 6000 rpm/ 98 lb-ft @ 5000 rpm	5-speed/ 3.25, 1.89, 1.26, 0.94, 0.77/ 4.25	2086
PONTIAC FIERO FORMULA	$10,999/$13,021	V-6, 173 cu in (2837cc), iron block and aluminum heads, GM electronic engine-control system with port fuel injection	135 bhp @ 4500 rpm/ 165 lb-ft @ 3600 rpm	5-speed/ 3.50, 2.05, 1.38, 0.94, 0.72/ 3.61	2778
TOYOTA MR2	$12,808/$15,468	4-in-line, 97 cu in (1587cc), iron block and aluminum head, Toyota electronic engine-control system with port fuel injection	115 bhp @ 6600 rpm/ 100 lb-ft @ 4800 rpm	5-speed/ 3.17, 1.90, 1.31, 0.97, 0.82/ 4.31	2466

C/D Test Results

	acceleration, sec						top speed, mph	braking, 70–0 mph, ft	roadholding, 300-ft skidpad, g
	0–30 mph	0–60 mph	0–100 mph	¼-mile	top gear, 30–50 mph	top gear, 50–70 mph			
HONDA CRX Si	2.8	8.6	28.0	16.6 @ 82 mph	10.3	11.4	121	176	0.79
PONTIAC FIERO FORMULA	2.3	7.9	28.2	16.1 @ 82 mph	12.5	13.8	123	197	0.83
TOYOTA MR2	3.0	9.2	34.9	17.1 @ 80 mph	12.5	13.0	118	168	0.81

low-effort it is. You'd swear you could steer it by thought alone. The stubby shifter moves with less resistance than a light switch. The smooth clutch takeup and the sharp throttle response let you snap off downshifts like Ayrton Senna. And the engine—now this is what sports-car powerplants are all about. It acts as if it were lined with Teflon, and the sound track it plays as it charges to its 7500-rpm redline is pure Formula 1. The only kinks in the MR2's elegant way with the road are a slight indecisiveness when bending into corners and less-than-average straight-line stability. The rest is unvarnished enjoyment.

Not only is the MR2 fun to drive, it's also comfortable enough for long bouts behind the wheel. It offers enough seat travel for Paul Bunyan, and plenty of footroom around the pedals. You sit surprisingly upright, and all of the controls fall to hand, finger, and foot as if they were custom-designed for you. Radar-detector users will find the console-mounted lighter awkward, but no interior is perfect.

As much as we revel in the MR2's zingy personality, two quirks blocked its way to victory. The first is its styling. Man does not live by performance alone, and our panel of judges rated the MR2's sex-appeal quotient the lowest of the group. More damning is its price. Stripped to the bare minimum, the MR2 is still about 25 percent more expensive than a base CRX Si. In this cost-conscious segment of sportscardom, that premium ought to buy you a lot more *something*. In Mister Two's case, it's yet another number that doesn't add up.

Honda CRX Si
First Place

The winner of this test swims upstream against the rush of tradition. The CRX Si is a magic combination of disparate entities—part front-wheel-drive economy sedan, part utility wagon, and part Ferrari. From its terrific styling to its clever cargo hold, the CRX Si strives to do more things well than you would expect of a two-seater. And it succeeds.

The CRX is all-new this year, and it's better than Honda's original snub-nosed bullet in virtually every way. Under the hood of the top-of-the-line Si is a new all-alloy, single-cam, sixteen-valve four-cylinder engine, developing 105 hp. The new suspension consists of a sophisticated control-arm setup in front and an elaborate multilink layout in the rear. All Honda has carried over from last year is its total devotion to low-mass design. The CRX Si, at only 2086 pounds, is the featherweight of this group.

You can feel its light weight in the way the Si moves: it's as wide awake as a Maxwell House addict. Snap the throttle wide open in any of the four lower gears and the sweet sixteen answers with an insistent "*Kwaaaa!*" and an instantaneous lunge. If you're not careful, the tach needle will bury itself in the red zone before you can catch it.

On the road, the Si's short gearing keeps the engine in the juicy part of its power band. As a result, the Si proved to be the most willing performer in this trio—a fact underscored by its sweep of our top-gear-acceleration tests.

The Si's reflexes are quick as well—maybe a little too quick. The steering is micrometer-accurate; in most situations, the CRX shadows your moves. Sensitive drivers and hard chargers might pick up an occasional tail feint or a hint of bobbing, though. The Si's impressive power and front-drive layout also hamper it in tight corners. If you're too aggressive with the throttle, the inside front tire will spin helplessly. All of this is enough to drop the CRX's back-road rating from "great" to "very good."

When you tire of two-lane, you'll find the CRX a worthy weapon for Interstate attacks. The steering that follows your lead so well in the turns locks onto straight-ahead as if it were laser-guided. The ride is reasonable, the noise level low.

The CRX's interior is roomy and handsomely tailored. Its new bucket seats are as solid as Recaros, and they do a good job of restraining you in off-ramp flings. The dash is a model of organization, and a standard electric sunroof brightens your day at the flip of a switch. You'll never have to worry about overpacking with this car: compared with the two mid-engined entries, the CRX is a moving van. It's also equipped with a well-designed cargo cover to keep your belongings out of sight.

About the only hitch to maintaining a long-term relationship with the CRX is its driving position. As in the original CRX, the new car's steering wheel is located so far away that you'll find yourself wishing for simian arms. No amount of fiddling with the seat will solve the problem.

Still, the CRX Si is one fine road rat. The Editors' Ratings box says that it's almost as much fun to drive as the MR2.

weight distribution, % F/R	dimensions, in				fuel tank, gal	suspension		brakes, F/R	tires
	wheel-base	length	width	height		front	rear		
62.5/37.5	90.6	147.8	65.7	50.0	11.9	ind, unequal-length control arms, coil springs, anti-roll bar	ind, trailing arm with 2 lateral links and 1 toe-control link, coil springs, anti-roll bar	vented disc/ drum	Yokohama AX-323T, 185/60HR-14
43.0/57.0	93.4	165.1	68.9	46.9	11.9	ind, unequal-length control arms, coil springs, anti-roll bar	ind, strut located by 1 trailing link and 2 lateral links, coil springs, anti-roll bar	vented disc/ vented disc	Goodyear Eagle GT+4 M+S, F: P205/60R-15; R: P215/60R-15
43.9/56.1	91.3	155.5	65.6	48.6	10.8	ind, strut located by a control arm, coil springs, anti-roll bar	ind, strut located by 1 trailing link and 2 lateral links, coil springs	vented disc/ disc	Bridgestone SF-406 M+S, 185/60HR-14

maneuverability, 000-ft slalom, mph	road horsepower @ 50 mph	interior sound level, dBA				fuel economy, mpg			racecourse, min:sec
		idle	full throttle	70-mph cruising	70-mph coasting	EPA city	EPA hwy	C/D 400-mile trip	
62.4	11.3	44	85	75	74	29	36	26	1:46.2
63.7	12.6	55	85	78	78	17	27	15	1:43.9
61.6	12.7	52	87	80	79	26	32	22	1:47.6

GEE FORCE

Two things keep this test from ending in a dead heat. First, the CRX has a great body. If Daryl Hannah were a car, she'd look like this. Second, and more important in this context, is that the Honda outbrakes the Toyota at the loan officer's desk. The CRX Si will make you grin just about as often as the MR2, but it costs thousands less. When the price tag says "Bargain Basement" and the fun meter says "Wow!" you know you've got yourself the ultimate Gee machine.

Editors' Ratings		engine	trans-mission	brakes	handling	ergo-nomics	comfort	ride	sex appeal	value	fun to drive	OVERALL RATING
	HONDA CRX Si	17	18	13	12	15	12	13	18	19	17	16
	PONTIAC FIERO FORMULA	15	12	12	15	9	10	13	15	15	13	11
	TOYOTA MR2	16	18	17	16	18	17	14	13	13	18	15

Four editors rated the cars in each of eleven categories on a 1-to-5 scale (5 being best). The numbers above are the simple additions of their ratings. (For example, if all four editors gave ratings of 5 to a car's brakes, it would earn a total of 20 points—the maximum possible.) The points in the Overall Rating column were assigned in the same fashion; they are not averages or summations of the other scores.

Plastic-bodied two-seaters like the Fiero have no future, say GM in the US. A warning for other car manufacturers around the world?

End of the road for Pontiac Fiero

GENERAL Motors in the US will be dropping their plastic-bodied two-seater Pontiac Fiero sports car from the range this September.

Since its introduction in 1983 the sporting two-seater Fiero has been credited with rebuilding the youthful image of GM's Pontiac Motor division. Fiero's best year was 1984, with the sale of 99,720. That dropped to 47,156 by the 1987 model year and sales for the 1988 model year were less than 10,000.

Several factors have helped to kill off the Fiero which, significantly, is being dropped rather than replaced. In 1983 when the first cars were launched they were underpowered. Later models were much improved, but it had been a tough job shaking off the car's reputation for poor performance. The Fiero is also in a sector of the market where competition is fierce and its major rivals include such cars as the Toyota MR2, Honda CRX and Mazda RX7. However, these Japanese rivals are experiencing a 40 per cent sales climb since the beginning of last year.

The Fiero also suffered bad publicity, received over the recall of 136,000 cars in November 1987. The recall was due to oil and coolant leaks which resulted in 260 engine fires and 22 injuries. GM didn't acknowledge a design defect in the recall.